UNDERSTANDING
ETHERIDGE KNIGHT

UNDERSTANDING CONTEMPORARY AMERICAN LITERATURE
Matthew J. Bruccoli, Founding Editor
Linda Wagner-Martin, Series Editor

Also of Interest

Understanding Adrienne Rich, Jeannette E. Riley
Understanding Alice Walker, Thadious M. Davis
Understanding August Wilson, Mary L. Bogumil
Understanding Colson Whitehead, Derek C. Maus
Understanding Edward P. Jones, James W. Coleman
Understanding James Baldwin, Marc Dudley
Understanding John Edgar Wideman, D. Quentin Miller
Understanding Michael S. Harper, Michael Antonucci
Understanding Randall Kenan, Andy Crank
Understanding Sharon Olds, Russell Brickey

UNDERSTANDING

ETHERIDGE KNIGHT

With a New Preface

Michael S. Collins

THE UNIVERSITY OF
SOUTH CAROLINA PRESS

Cloth edition published by the University of South Carolina Press, 2012
Ebook edition published by the University of South Carolina Press, 2013
Paperback edition published in Columbia, South Carolina,
by the University of South Carolina Press, 2023

uscpress.com

Manufactured in the United States of America

32 31 30 29 28 27 26 25 24 23
10 9 8 7 6 5 4 3 2 1

Library of Congress Cataloging-in-Publication Data can be found at catalog.loc.gov/.

ISBN 978-1-61117-066-5 (cloth)
ISBN 978-1-61117-263-8 (ebook)
ISBN 978-1-64336-439-1 (paperback)

Excerpts from "It Was a Funky Deal," "The Sun Came," "A Poem for Black Relocation Centers," "For Freckle-Faced Gerald," "The Warden Said to Me the Other Day," "Hard Rock Returns to Prison from the Hospital for the Criminal Insane," "Another Poem for Me," "On Watching Politicians Perform at Martin Luther King's Funeral," "Belly Song," "Green Grass and Yellow Balloons," "One Day We Shall Go Back," "The Bones of My Father," "Cop Out Session," "For Langston Hughes," "Welcome Back, Mr. Knight: Love of My Life," "A Poem for Galway Kinnell," "We Free Singers Be," "And Tell Me Poet, Can Love Exist in Slavery," "My Uncle Is My Honor and a Guest in My House," "I and Your Eyes," "Poem for the Liberation of South Africa," "A Black Poet Leaps to His Death," "At a VA Hospital in the Middle of the United States of America," "Rehabilitation and Treatment in the Prisons of America," and "Various Protestations from Various People," from *The Essential Etheridge Knight,* by Etheridge Knight, © 1986, are reprinted by permission of the University of Pittsburgh Press.

Broadside Press has granted permission for this book to excerpt the following poems, which were first published by Broadside: "To Make a Poem in Prison," "It Was a Funky Deal," "The Sun Came," "For Langston Hughes," "Hard Rock Returns to Prison from the Hospital for the Criminal Insane," "For Freckle-Faced Gerald," "Cell Song," "The Idea of Ancestry," and "2 Poems for Black Relocation Centers" (all first appeared in *Poems from Prison,* by Etheridge Knight, © 1968 by Broadside Press); Broadside has also granted permission for this book to excerpt "Genesis," "Huey," "A Poem to Be Recited," "On Watching Politicians Perform at Martin Luther King's Funeral," "Belly Song," "Green Grass and Yellow Balloons," "The Bones of My Father," "This Poem Is For," "My Life, the Quality of Which," "Cop-Out Session," "A Love Poem," "For Mary Ellen McAnally," "For Eric Dolphy," and the introductory letter in *Belly Song* (all first appeared in *Belly Song,* by Etheridge Knight, © 1973 by Broadside Press).

The *Worcester Review* has granted permission for this book to quote from Knight's poem "Behind the Beat Look Is a Sweet Tongue and a Boogie Foot (for those who see me as a tragic figure)."

The *Painted Bride Quarterly* as well as Knight's literary executor, Janice Knight-Mooney, have granted permission for this book to excerpt the following Knight poems: "Things Awfully Quiet in America," "Who Knows???," and "Dearly/—Beloved/—Mizzie."

CONTENTS

Series Editor's Preface *vii*

Preface *ix*

Acknowledgments *xvii*

Chapter 1
Introduction: Knight's Resurrections *1*

Chapter 2
Knight in the Aleascape *33*

Chapter 3
Black Voices from Prison *51*

Chapter 4
Belly Song and Other Poems *72*

Chapter 5
Born of a Woman: New and Selected Poems *98*

Chapter 6
The Essential Etheridge Knight *122*

Notes *139*

Bibliography *153*

Index *157*

SERIES EDITOR'S PREFACE

The Understanding Contemporary American Literature series was founded by the estimable Matthew J. Bruccoli (1931–2008), who envisioned these volumes as guides or companions for students as well as good nonacademic readers, a legacy which will continue as new volumes are developed to fill in gaps among the nearly one hundred series volumes published to date and to embrace a host of new writers only now making their marks on our literature.

As Professor Bruccoli explained in his preface to the volumes he edited, because much influential contemporary literature makes special demands, "the word *understanding* in the titles was chosen deliberately. Many willing readers lack an adequate understanding of how contemporary literature works; that is, of what the author is attempting to express and the means by which it is conveyed." Aimed at fostering this understanding of good literature and good writers, the criticism and analysis in the series provide instruction in how to read certain contemporary writers—explicating their material, language, structures, themes, and perspectives—and facilitate a more profitable experience of the works under discussion.

In the twenty-first century Professor Bruccoli's prescience gives us an avenue to publish expert critiques of significant contemporary American writing. The series continues to map the literary landscape, and provide both instruction and enjoyment. Future volumes will seek to introduce new voices alongside canonized favorites, to chronicle the changing literature of our times, and to remain, as Professor Bruccoli conceived, contemporary in the best sense of the word.

Linda Wagner-Martin, Series Editor

PREFACE

While writing the first edition of this book, I felt like someone mapping a new country on a very tight deadline. I was a happy mapper, however. After Linda Wagner-Martin, editor of the University of South Carolina Press's *Understanding* series, gave me the green light, I plunged into the project, returning to a trove of Knight material I had previously gathered at the Knight archive at the University of Toledo in Ohio and traveling to other Knight archives in Indianapolis, Indiana—the river-fed city that was the poet's home for most of his life.

As I probed the sources of Knight's poems about prison, psychosurgery, love, Black liberation, self-loathing, and much else, I found myself in the prehistory of the era of mass incarceration—a period that in the 2010s had begun to wind down until, with the political aphrodisiac of elections in the air, Biden-era conservatives began injecting the electorate with a sort of speedball: the conviction that crime is widely out of control and in need of a response as iron-fisted as ever.

Sometimes, in and out of the archives, I found myself wandering in a zone of kindness: Knight's sister Eunice Knight-Bowens, helped by an assistant, took me on a small tour that included Knight's modest grave—among the hills and grand mausoleums of Indianapolis's storied Crown Hill Cemetery. Also, out of the blue, Knight's literary executor and friend Fran Quinn contacted me and poured tales of Knight and his relationships into my ear.

My research also took me into force fields of wariness thrown up by some who loved Knight and did not know me from Adam or were nervous about the delicate politics of a Black poet's legacy in a country often hostile to such people. If I had had world enough and time, I would have tried to do more to cultivate trust, and to reach out to many more from Knight's orbit, but the deadlines for returning to teaching and for turning in my manuscript rang down one after the other.

After the book appeared, it became clear that it was part of a modest Knight renaissance. In 2014, the former US poet laureate Donald Hall (one of those I wish I had had time to contact while writing the first edition) told me that after "a poet dies, there is immediate attention to him. But then people stop talking about him. For many poets, they never start again. I have heard more about Etheridge Knight in the last year or so than I have for a long time."[1]

One of those invoking Knight's name in the period Hall referred to was Reginald Dwayne Betts, who was incarcerated on a carjacking conviction at the age of 16 but started writing in prison and compiled such a record of achievement that in 2021 he received the MacArthur Foundation "genius" award. Betts opens his 2009 memoir with a variation on the opening of Knight's poem "For Freckle-Faced Gerald," and Betts traces his origins as a mature poet to a jailhouse encounter with Knight's work. Reading voraciously behind bars, Betts noticed that prisoners' lives

> weren't written about in most of the books I'd read. For moment, reading Etheridge Knight, I began to figure that I could fish for the gray in the lives around me and write the life I didn't see in books. Etheridge Knight weaved prison's hurt into poetry, and for the first time I wanted to write a poem that wasn't for women. A poem that was for the dudes around me, carrying time like the heaviest albatross around their necks.[2]

In 2018, another MacArthur Fellow, Terrance Hayes, published *To Float in the Space Between: A Life and Work in Conversation with The Life and Work of Etheridge Knight*. The title *To Float in the Space Between* is taken from a line in Knight's much-anthologized poem "The Idea of Ancestry," and in the book itself, Hayes uses Knight's life, work, and poetics—including their tremendous differences from his own—as a scaffolding within which to build an account of his own life, work, and poetics. Knight's meditation on ancestry, for example, inspired Hayes to undertake a "family inventory" of his own.

Hayes's journey to his book is further evidence of Knight's magnetic effect on others' imaginations. For, when he was offered the opportunity to meet Knight by Fran Quinn, he failed to take the chance before Knight died because he knew his mother, an employee of the South Carolina Department of Corrections, would disapprove of his associating with an ex-convict.[3]

Still, Hayes writes, "[m]y coming-of-age story begins unheroically with me on a college bunk reading 'The Idea of Ancestry.'" Hayes's book, memorably illustrated with his drawings of Knight himself and of images from or inspired by Knight's work, grew out of Hayes's career-long pursuit of Knight as "muse and mystery."

Further evidence of Knight as magnet for others' imaginations and projects came in early 2022, when poet and professor Norman Minnick got in touch with me to ask for a blurb for *The Lost Etheridge: Uncollected Poems of Ether-idge Knight*, a 255-page gathering of Knight's unpublished and out-of-print poetry (along with a few examples of his prose). This welcome volume expands the published Knight canon with magnetic masterpieces like "O Elizabeth," written when Knight knew he was dying to Elizabeth McKim, the "wife of [his] comings and goings."

"O Elizabeth" is a love poem that exemplifies Knight's ability to put every-thing—from relationships as vast in their complexities as snowstorms, to self-celebration and self-blame, to illness and death—under a level of imaginative magnification that brings new aspects of those subjects into view, and in doing so, gets under the skin of writers like Betts and Hayes. "Woman of my wander-ings," Knight writes,

> Wife of my comings and goings–
>
> . . .
>
> You bless my 58th year, tho
> I be / here / in this Domain
> of Death and Excellent Pain
> I languish. I suffer. I exalt–
> Do you still love me? Is–
> my smoke still in your
> fire? How can you love me?
> Me: liar cheater and dirty
> mistreater / I love you
> I, man of the high step
> and the long-laugh.
> Despite the rocks and
> shoals and silver water
> falls, our rivers flow
> together. Who knows
> what the weather / will
> be tomorrow, we row
> for sunshine, not storm . . .

There is also a poem for McKim's daughter, Jenifer, now a journalist, who in-terviewed me in 2021, and expressed the distress that her mother (who is white and who has a book about her time with Knight in the works) felt at something Hayes reports: That one of Knight's sisters identified Sonia Sanchez, Knight's first wife and a legendary poet in her own right, as her eternal sister-in-law and Knight's one true love, but added, "I don't know about all them white women after Sonia."

Whatever differences may have existed in the depth of Knight's feelings
for the women in his life over the years—differences that can arise out of the
same fusion of chance, history, and desire that binds people in the first place—
Knight enters full stepfather mode in the poem to Jenifer McKim by turning
his own youth, in his first stanza, into a mirror where the young McKim might
see herself:

> When I was twenty–
> Like you:
> I knew plenty
> That's tru
> And I too
> Was full of breath

The unflinching frankness, leavened by wit and metaphysical insight, that
Knight shows in the poems to the McKims, and just about everywhere else
in his oeuvre, are part of what draws readers and successors into his orbit.[4]
Indeed, Knight's impact as a man and poet can be measured in part by the
possessiveness of those who loved him while he was alive or who, like Hayes,
plunged "into the slants and shades" of his lifework after he died.

The city of Indianapolis itself has been drawn to a degree into Knight's
chronicles of the journey between what he once called "the illogic of birth and
the absurdity of death."[5] This is in part because his mother Belzora and his
sister Eunice Knight-Bowens took care to institutionalize him by launching an
annual Etheridge Knight Festival of the Arts in Indianapolis in 1992. Over the
years, a who's who of African American poetry and criticism has participated
in the festival—Gwendolyn Brooks, Amiri Baraka, Mari Evans, Henry Louis
Gates Jr., Houston Baker, Yusef Komunyakaa, Michael Harper, Lamont B.
Steptoe, Haki R. Madhubuti, and others.

Powered by Eunice Knight-Bowens, the festival sought to be a community hub for at-risk youth, the elderly, the incarcerated, and art-starved poor
neighborhoods. It sought, too, to transcend racial divisions: "For starters, my
brother didn't abide by that color thing," Knight-Bowens said in 1998; "so if
this festival is going to be anything like Junior [the family nickname for Etheridge Knight], it has to be the way Junior was, which is colorblind."[6]

When, nine years after the passing of Eunice Knight-Bowens in 2013, I
briefly visited Indianapolis it was clear that Knight is increasingly part of what
the city chooses to celebrate about itself. The Indianapolis Public Library had
teamed up with Butler University to open an exhibition called the Etheridge
Knight Project, which grew out of a $10,000 grant to Butler secured by a team
that included Sally Childs-Helton, the award-winning percussionist and star of

filk music who heads the Butler special collections library that includes one of Knight's archives.[7]

As part of the project, students were hired to study and respond to the Knight archive. Six Butler classes incorporated Knight's work into their assignments, and, in one case, incorporated interviews with members of his family. Nicholas Redding, one of those who used Knight's writings in his class, required students to write a five-to-seven-page essay on Knight and found that those students, on a campus that was 82% white, initially saw Knight as "a black man, a convict, and an addict—and felt distanced." Yet Knight magnetism prevailed because, by engaging with Knight's work and with Terrance Hayes, who visited the campus while the course was being taught, students ended up feeling kinship with Knight.

I saw this kinship—as well as the special door the Knight archive opened for black students—after I arrived at the Indianapolis Public Library and climbed the steps past the statue at the top of a powerful buffalo beside a massive open book (perhaps a riposte to the Indiana state seal, which features a buffalo fleeing a forest being put to the axe). I went inside and found (with help from a kind librarian) what had been wrought by Childs-Helton, Butler colleagues of hers, students hired one summer to scour the Knight archive, and Knight's own family led by his glowing-skinned great niece Hanako Gavia.[8]

The exhibit consisted of free-standing, approximately eight-foot-tall blue panels, each curated by a Butler student, that treated the viewer to selections from Knight's letters, poems, drawings, and essays. Also featured were letters *to* Knight and work inspired by him—not least the students' own observations.[9]

One highlight of the exhibition was a reproduction of Knight's account of the effect on him of his first-ever acceptance letter for a poem. The letter came while Knight was still incarcerated and feeling immersed in rejection at the Indiana State Prison on the south shore of Lake Michigan. But, for "the next 4–5 years, until I was released from prison, my 'doing time' was different," Knight recalls:

> I saw the sky in different shades of blue, my sense of my / self / changed, and therefore my view of the world. As I struggled with the language and the discipline of poetry I was forced to re-examine, and re-structure, my relationships: with myself, with family and friends, with society, and with nature / god.

Butler class of 2020 student Nate Leman, a young man with a neat mustache and John Lennon glasses, includes Knights account in his panel.

Presenting during the virtual celebration that launched the exhibition in May 2021, Leman called attention to another remarkable document—a

Knight letter supporting the release from prison of John Paul, an alumnus of a prison workshop Knight had conducted some years before. "I personally am convinced it was poetry, and my defining my/ self/ as a poet, that caused me to change," to live in a non-criminal way, and to relate myself to others in a non-destructive manner Knight wrote. "And I feel very / strongly that John Paul has made that change too."[10]

The highlight of the online launch where Leman spoke was the presentation by Knight's nephew, Floyd Knight Jr.—a bearded, handsome, jovial pastor. Offering context before reading a eulogy where a Knight-like figure says he wants to "drive to hell in style," the pastor spoke of the efforts he and other family and friends made to get the chronically addicted Knight to complete a rehab program during his lifetime. Such a program might have helped Knight come to terms with religious values that he absorbed from his mother, Knight Jr. suggested; it may have helped the poet see past the "hypocrisy in the church and the mean-spirited Christians." Knight might have been "surprised by those who would have forgiven him," the pastor said. Indeed, after completing the program and making the proper amends, Knight might have managed an unexpected last step into self-acceptance, the poet's nephew added.

Knight nevertheless reflected on his roads not taken deeply enough to have the aforementioned magnetic effect on others. Indeed, he all but portrays himself as one of nature's magnets in "I am a Tree, My Lovers Fly to and from Me," a poem chosen for her library exhibition panel curated by Chris Strong (a student whose exhibition photograph showed her sporting a fluffy afro and translucent-framed glasses over big kind eyes). "I am a Tree" shows off a love affair's wild peaks and burnt-out coals—and his genius, clearly, for capturing the imaginations of young people.

This effect on young people is underscored by Pulitzer Prize-winning poet Yusef Komunyakaa in his preface to *The Lost Etheridge*. There Komunyakaa reports that his talks with young poets make it clear that the Knight who died in the last century remains a potent force in this one.[11]

Indianapolis' slow turning toward Knight is further evidenced by Bookmark-Indy, an online guide that highlights "points of inspiration" associated with Indianapolis authors Kurt Vonnegut, Booth Tarkigton, Maria Evans, and now Knight.

To cap it all off, a downtown mural of Knight is in the works in an effort being led by Hanako Gavia, who is not only Knight's great niece but also assistant director of Butler University's Center for Citizenship and Community. In fact, Helton says, Gavia is the sparkplug for all the efforts to weave Knight more tightly into Indianapolis life. (Gavia herself wrote in an email to me that she was "voluntold" by her family to take the sparkplug role. But her joy and pride in what she is achieving is quite evident).[12]

In short, Knight, who when his mail was delivered to him in Michigan City was called not by his name but by his inmate number—30562—is gradually becoming, under his own name, a larger-than-life presence in Indianapolis and beyond. His transformation flows from a redefinition process that he himself described during a 1980 reading at the Scranton, Pennsylvania Public Library: "Definitions," he said,

> are very powerful things and a lot of men, especially young men in prison who wouldn't go along with all the bullshit would be thrown in the hole in solitary confinement, and if that didn't teach them their lesson, then they would be defined as crazy and they would be sent to mental institutions where ugly things would be done to their heads. It's very easy to define a person in prison—or if you are a woman . . . a brother can have a sister defined as crazy, a husband can have a wife defined as crazy *I want her locked up, she's crazy, she's hysterical, she's demented. . . .*[13]

The first edition of this book was my effort to define Knight as a major American poet and intellect—someone whose work and thought have flown like sparks through the American night, lighting the locked interiors of prisons and traumas, lighting truths at cross purposes with the nation's preferred mythologies, and, not least, spotlighting bad patriarchal habits (for Knight in his writing and professional utterances was no small feminist). The present edition corrects key errors and omissions in the first while leaving the original text largely intact.

February 25, 2023

Notes

1. Michael Collins, "'God—*his uniqueness*': Donald Hall remembers Etheridge Knight," *Worcester Review* no. 36, 1/2 (2015), 144.

2. Dwayne Betts, *A Question of Freedom: A Memoir of Learning, Survival, and Coming of Age in Prison* (New York: Avery, 2010), 165.

3. Terrance Hayes, *To Float in the Space Between: A Life and Work in Conversation with the Life and Work of Etheridge Knight* (Seattle: Wave Books, 2018), 35.

4. See Carolyn Warfield, "Love and Freedom are One." *Indianapolis Recorder*, April 25, 1992.

5. Etheridge Knight, "Eulogy for Wes Montgomery," *Lake Shore Outlook,* July 1968. Accessed at the Knight archive at the Indianapolis Historical Society.

6. Charles Sutphin, "Universal Etheridge," *NUVO Newsweekly* 9.3, March 26–April 2, 1998. Accessed at the Knight archive at the Indianapolis Historical Society.

7. Sally Childs-Helton, "Humanities Research for the Public Good: Council of Independent Colleges Grant Outcomes at Three Indiana Institutions," presented at the

Society of Indiana Archivists Spring Meeting, April 29–30, 2001; Sally Childs-Helton, "'His Kindness was Overwhelming': The Etheridge Knight Collection and the Transformational Power of Primary Sources," presented at the Midwest Archives Conference Spring Meeting, May 5–7 2022. Other facts about the Etheridge Knight Project and related ventures that are presented in this preface were obtained in email exchanges with Knight-Helton, Hanako Gavia, and Norman Minnick.

8. Amira Malcolm, the Interim Manager of the library's new Center for Black Literature and Culture, also had a hand in the exhibition.

9. One student, Scholar Idjagboro, a Baylor Dance Performance and International Relations major, is in charge of publicizing the Knight Project with efforts that include Facebook and Instagram accounts (@EKFREEPEOPLESBE) and the relaunching of the Free People's Poetry Workshop, a Knight institution the poet convened during his lifetime in cities from Memphis to Indianapolis. (The workshop has spread through a one-time Knight student, Kenneth May, all the way to South Korea.)

10. "CLBC Presents a Virtual Celebration of Poet Etheridge Knight," accessed September 10, 2022, https://www.youtube.com/watch?v=zsvKBecrTZY.

11. Yusef Komunyakaa, "Foreword," in Norman Minnick, ed., *The Lost Etheridge: Uncollected Poems of Etheridge Knight* (Athens, GA: Kinchafoonee Creek Press, 2022), xix.

12. A panel that includes Gavia, Sally Childs-Hilton, Norman Minnick, and others is, at this writing, in the process of selecting the artist who will paint the mural.

13. "Etheridge Knight reading [FULL] @ Scranton Public Library," thepostarchive, accessed July 9, 2020, https://m.youtube.com/watch?v=uFNyUX8_GDo.

ACKNOWLEDGMENTS

I am grateful to Daying and Tianchen, my wife and son, who bore with me while I worked on this book and related projects. I am also grateful to the late, great Sybil Ford, my grandmother, who used to pour out wisdom for hours while she cooked in her kitchen and I sat and listened, and who was always rooting for me.

I also thank Eunice Knight-Bowens, who not only answered my questions about her brother but showed me the meaning of hospitality as she took me on a tour of everything from her brother's last address to the family plot where Etheridge Knight is buried; Janice Knight-Mooney, her brother's literary executor, who granted me permission to quote from Knight's out-of-print poetry collections, from his uncollected poetry, and from material in Knight archives at Butler University and the University of Toledo; the Rev. Dr. Mary McAnally for allowing me to quote from her chronology of her marriage to Knight, for educating me about her own life, and for granting permission for me to quote from Knight correspondence that belongs to her; Roberto Giammanco, one of the early nurturers of Knight's work, for granting me permission to quote from his letters to Knight; Steve and Francy Stoller, who graciously answered my questions about the Knight they knew; Fran Quinn, who contacted me, educated me about the Knight he knew, and sent me a copy of the *Worcester Review* Knight issue that he midwifed; Sonia Sanchez, who permitted me to quote from a letter she wrote to Knight; Rodger Martin, who allowed me to quote remarks he made about Knight during a phone conversation; Sally Childs-Helton of Butler University's Irwin Library, who gave me access to the materials I needed from the Knight archive at Irwin, educated me on copyright law, and generally talked me through the process of obtaining permission to quote from Knight's writings; Barbara Floyd, who helped me get the materials I needed from the Knight archive at the University of Toledo in Ohio, and who told me how to get in touch with Mary McAnally; Professor Nancy Bunge, who allowed me to quote from published and unpublished portions of an interview she did with Knight; the Institute for the Medical

Humanities at the University of Texas Medical Branch (IMH-UTMB), which awarded me a position as a visiting scholar for the summer of 2010 and arranged for me to present a portion of this book's second chapter to the institute's faculty and students; IMH-UTMB's Dr. William Winslade and Dr. Howard Brody, for the hospitality they showed me while I was there; Texas A&M University's Dr. Karan Watson, who when she was dean of faculties provided seed money for the research that led eventually to this book; Dr. Paul Parish, who while he was head of Texas A&M's Department of English made me aware of the funding that allowed me to make my first trip to Knight archives in Indianapolis; the editors and anonymous readers of *PMLA*, where the essay that is the basis of this book was published in 2008; Erich Wirth, the *PMLA* assistant managing editor, who suggested the device of using double slash marks to indicate Knight line breaks and avoid confusion with his intralinear slash marks; the *Worcester Review* and *Painted Bride Quarterly*, for allowing me to quote from uncollected Knight poems that originally appeared in their pages; Margie K. Bachman of the University of Pittsburgh Press, for allowing me to quote from Knight poems published by the press; Dr. Gloria Aneb House, vice president, Broadside Press, and Aurora Harris, secretary, Broadside Press, for their response to my request to excerpt poems from Knight's Broadside books; and Gabriel Hillel Kaimowitz, who has explained his view of *Kaimowitz v. the Department of Mental Health of the State of Michigan* in a series of e-mails that will be the basis of a future project. Last but not least, I thank Beverly, Raymond, and Camille Collins, my mother, father, and sister, respectively, who bore with me while I worked on this book and related projects.

CHAPTER 1

Introduction
Knight's Resurrections

Etheridge Knight is a mighty American poet who is relatively little known. He and Wallace Stevens stand as "two poles of American poetry," according to his better-known fellow writer Robert Bly.[1] Knight is no doubt a south pole to Stevens's ice cream emperor's north. Or, rather, Knight was, as he often said, a poet of the belly: a poet of the earth and of the body, a poet of the gut feelings from which cries and blood oaths and arias come, while Stevens was a poet, arguably, of the ache left in the intellect after it tears itself from God. "Ideas are not the source of poetry," Knight told one interviewer. "For me it's passion and feeling. Then the intellect comes into play. It starts in the belly and then [moves] into the head."[2] For Bly, Knight's work awakens the mind's "truth receiver," bringing us out of the "ordinary trance, in which we are inured to lies."[3]

The poem that awakens its reader or auditor, of course, can come as a shock. Fran Quinn, the poet and friend whom Knight made his literary executor, recalled that he had been warned before they met that Knight was a junkie con man to be avoided at all costs. But after hearing Knight perform a poem, Quinn decided, "I don't care if he is Beelzebub himself—I've got to get to know this guy."[4] Of *his* first encounter with a Knight "drunk but ready to poet" in a Philadelphia bookstore, Lamont B. Steptoe (a poet who credits Knight with a portion of his initiation into the art), wrote that he was shocked to come face to face with a "God of thunder."[5] Yusef Komunyakaa, the poet, playwright, and Pulitzer Prize winner, believed Knight was a Lazarus full of biting irony with "the tongue of a two-headed man . . . urban and rural in the same breath."[6] Haki R. Madhubuti, an early mentor of Knight and a poet, summed up the contradiction between Knight's truth-telling lyrics and his much more ambiguous life by arguing that Knight was "a genius with no place to go, a Black walking book full of unmade poems in an America that said 'no' so often that he felt it was part of his name."[7]

Though comparatively small—and very much smaller than that book of unmade poems—Knight's corpus touched upon a wide range of subjects, from childbirth to drug overdoses to war to, yes, the belly, locus of "the only universality" Knight thought real: "the universality of feelings."[8] But it is Knight's portrayal of what might be called the culture of incarceration (often referred to as the prison-industrial complex) that makes his writing alarmingly relevant in the twenty-first century.

Few other American writers have so carefully outlined the ways in which America's get-tough-on-crime "prison-industrial complex" becomes a debilitating *psychological* complex worthy of Jung—both for the inmate and for the society that imprisons him. It is for this reason, as well as for reasons of raw two-tongued literary merit, that Knight's best work deserves to be read by all those affected by the culture of incarceration: those who are incarcerated, and those who do or who applaud the incarcerating.

Knight's most obsessive theme, however, is not incarceration but the all-American one of freedom. To achieve it for himself and his community, he aimed to create a revolution in American thought, warped as it is by conceptual survivals from the age of slavery. He believed, in fact, that "the American revolution is still going on"—in language: "We [have] the widest language to communicate with and express ourselves in that exists on this planet—connotatively, the intonations, the inflections, the nuances."[9] Knight wanted to guide the revolution in language like a missile that would break American thought open and release the creativity he heard trapped within it. If not a Whitmanian barbaric yawp, he wished to create an Etheridgean noise: in his poem "Things Awfully Quiet in America (Song of the Mwalimu Nkosi Ajanaku)," he explains that it is "Much too quiet in America. . . . In America 'Revolution' is never heard. . . . Empty bellies ache at night in America. . . . There's a war going on in America, // And we're killing our sons in America, // In many, many prisons in America. . . . Need to 'Raise a Ruckus Tonight' in America. . . . We/gonna set things right in America."[10] Knight is writing here of a revolution in correctional culture. He wants to raise a "Ruckus" that will shout down the culture's quiet, half-conscious endorsements of the killing of "our sons . . . [i]n the many, many prisons in America," a ruckus in which the oldest equation—"Power equals Law equals Right as defined by whoever has got the guns"[11]—no longer holds.

Knight's Life

Etheridge Knight was born April 19, 1931, in Corinth, Mississippi, to Belzora Cozart Knight and Etheridge "Bushie" Knight, who were parents of five other children. According to the journalist Gladys Keys Price, the father "followed jobs from city to city, uproot[ing] and re-locat[ing] his family whenever a situation looked particularly promising. In this manner, Etheridge, having started in Mississippi, moved to Kentucky and on to Indianapolis, from poverty to poverty."[12] But Eunice Knight-Bowens, one of Knight's younger sisters, disputed this characterization, suggesting that her brother may have been telling Price what she wanted to hear. Etheridge Knight told Price and, later, the *Memphis Commercial Appeal,* that his father worked construction and moved to Paducah to labor on the building of the Kentucky Dam. But Knight-Bowens remembers her father as a railroad worker who followed the rails to Paducah, where she was born, and then to Indianapolis.

She does recall though, "My mother actually said she didn't know anything about being poor until she married my father," whose family was poor. Belzora Knight's relatives, on the other hand, had land "as far as the eye could see," the "land where Etheridge was born," and they were founders of the community of Wenasoga north of Corinth in Alcorn County, Mississippi. They were "very well educated and . . . were fine artists" and musicians. Knight's mother herself was a poet and songwriter.[13] Still, after her parents' marriage, Knight-Bowens concedes, "I think . . . people would have classified us as poor, especially by today's standards. But I don't remember it like that. . . . If I needed clothes, mama could sew clothes. I was never hungry. . . . Now we knew we were not as well off as others. . . . But it wasn't a thing like being homeless and raggedy."

Relative poverty, or at least diminishment of economic status, then, came into Knight's mother's life with the marriage. Perhaps chafing under this perceived diminishment as communicated by his mother, and certainly chafing at the status injuries African Americans suffered during the era of segregation, Knight repeatedly ran away from home. As he told one interviewer, "My old man didn't talk much. He was physical. We'd get into it and I'd say, 'You think I'm going to stay here and grow up like you?' Then I'd take off [for a while]."[14] He nevertheless maintained an A average in school and was valedictorian of his junior high school class, according to Price. But in the ninth grade he decided school was "irrelevant" and dropped out.

Outside of school he had already entered the workforce as a shoeshine boy: "My first job was in a small town in Kentucky," he told Nancy Bunge in 1986, in the course of an explanation of how he came by his sensitivity to language. "You can imagine a little black boy down on Market Street, down near the river, down where these farmers and townspeople buy their groceries and there [were] taverns and juke joints and when you're a black boy growing up in the south where violence is always. . . . You pay attention because you can get kicked in the ass. You listen to every nuance. . . . 'Shoeshine, mister?' 'NO!' You have to watch out for some who are a little perverted; they want to play with you and you have to pick that up quickly. You can have your head down shining shoes and you'll still be listening to how he's talking to you. . . . A little black boy out there . . . he's vulnerable."[15]

Vulnerability and devotion to listening probably catalyzed another powerful though problematic aspect of Knight's creativity. He became "a lot like a chameleon," Knight-Bowens recalled. "Depending on what environment he was in, what social setting he was in," he could reconfigure himself and hold his own in anything from a conversation with "men sitting in the corner by a liquor store drinking shooting dope" to, if the opportunity had come, an exchange with Barack Obama. "Whatever that environment is at that time, that's what he could do. . . . He was the type of person that could immediately assess his environment, and any situation, and adjust himself accordingly."[16] Komunyakaa speculated that the snake-tongue doubleness and swiftness of Knight's lines may have "evolved from the necessity of switching codes in . . . [segregated] Mississippi, [from] having honed his ability to talk to whites and blacks simultaneously."[17]

Knight entered the army in 1947 and scored so high on intelligence tests that "authorities at Fort Knox questioned his integrity and reexamined him but failed in their search for . . . dishonesty."[18] After leaving and then reenlisting, he was sent as a medical technician to the Korean War, where he sustained a tremendous "psyche/wound"[19] "There was a whole lot of dying and blood," he told the *Rocky Mountain News*. "No 17-year-old is ready for that. So I started using morphine. I started using drugs because it killed the pain."[20]

It has been suggested that Knight may have been an addict prior to joining the military, and the poet himself once said that, in his youth, the mentor who introduced him to his first art form—the "toast"—was "a wino named Hound Mouth" whom Knight and his friends paid in alcoholic drinks and listened to "in the park [while] smoking grass."[21] On the other hand, there is no hint of "hard drug" use, and Komunyakaa, a Vietnam War veteran, has argued that if Knight "had an addiction before, I don't see how he would have gotten into the military."[22]

The fragments of Knight's military records that survived a 1973 fire at the installation where they were housed indicate that he served in the army from February 23, 1950, until November 17, 1950, after serving previously from

June 24, 1947, to June 7, 1949. He was honorably discharged each time. The legible portion of one burned document indicates that his separation from the military was due to "Disability" and that he had been hospitalized. Other documents report that his character and efficiency rating while in the military were both "Excellent," and that in both 1948 and 1950 he was favorably considered for a good conduct medal. The remains of the report on a physical and psychological evaluation of Knight indicate, among other things, no "personality deviation." However, documents or portions of documents that would have provided definitive details of his service in Korea were destroyed in the fire.

Nevertheless, by the time he left the army, Knight was hooked on opiates. He became an artful forger of prescriptions—"scripts"—for himself and other users, and became a "usual suspect" for the police whom, according to his sister, he often outwitted. "I remember times when we were kids," Knight-Bowens recalled, ". . . the police would come to the door, looking for Junior [Etheridge Knight]. And my mother would say, 'what do you mean, you're looking for him? He's downtown in jail. . . . And so, they'd be looking for Junior. Because someone [had] done something similar to what Junior would do. . . . A lot of times I think Junior would be in jail telling people what to do on the outside. . . . So it would be sounding like something Junior did. So that means they didn't have sense to see that they already had him locked up."[23]

When police both had Knight in custody and *remembered* that they did, his sister suggested, "they didn't have any problems beating him up. . . . Downtown in the jailhouse [where prisoners were held while awaiting trial], they didn't have any problems beating Junior up." This may be one of the reasons why Knight's mature face was "rough and scarred."[24]

One of Knight's encounters with police for which a record exists began in June 1958, when a police officer observed the future poet leaping from a second-story window of the Indianapolis General Hospital with what turned out to be a bottle of medicine infused with cocaine on his person. When he eventually pled guilty, Knight told the judge he had "been arrested about 10 times for larceny and narcotics." He was given a one- to ten-year suspended sentence along with fines, liability for court costs, and a warning of stronger consequences if he failed henceforth to leave all laws he touched intact. Knight was not so lucky when, on December 6, 1960, he and two associates "unlawfully, feloniously, forcibly by violence" put one Lillian Robertson "in fear" in order to rob her of what turned out to be ten dollars.

After his arrest for this crime, Knight, according to his prison associate and fellow writer Art Powers, "lay in jail for more than a year angling for a short sentence, but the police, the judge, the newspapers, and the public were insistent that only by meting out the full measure of 'justice'—a ten- to twenty-five-year term—could the best interests of society be served."25 Knight-Bowens also recalls a political element in Knight's sentence: "His attorney—I think his name was Owen Mullins . . . I think he was running . . . for some kind of office. And I think Junior actually got hung up in the politics."26

After his December 1960 sentencing, Knight "didn't have much going for him," according to Powers. "His work record was spotty; he had a limited education; and his outlook on life was blackened by his sense of injustice. He was assigned to menial jobs and was in and out of the hole [solitary confinement] for refusing to work. His friends called him a 'low rider,' a real son-ofabitch. . . . It wasn't long before officials transferred him from State Reformatory to the prison as an incorrigible. . . . He told me time and time again that he had almost no recollection of his first few months in the reformatory, he was so angry."27

After going through the stages of grief for his lost freedom, Knight began to reorient himself, like Dante and Virgil on the body of Satan: "He read books like they were going out of style," Powers wrote, "and applied himself in many areas—philosophy, art, science, and religion. In five years he covered a wide field, and he found a bit of Etheridge Knight in all of them. He found a sense of worth. . . . In his discovery he became an articulate spokesman for the prison Negro population. . . . He became the Negro voice for 'telling it like it is.'"28

Knight emerged as a letter writer for other inmates, who lined up for his services, and as a journalist for prison publications, such as the one where he met and worked with Powers. He began submitting work outside the prison and, starting in 1965, published a flurry of poetry and fiction in Negro Digest. "I watched him furtively, many times," Powers noted, "a gaunt hulk of a man with hamhock hands and stubby fingers, hunched over his typewriter digging at the keys in utter consternation, and I thought, 'If that bastard is creating something, I'll eat my hat.'"29 Yet when Knight granted Powers's requests to see what he had written, Powers always found "a thing of perfection" in his hands.

Knight also left people beyond the prison walls marveling. In August 1966, Negro Digest editor Hoyt W. Fuller took the unusual step of running, in the same issue in which Knight's short story "The Next Train South" appeared, a short profile announcing that "Mr. Knight has justified the editors' faith in him" by not letting publication go to his head and continuing "to learn, to read, to analyze, to question" (94). The renowned African American poet Gwendolyn Brooks either contacted Knight or was contacted by him (there are different versions of the story). In any case she visited him in prison (through on her first attempts the place was locked down, according to Knight-Bowens). Brooks immediately recognized his "genius," as she called it in one letter, and began guiding that genius with acute critiques. Another early fan was Dudley Randall, the poet who founded Broadside Press, which published Knight's first two books of poetry. Randall became perhaps Knight's most constant mentor, corresponding with him, twice visiting him in prison, and advising him on phrasing. In this way Knight, who said he died in Korea but was resurrected by narcotics and died again in prison, only to be revived by poetry, stayed alive.

Brooks, Fuller, and Randall, of course, were far from alone in recognizing his talent. The poet Sonia Sanchez, who married Knight shortly after he was paroled, told him in one 1968 letter, "take care of yr/self—u must survive to tell the world abt itself."[30] His writing was otherwise affirmed from across the seas, when on June 8, 1967, a letter was posted to him by Roberto Giammanco, a self-styled "non-white white" person who had translated *The Autobiography of Malcolm X* into Italian and used lines from Knight's poem "It Was a Funky Deal" as an epigraph to his preface. Knight was a voice of "the wretched of the earth" and a major talent, Giammanco declared.

In a September 1967 letter, Giammanco described a trap Knight had probably already stumbled upon—and that Knight later painted powerfully in his poem "The Point of the Western Pen"—but which Giammanco feared Knight's work showed signs of falling prey to: the trap of "Bourgeois age" ideas about "legitimate" art. Such art, Giammanco cautioned, assumed

a society in which the private individual is the master of his own destiny and comes to grips with the society by his own efforts. He expresses his own experience of this process as a reflection of his self, his ego. The great art and poetry of the Bourgeois age rests upon this assumption. In other words, the aesthetic dimension had to be separated from all the others, in order that undesirable conclusions might be avoided. Thus the poet was restricted to the beautiful (himself and what he saw), his task was to edify the listener, to make him see the . . . beauty . . . of the world. This conception of beauty was financed by the slave trade, the sale of opium to colonies, the extermination of the Indian, etc, etc, etc. The society does not kill its poets. It kills the ones who do not accept its assumptions. It defines the poet as one who accepts its assumptions in a certain way. If you don't accept the society, how can you accept the forms it sanctions? To adopt the traditional poetic forms means to accept the slave trade, the drug traffic, the treatment of the black man in "your" country. . . . What is needed is a new kind of "poetry" which represents the complete rejection of the whole system. The simple narratives of the 'inarticulate cats' that Knight had collected and sent to Giammanco for inclusion in what became Knight's edited volume, *Black Voices from Prison*] express this rejection as the logical conclusion of their experience of life in a society which does not allow them to live. (After all, who are the criminals . . . ?)[31]

Giammanco went so far as to send Knight books by Jean Genet, counseling Knight to avoid following Genet into the trap of "sickness disguised as art, masturbation disguised as creativity, narcissism that creates an alibi to the worst horrors," and, above all, the "literary glorification of crime" that "makes crime universal . . . and thus deprives man of the possibility of understanding crime's social roots." *Black Voices from Prison*—a collection of writings by Knight and other inmates with a preface by Knight and an introduction by Giammanco—emerged directly out of their correspondence. But Knight continued to deploy—and to insist that his students deploy[32] traditional forms and other elements of "legitimate" aesthetics. One of his favorite forms throughout his career was the haiku, adopted from Japan by "bourgeois" westerners.

Indeed, after he was paroled, Knight was befriended and aided in his career by such masters of "legitimate" aesthetics and stars of the white poetry world as Donald Hall, Galway Kinnell, and Robert Bly. After hearing Kinnell read from Knight's work in 1969, Hall immediately invited Knight to the University of Michigan for what may have been his first official poetry reading.[33] (Earlier, while Knight was still in prison, Randall taped him reading works Randall was publishing. Randall thus captured the sound of Knight's resurrection in a penitentiary room usually "reserved for consultation with death row inmates.")[34]

In 1976, Quinn says, he and Knight met when both were invited to Bly's second "Great Mother Conference"—an event inspired in part by Erich Neumann's 1955 book *The Great Mother* and by Bly's concern with finding a way to nurture and ease the readjustment of soldiers returning from the Vietnam War. After Quinn's "even if he is Beelzebub himself" moment, Knight and Quinn became close, and through Quinn, Knight met two of the loves of his life—Charlene Blackburn, the mother of his only biological child, and Elizabeth McKim, in whose arms he died. ("At 11:00 A.M. on March 10, 1991," McKim has written, "he went to the *faraway country*, which was how he referred to his death. It gave us a way to talk about it. '*Now lady, what's gonna happen to you after I go to the faraway country?*' . . . My arms circled him from behind, and my hand was on his heart. I felt his breathing go shallow. I felt him leave.")[35]

Knight's major relationship between those with Blackburn and McKim was with the activist and writer Mary McAnally, whom he married on June 11, 1974. In 1972, in anticipation of their marriage, McAnally adopted two children—Mary Tandiwie and Etheridge Bambata. She did so "as a single woman because Etheridge and I weren't yet legally married . . . and because I knew the adoption agency would never approve Etheridge with his prison record."[36] The relationship with McAnally, and with the children, was hounded, before and after the marriage vows, by Knight's addictions.

In 1971 he was arrested for drug possession soon after absconding with McAnally's car. He was thrown into the Bridgeport, Connecticut, jail, and slapped with a five-year sentence suspended on condition that he enter a rehabilitation facility. McAnally wrote in her family chronology that in August 1972 she was "busted for possession; EK had stashed reefer in her luggage."[37] In a 1973 letter to Dudley Randall, Knight reported being fired from a job at Lincoln University because "some of the old guard faculty and staff . . . conspired to 'run me out of town' and they succeeded because I gave them plenty good reason, by acting like a drunken, damn fool poet."[38] In April 1974 Knight won a twelve-thousand-dollar Guggenheim Fellowship, bought a new car, and soon was "strung out on dope again," according to McAnally. Between 1975 and 1977, McAnally and Knight lived separately. Knight was "on methadone maintenance but regularly shooting dope, drinking, being arrested, car wrecks, fights, hospitalizations during this whole period, as [was] also . . . the history [previously]," McNally wrote in her chronology.[39]

Beyond the addiction-related disasters, the Knight-McAnally marriage was likely strained by differences in their experience of the era's racial dogmas. In 1968 McAnally had been ejected from apartheid South Africa, where she had gone to research her Columbia University doctoral dissertation on what the apartheid government called "Bantu Education." She was thrown out, she asserts, because she openly defied the system. She not only delivered "money from the World Council of Churches to the South African Council of Churches . . . for . . . defense and aid of political prisoners such as Nelson Mandela" but also led founding workshops for a new University Christian Movement—"later banned as an antiapartheid and multiracial group"[40]— that elected the now-legendary antiapartheid leader Steve Biko as its first president. (Biko later traveled to the United States to raise money for the group at McAnally's invitation.)[41]

This is not the whole of McAnally's activism. On the way to South Africa, she befriended Amilcar Cabral and other fighters for the decolonialization of Guinea-Bissau. When Cabral traveled to Lincoln University to accept an honorary doctorate in 1971, she was asked to find bodyguards for him, and she recruited Knight among others.[42] Gil Fernandez, who represented first Cabral's rebels and then the liberated Guinea-Bissau at the United Nations, is the godfather of McAnally's and Knight's adopted children.[43]

Yet, in a 1982 letter to her, Knight refused to yield McAnally an iota of authority on the subject of black liberation: "You 'Africanists' have never forgiven Black Americans for telling y'all to go / fuck / off for telling y'all that you were not authorities. . . . Like so many liberal intellectuals, I think you've always resented and probably envied the fact that I was publishing and people were listening to this 'unlettered' convict, junkie, thief, liar, 'womanizer' black male, while you, white, 'educated,' female, godsent, honest, kind . . . went unheard and unseen." Lest his own sins be used to refute his argument, Knight added assertions that could serve as his motto: "Freedom is an inalienable right, unattached [to] anybody's or group's moral concepts. . . . Even an idiot slobbering with a syphilitic brain has the right to / be/ free."[44] All this suggests that Knight struggled to assert his vision of things at all costs, and that, for him, even a freely chosen mutuality could congeal into something like a prison.

After the final collapse of the McAnally relationship in the late 1970s, Knight was "periodically hospitalized in Memphis, St. Paul, Indianapolis for recurring acute pancreatitis, alcoholism and related problems," according to the chronology. Between 1977 and 1982, he underwent "temporary drying-out spells" but was "back on booze and dope" as soon as he was released from hospitals. Yet in the same period, Knight pressed forward artistically, and had "common law marriages," McAnally wrote, "to Charlene Blackburn, Evelyn Brown, Elizabeth McKim, etc."

Lost in the maze of his own contradictions, Knight remained "a good man struggling with addiction" who "always kept his humor and good nature," according to *Worcester Review* managing editor Rodger Martin.[45] In a 2011 letter McAnally herself concluded that "Etheridge was a mixed bag of treasures . . . and talents. A deeply-compassionate man, prone to violence when on alcohol, but amazingly creative when free of drugs. A man of the old school with a few new age inklings."[46]

The relationship with Charlene Blackburn—a onetime Fran Quinn student with whom Knight became involved in Massachusetts and whom Knight refers to as his third wife in one publication—was the next to leave a substantial mark on Knight's poetry. When Knight announced his intention to return to the South—to Memphis—in 1977, Blackburn decided to go along and bring her son from a previous relationship. "You are giving up your entire life and putting him in charge and he *can't* be in charge," Quinn told her.[47] As Quinn explained in 1998, "you had to protect yourself when [Etheridge] was using. . . . If you moved in too close and didn't keep your guard up, you could lose a lot including his friendship (because you could [not] afford to keep it). If you distanced yourself too much, you would miss the talent and the understanding that Etheridge had not only of the world he lived in, but of . . . language and poetry."[48]

In 1978, while they were in Memphis, Blackburn gave birth to the poet's only biological child, Isaac Bushie Blackburn-Knight. (Knight chronicles Blackburn's labor in the triumphant poem "On the Birth of a Black / Baby / Boy.") Nevertheless, Quinn's prophecy proved accurate: Knight's addiction seized him, and, a few months after she gave birth, Blackburn left Memphis broke and by bus. (After being put up by Quinn [along with her children] for two weeks, the resourceful Blackburn landed both a job and an apartment.)

Clearly Knight was a man fraying like a ripped sweater—and often leaving those closest to him in the cold. Yet when he seized control of himself, he was enormously giving, according to Quinn, and could have a positive, transforming effect on other people's lives. Ellen Slack, a folklorist and poet who drove Knight on a 1979 trip to Corinth, Mississippi, in search of his centenarian relative Pink Knight, recalled that in "one sense I was doing him a favor by driving and taking the pictures, but that afternoon gave me back far more than I ever put into it. Etheridge is seldom *not* teaching. . . . Central to the course of study is learning to survive in this world without being crippled or ground to a pulp by it."[49]

Slack (who snapped the photographs that appear on the front and back covers of Knight's 1980 collection *Born of a Woman*) offers a glimpse of a Knight in full self-command that, in the context of his collapses, is quite poignant: "The last time I saw Etheridge, a year or so ago, he seemed . . . more accepting, less contentious, drinking only water. I began to think that the man might actually make it to old age. I had always thought that the thing most likely to kill him would be his belief that nothing could kill him."[50]

Another Fran Quinn friend, Elizabeth Gordon McKim—the companion about whom Knight wrote that if she stopped loving him, "My heart would quiver, and break, // Like a Florida oak in a hurricane"[51]—has written that the Free People's Poetry Workshops, which Knight founded and called into being around him in various cities, taught "many young poets . . . to . . . trust their voices. . . . Ask the poets in Memphis or Minneapolis or Toledo or Worcester or Philly. Or Indianapolis during the last year and a half before he passed."[52]

Stephen Stoller, primarily a visual artist, captured a Free People's Poetry Workshop in a painting that is reproduced in *Freedom and Fame,* a chapbook he and Knight coauthored. Stoller wrote in the chapbook that his hand had "ached to paint" Knight, so great was the poet's work and vision and will, and so great was his impact on audiences.

A case in point is Knight's effect on two people drinking in a bar where a workshop was held. The two, who Stoller says were mute and probably deaf, were "blown away" by Knight's performance of his poem "The Sun Came." When he finished, "they were exuding sounds to each other [that] were just brilliant."[53] Stoller was inspired to write in their chapbook, "He makes the mute speak, the deaf hear and the blind see."[54] To this day Stoller asserts, "I have never known any poet with this type of strength of being, this type of art." Stoller recalls that while they were preparing *Freedom and Fame* as a companion to a show of Stoller's work and readings by Knight, Knight learned that he "was dying . . . of cancer. And I was ready to give up. . . . [But] no matter how difficult things got, [Knight's] grip just became more solid. I have never seen that type of tenacity in my life. And so, added to his work as a poet, [is] his work as a man and as a man of urgency."[55]

A major feature of the Free People's Poetry Workshops was Knight's insistence that participants—including those he taught in prisons—commit themselves to nonviolence, for at least the periods they devoted to writing. In this way, Knight believed, each time he "got 10 or 12 guys or women committed to nonviolence even after they leave the [Workshop]."[56]

Stoller's wife, the poet Francy Stoller, wrote in 2011 that her aesthetic was altered by participation in the workshops. She recalled how Knight, who insisted that workshop members "write what presses on you," confronted her, demanding to know, "was I a valid woman. Did my acting career mess me up [since] memorizing has nothing to [do] with saying a poem from the heart?" He insisted that she "go deep beneath the clear lake in the belly—beneath the demons—fight—squeeze the ball—worry—fret—fight to do your work." Stoller "dedicated [herself] to the Oral Tradition" Knight championed.[57]

Wherever he was on his roller coaster journeys from "only water" to heroin or hard liquor, from Free People's Poetry Workshops to the New York homeless shelter he lived in for a time in 1989, Knight kept sending poems up like flares that illuminated his deepest self, the turmoil of the world around him, and areas of the human spirit that his fellow poets peered over his shoulders to see. As a result, a decade after the 1974 Guggenheim, he was awarded the Shelley Memorial Award, "given to a living American poet selected with reference to genius and need." In 1980 he was awarded the second of two

National Endowment of the Arts Fellowships. (The first was awarded in 1972.)[58] In 1987, seven years after the appearance of his third volume, *Born of a Woman*, he won the American Book Award for his last collection, *The Essential Etheridge Knight*. During these years, Knight earned a living by "poeting," as he put it—giving readings, holding workshops, and intermittently securing poet-in-residence positions at places like the University of Pittsburgh (1968–69), Connecticut's University of Hartford (1969–70), and Missouri's Lincoln University (1972). Knight also worked (from 1969 to 1970) as an editor for *Motive* magazine (whose editor introduced him to Mary McAnally) and as a contributing editor for *New Letters* in 1974.[59]

Knight appeared to close the distance between himself and stability in 1989, when income from royalties and the sale of his papers to the University of Toledo gave him a substantial cushion of savings, a position at Boston's Roxbury Community College gave him employment, and Elizabeth McKim, at his side, gave him love. From that height, Knight fell into a whirlpool of heroin and alcohol use that sucked away twenty thousand dollars in three months. When he turned to forging McKim's signature on her checks, she ordered him out of her household.

One possible impetus for this downward spiral was a November 1988 accident in which Knight was struck by a hit-and-run driver. The accident broke Knight's previously indestructible health, according to Quinn. It left him immobilized at a time when he was trying to write a manuscript called *Running with the Wild Ones*. Suffering through two skin grafts and barely able to use his writing hand in the Indianapolis VA hospital where he was finally moved, he was, in effect, in prison again and feeling "angry, violated," according to journalist Dan Carpenter.[60] His frustrations were probably deepened by a lawsuit he filed in relation to the accident that seems to have gone nowhere. Nevertheless, he warned "those who see me as a tragic figure" that "there is glee in my teeth, and mirth in my mouth."[61]

Following the temporary break with McKim in 1989, a flare-up of phlebitis sent Knight once again to a Veterans Hospital. After his release, he ended up homeless, "strung out and broke," and resided for a time in New York City's Fort Washington Men's Shelter.[62] According to Knight-Bowens, their mother later asked the poet, "Why didn't you call? We could have sent you a ticket to come home." But, Knight-Bowens reflected, it may have been that "whatever he was doing he was so into that—he knew he couldn't do it once he came home. Because . . . Mama just didn't allow it."

While at the homeless shelter, he joined a group of shelter residents who accepted an invitation to read poetry at New York's Society for Ethical

Culture. At the event an organizer took a look at him and, fearing he might be "incoherent," demanded to see a sample of his work before he read it; she was "embarrassed" when she registered its brilliance.[63]

Back in Indianapolis at the end of the 1980s, Knight began another upward swing after forming a close bond with Stephen and Francy Stoller. "Always teaching," Knight passed on lessons from his own life. He told the couple "how important it was to him that we maintain our lives as artists" but also keep "our family intact," Stoller says. (At this time, Knight's children "had sort of fallen away," Stephen Stoller recalls. "And it hurt him terribly.") The Stollers were raising six children and were struggling financially, but they and Knight found in each other "a recipe for continuing on," in Stoller's words: "We gave him faith that he could tie his life back together and he gave us the faith that we could keep marching on." This is indeed what happened for one final time in Knight's life: McKim reunited with him. "Etheridge started having more readings," and the art gallery the Stollers ran became "a hot spot—a center for not only art but poetry," according to Stoller. Sleepy Indianapolis "got turned on" artistically, and the gallery was "one of the main circuits of that activity."[64]

Near the end of his life, Knight taught and took courses at Indianapolis's Martin Center College. The college awarded him both a bachelor of arts degree and its inaugural poet laureateship in 1990, when, aged fifty-nine, Knight was fighting lung cancer, albeit continuing to smoke while doing so.[65] In this final period, Knight arranged for a portion of his papers to be sold after his death (by Fran Quinn) as a way of raising money for his children. "This was what he was hoping to be able to leave them," Quinn says. "He knew he had been a bad father."[66]

This is how Quinn ended up closing a parenthesis that was opened on October 2, 1975, when Ezra Pound–specialist Noel Stock wrote to ask Knight if he was interested in selling his "literary papers (letters, manuscripts, proofs, etc.)" to the University of Toledo. Knight was astonished by Stock's offer, and though he was desperate for money, he felt the need to pause and ask Hoyt Fuller and Dudley Randall what he should do.

On the one hand, the offer was a "real ego/trip" and a financial godsend, Knight wrote Randall. But, he added, "I don't wanna be like Charlie Parker, and thousands of other/artists who had to sell their art and their blood for a few pennies; I'm also considering what it means in terms of black art and our people. In other words, I'd hate for my 'papers' to/be bought by a school that was essentially John Birch (assuming that there are some white schools that are/not)."[67] Randall represented Knight in the subsequent negotiations.

After Knight's death, Quinn had the papers that had accumulated since the Toledo deal appraised and was told they were worth thirteen thousand dollars. Since Toledo had the right of first refusal, Quinn turned to them first in his search for a purchaser—although he was hoping to keep the documents in Indianapolis in an attempt to fight the city's habit of "obliterating its history." Because Knight had "scammed" the Canaday Center, according to Quinn, by sometimes sending and accepting payment for boxes that, when finally unpacked, turned out to contain nothing but "newspapers and telephone bills" and the like, and since the then-head of the Canaday Center was not only apoplectic with anger about this but also of the belief that he already had the cream of the crop of Knight's papers, Toledo declined to buy the new material.[68] Quinn turned happily away, and eventually sold the papers to Butler University (where he had a position at the time) for fourteen thousand dollars.

This little drama raises a question: was Knight's decision to "scam" the Canaday Center part of a lingering distrust or resentment of a white institution? There is, of course, now no way of knowing; but Knight *did* tell the scholar Nancy Bunge that an oppressed person must subordinate all else to the struggle for freedom: "I question," Knight said, "that the slave who follows all the rules is being responsible."[69] He spells this out even more clearly in a 1968 letter, where he writes that a society built on laws that treat people like himself as "not quite" men is a society where "obedience to the spirit of the law would be to follow the path of non-existence," and "all men resist such a death, each according to his own light."[70]

Whatever the truth behind Knight's scam artistry, the whole Toledo-Knight saga underscores the literary politics of the late 1960s and early 1970s—and underscores the glacially shifting balance of star-making power that, despite a Black Arts movement whose fruits include the Broadside Press and its dedication to publishing black authors, remained in white hands, hands that, for Black Arts founders like Amiri Baraka (formerly LeRoi Jones), by definition could not be trusted. That Baraka had a point is clear from Hoyt Fuller's demonstration, in the January 1968 *Negro Digest*, that those in charge of the prestigious *American Literary Anthology* relied on editors who had no idea "that the white angle of vision is not the only valid perspective on the world." Fuller's exhibit A is the observation by one of those editors, Louis Simpson, that it might not be "possible for a Negro to write well without making us aware he is a Negro," and yet, "if being a Negro is the only subject, the writing is not important."[71]

The Toledo-Knight exchange, alleged scams and all, has to been seen against the backdrop of the remarks by Simpson and others like him. But it is also consistent with the chameleon-like element Knight's sister saw in his character and with the seismic intellectual changes that were part of his emergence as a major writer. The arguments and debates published in the pages of *Negro Digest* were among the drivers of these intellectual changes and chameleon-like shifts.

In the same July 1965 issue in which one of Knight's early works appeared, for instance, the editors published Jean-Paul Sartre's preface to Frantz Fanon's *The Wretched of the Earth*. This may be why some Knight writings bear Sartre's mark. Yet at the same time, issues of *Negro Digest* from the later 1960s increasingly featured proponents of the Black Arts movement, some of whom condemned white influences and black-white collaboration. In his untitled response to a 1968 *Negro Digest* questionnaire, Knight himself asserted that unless "the Black Artist establishes a 'black aesthetic' he will have no future at all," and, further, "the Black Artist who directs his work toward a white audience is guilty of aiding and abetting the enemy."[72] Such assertions make perfect sense in the Louis Simpson context, but not necessarily in the Sartre context. They especially do not make sense in light of the fact that, elsewhere in his response, Knight lifts, word for word, passages from the September 29, 1967 letter from Giammanco quoted earlier in this introduction.

This particular bit of scamming is especially complex psychologically, but the *Negro Digest* editors are among those who are being played. Knight's choice of venue for the co-option of a nonwhite white person's pro-black text suggests that he was either so impressed by Giammanco's argument that he believed he could not improve upon it or so deeply ambivalent about the Black Aesthetic in its most uncompromising forms that he felt he could not fully subscribe to it. After all, the intensity of the Black Aesthetic movement was such that Knight was nervous at times about his debt to Sartre.

One sees the chameleon between colors in the mid-1970s. In an interview Knight gave to the editor of *Callaloo,* a journal of black diaspora arts and letters, Knight spoke regretfully of having begun writing under the aegis of "European definitions" of art[73] and only subsequently having begun to understand "what black art—really all art—is about." When he referenced Sartre, Knight immediately added a qualifier: "I always use him, because people accept him as an authority." In a 1982 *Callaloo* interview, Knight again cited "Sartre—or whatever his name is."[74]

Yet whatever protective coloring his phrases take on, whatever double game he felt he had to play, Knight retained certain core concerns. Prominent among these concerns is the thought that an artist's mind can always be trapped and imprisoned. And behind this concern is Knight's overwhelming desire not to be caught, even by himself. In a 1987 conversation among

himself, *Painted Bride Quarterly* editor Lou Camp, and Elizabeth McKim—
a conversation that took place the morning after Knight received the 1987
American Book Award—Knight stressed the importance of the "break." While,
as will be shown in a moment, his primary reference was to musical breaks,
Knight—a devotee of the resonances and multiple inflections of words—would
have been toying at some level with some of the word's overtones—*break
away, prison break, breakthrough*. Dipping into his era's African American
vernacular, Knight noted that "when you go into the break, you out there
by yourself. The more . . . you get enmeshed in the credit card thing [a secure
social position], the less chance you get to take that break—because you never
get that creative gig [that creative burst]. . . . When you go into that break
and improvise—you're depending on what's happening now. The authority
does not come from that big band back there—the authority comes from
you."75

The break as musical miracle making, as breakaway and as breakthrough:
that is what Knight sought in his poetry, in his life, and even in his sometimes
apparently self-destructive activities. Knight was, to borrow Cornel West's
autobiographical words, "very much a brother on the run." He was on the
run most of all from the feeling of being in a concentric set of prisons designed
to keep black males like himself away from a proper set of opportunities—
away, precisely, from breaks. There may have been some paranoia in his
assessment, but for an African American born in the South in 1931, there was
much hard evidence, too. Knight once summarized this paranoids-have-
enemies-too paradox in a joke about a patient who asks his psychiatrist,
"Doc, . . . when you think people are out to get you and they're not, you're
paranoid, right?" When the doctor agrees, the patient asks, "Well, what do
they call you if you think everyone is out to get you and they are?" "That,"
the doctor replies, "means you're black."76 The combination of fearing that
one is paranoid and yet having real reason to worry is in itself a source of distress that, added to many others, provoked Knight poems like 1972's "My
Life, the Quality of Which," where he declares that his life can be summed up
in "the one word: DESPERATION."

Much of Knight's commitment to achieving the breakaway, the breakthrough, the time-stretching, Charley Parker–esque musical break, can be
viewed as the positive response to "DESPERATION," itself a manifestation of a
heightened and prolonged fight-or-flight response—a response that seems to
have contributed to everything from the intensity of Knight's poems to the
persistence of his substance abuse problems to a late-life bout with phlebitis—
a condition involving blood clots and vein damage that can be brought on by
smoking, by injury due to the insertion of intravenous tubes or intravenous

drug use, and by stress, the precursor and fuel of desperation. Of African American stress, Knight himself once said, to Walter Ray Watson Jr. of the *Pittsburgh Courier Entertainer,* "People say 'it's the diet that's wrong: they eat too much salt . . . it's this or that or it's inherited.' That's b.s. In the South, poor whites eat the same diet as Blacks do. Brothers in Africa don't have high blood pressure. Nobody talks about the political or sociological factors—all of the stress in being a black man in this country."[77]

As Richard Wilkinson has argued, "In a process triggered by perceptions of danger or threat, the body is prepared for fight or flight by both the nervous system and the endocrine system. . . . The sympathetic nervous system is linked to all the major organs. . . . When activated, the system causes the release of adrenaline and noradrenaline (epinephrine and norepinephrine in US usage), which contribute to the body's arousal and activation. . . . Serious consequences for health arise when anxiety and physiological arousal are sustained or recur frequently over weeks, months or years. . . . The accumulated physiological impact of chronic stress has been called 'allostatic load.' . . . The higher the load, the greater the risks of cardiovascular disease, cancer and infection. . . . There are also processes linking current stress to . . . increased risk of infection or blood clots."[78]

The Prison-Industrial Complex

Societies also have their versions of "allostatic loads"—loads that have their origins in perceptions of threat. Knight's desperation is motivated in large part by his perception of his place in an American society he views as sometimes, or even often, "out/to/get/US," as he writes in one letter.[79] The visual pun of "US" and "U.S." suggests that American society in its anti-black, anti-outsider predatory modes is also out to get itself.

One of the instruments America uses to "get us" is what has been called the prison-industrial complex. The rise of this complex—the multiplication of its cells like the cells of some vast animal—is evident when one considers that in 1966, toward the end of Etheridge Knight's time behind bars, there were 199,654 inmates in state and federal prisons. At the beginning of 2008, 2.3 million inmates were locked in America's prisons.[80] U.S. incarceration rates had increased 600 percent since the late 1970s, and the Pew Center found that while "one in 30 men is behind bars, for black males in that age group the figure is one in nine."[81]

Those who promote the term "prison-industrial complex" have a theory about this. Angela Davis explains that the use of the term by scholars and activists "has been strategic, designed precisely to resonate with the term military-industrial-complex. . . . In fact, many young people—especially young people of color—who enlist in the military often do so in order to escape a trajectory of poverty, drugs, and illiteracy that will lead them directly to prison. . . . Imprisonment is the punitive solution to a whole range of social problems that are not being addressed."[82]

Whether or not one accepts Davis's premise in its entirety, there is no doubt that the incarceration boom of recent decades has been presented as a cure for much of what is said to ail America. A well-known case in point is the "war on drugs,"of which a June 1988 report of the White House Conference for a Drug Free America was an early volley. Drugs "threaten to destroy the United States as we know it," the report's preface declares. The report includes a diagram with "illegal drug use" lurking like a Minotaur at its center as a driver of the federal deficit, child abuse, AIDS, loss of individual freedom, diminished public safety, and impaired national defense, among other ills.[83]

Much of the reality of the next two decades is prefigured in the demands of the conference's recommendations. They include the demand that prosecutors stop viewing "drug users apprehended with small amounts of drugs . . . as [people who were not] serious criminals. . . . Prosecutors must make every attempt to bring drug user cases before the courts."[84] In 1989, the year after the report appeared, "states and the federal government spent some $5 billion on prison construction," according to Paul Scriven.[85] As important, the rhetoric of the report became part of the national media narrative and, therefore, part of the way the United States saw itself and its problems.

Admittedly this rhetoric is rooted in much genuine information. But it is also shot through with out-of-context facts fused with unexamined fears and prejudices, political dog whistles, and ratings-seeking media sound bytes that created such folk monsters as the crack baby, the welfare queen, and the crime-prone black male. The traditional term for this sort of amplified distortion is *propaganda*. But this book will use the term *spin-formation*, since it highlights the fact that, properly spun, the most innocuous piece of information can be turned into a cognitive explosive that, lit by half-truths and myths, can detonate hysterias great and small.

Though he of course did not use the term, one of Knight's great themes is that nothing has damaged African Americans more—or endangered the planet more—than spin-formations. Hence his emphasis on un-spinning them with well-turned words: "the key to human feeling, thinking and believing is in the language," he told Nancy Bunge. "I believe that words are magic, that when you use a word there are physical changes in you. . . . Psychiatrists know it, preachers know it. . . . It's tricky, like limited nuclear war. Once the debate was nuclear war or no nuclear war, then it shifted to [the fig leaf of] limited nuclear war. . . . Hey! I watch the language; I watch what people say."[86]

An example of Knight moving to undo a dangerous spin formation is a 1983 proposal he coauthored on behalf of an Indianapolis group called People against Crime. Knight and his collaborator, John E. Sullivan, outlined a plan to reach a "historically 'unreachable'" population with vignettes to be written and directed by Knight. The "unreachable" target audience included youth on a collision course with the criminal justice system—youth caught in a terrible "life script" for "a multitude of social/ psycho/ spiritual reasons." Knight and Sullivan planned to reach into and revise the terrible "life scripts" with street corner, park, and community center performances of Knight's vignettes.[87] The impulse behind the proposed vignettes was identical with the one behind the Free People's Poetry Workshops and Knight's prison-related and political writings. It was an impulse to use art to unspin poisonous "social/ psycho/ spiritual" formations.

In the workshops, which he liked to convene in bars in such a way that customers heading for the bathroom would pass him and his students, Knight taught that one index of the power of a poem was its ability to "stop a man with a full kidney of beer heading for the men's room," according to Fran Quinn.[88] Despite the humor of this anecdote, its celebration of the power to change the direction of a natural impulse suggests a kernel of realism in Knight's ambitions for his poetry and for life-script-changing vignettes.

Had they been staged as Knight and his partner wished them to be, the vignettes might have reached those who witnessed them more effectively than the "war on drugs" that actually swept Indianapolis, Indiana, and the rest of the country at the time.[89] Indeed, after more than twenty years of following the report's recommendations, a large number of states find that they have over-indulged. In 2010, Indiana, where Knight did his time for robbery, reported that it could "no longer afford to support its growing prison population."[90]

Randy Koester, the deputy commissioner of the Indiana Department of Corrections, was forced by money woes to make a point that Knight and others advocating prison reform were making decades earlier: "It may sound maudlin these days, but it helps to remember that our state's penal system was founded not on vindictive justice, but on the concept of restoration."[91] A "frequently asked question" on the Indiana Department of Corrections website—why, if "people are sent to prison for punishment, . . . they [are] allowed television, radios, free education and access to gymnasiums, and libraries, as well as medical and dental care?"—receives a similar answer: the Indiana state constitution stipulates "that the penal code shall be founded on principles of reformation, and not of vindictive justice."

Decades earlier Knight made the same point with a line that takes the biblical verse "Vengeance is mine, saith the Lord"[92] and replaces "Lord" with

"Law." If vengeance is the Lord's, the replacement implies, legal vengeance is blasphemy. The U.S. prison's system's current financial woes suggest that vengeance is also self-defeating. The decades and billions of dollars it took for Indiana and other states to learn this lesson are strong reasons why it makes sense to study and build on Knight's most honest insights.

The play of forces seeking to control behavior (forces that include the legal system without and the will within a person) and forces seeking to expand the sphere of behavior (forces that include schooling and other training without and ambitions within a person)—such a play of forces is at the root of all debates about incarceration, vengeful or otherwise, and it is one of Knight's great subjects.

"Poets are meddlers," he wrote in the preface to his 1980 poetry collection, *Born of a Woman*. "They meddle in other people's lives and they meddle in their own. . . . One of the main justifications for a poet's meddling is loving concern. . . . The poems you are about to read come into being during the past fifteen or so years of meddling. In prison, outta prison. In pool halls, college campuses, street corners."[93] Knight's meddling is an attempt to manage the play of forces.

In a prison newspaper column Knight wrote in response to a hate letter, for instance, he meddled subtly with the prison system both inside and outside the skull: "I realize that I am . . . a highly visible and real target, and that it is easier to vent green anger and frustration upon me than it is to face the frightening intangibles of your own mind and the awesome, and capricious realities of so/ci/ety. But face them you must. . . . It would seem that the misery of prison existence would form a common bond. . . . But [your] eyes are shut tight in exquisite pain. Open them and look around you, man. Ain't nobody here but us poor folks. Now don't that tell you something?"[94] Knight's two closing sentences could serve as a motto not only for prison reform, but for many social reform movements.

The Black Arts Movement

Though Knight spoke beyond race in the just-quoted passage, one of the sources of the oracular confidence he exhibited was the Black Arts movement—the movement on whose axioms his *Negro Digest* survey response (ambivalence, lifted passages, and all) is based. The movement grew out of the words, the public persona, and the martyrdom of Malcolm X. Amiri Baraka recalled that "Malcolm X put words to the volcanic torrent of anger and frustration many of us felt with the civil rights movement [and its] 'turn the other cheek,' 'non-violent' approach. . . . We did not understand why we must continue to let crazed ignorant hooligans attack us to show we were noble and deserved to be citizens. . . . So when Malcolm stepped forward and began to teach Self Determination, Self Respect and Self Defense, it struck a chord. . . . We wanted a Malcolm art, a by-any-means-necessary poetry. . . . We wanted ultimately, to create [art] . . . that would help bring revolution!"[95]

Knight acknowledged Baraka and Gwendolyn Brooks (herself a predecessor of, as well as a convert to, the Black Arts) as major influences—even asserting once (unfairly to himself in this case) that his use of Brooks-inspired poetic approaches bordered on plagiarism. But on other occasions, Knight numbered Whitman among his major influences, and he diverged from the Black Arts focus on black writing for black audiences by conceiving of his audience as consisting of concentric rings of people that could include non-blacks and, ultimately, any human being who had experienced fear and other basic emotions—Knight's version of the universal substance.

While still in prison, Knight answered a fellow inmate who had called him "Brother Tom" (a race traitor) and who then asked, "Just who in the fuck are you speaking FOR? And just who in the fuck are you speaking TO?" Knight answered,

> (1) I/am speaking to, and for, my/own/self, and (2) I/am speaking to and for selves like my/self—and that/is/you, and third, I/am speaking to and for the/other/selves, who/are essentially like you and me, but whose existence is not like ours. . . . Now take your/self—you/are (me, too) in the most oppressive, enslaving situation in the world—other/than the graveyard . . . because you/are unable to move further than six feet in any direction, and you/are unable to speak, to talk, to any/one in a real sense. . . . In politics it's called 'exile' or 'enslavement,' in religion, it's called 'excommunication' or 'punishment,' in economics, its called 'bankruptcy' or 'being broke(n).' . . . The third, and last, self that I/am speaking to and for/is/the general, the Other—the essential human/being—"the Universal"—(the most favored phrase of the imperial academicians). My/address—and the communication—with the general can only/be created from my/own specific point of departure, which, if valid, must necessarily include common/human essentials: fear, hate, love, war, humor, humility.[96]

What Knight shared with less divided practitioners of Baraka-style "Malcolm poetry" was a certain "anxiety of influence," to borrow a phrase from Harold Bloom, that did not focus primarily on a poetic precursor—whether Brooks or Whitman—but on an entire culture: the culture whose language African American poets wrote in but which, as Dudley Randall suggested in the preface to his 1971 anthology *The Black Poets,* they found inhumane and uncivilized: a kind of Saturn devouring his children—his kidnapped children, the Black Arts poets would say.[97] Knight's was an anxiety of being co-opted by those who sought to own the universal and thereby reserve for themselves the right to decide who could enter it and who was by birth excluded from it.

A vivid representation of this anxiety was put on paper by Jean Genet, who, despite Giammanco's warnings against him, seems to have found in the Black Power movement the same call to action by "non-white whites" that Giammanco did. Genet wrote, in his introduction to *Soledad Brother: The Prison Letters of George Jackson,* a concise theory of the contortions required to make "white" language tell the truth about the black experience.[98] Tapping into the Manichaean rhetoric deployed by some in the Black Power movement and giving it his extra outsider's twist, Genet argued that a prisoner-writer like Jackson "must use the very language, the words, the syntax of his enemy, whereas he craves a separate language belonging to his own people."[99] The unsatisfactory but nevertheless heroic solution is to remake the language from within: to "accept this language but . . . corrupt it so skillfully that the white men are caught up in his trap."[100]

In his poetry, prose, and letters, Knight "corrupts" the language he finds in order to expand the "say" of people who are in the act of being silenced or trapped in a diminished realm of expression and conduct—trapped, in short, in a species of prison. In the process Knight diverts, like a river, not only the resources of what Genet labels "white" language, but also poetic devices like the intralinear slash marks found earlier in the works of white poets. Though Knight seems to have adopted the slash mark device from the writing of Sonia Sanchez (who used slashes to pace some of the letters she wrote him while he was in prison), he made it his own, using it to break up the rules and culture of American mainstream English—"Mainstreamese," in the clever coinage of novelist Gish Jen.[101] In this way Knight joins the long African American tradition of impregnating mainstream language and culture with alternative inflections, locutions, rhythms, and usages. Long before the Black Arts movement, this tradition was well established: in his 1973 anthology and treatise, *Understanding the New Black Poetry,* Stephen Henderson conceded that black poetry incorporates techniques from white poets like E. E. Cummings and Paul Blackburn,[102] but he stressed that the poetry also taps a unique font of originality—the black vernacular that constantly bubbles up in "Black Speech and Black music."

For Knight the potency of vernacular oral culture means that dictionary English is a dead thing, deprived of the breath in which language actually lives. "We don't speak English," he said in a 1987 talk. "That's a political misnomer. We speak American. This language we speak has been informed by a whole number of people, and the breath patterns of English are close to the

breath patterns of the Japanese. People who live in tight places take in air differently than people who live in wide-open spaces. And how we take in air
determines how we vocalize. The English might breathe in iambic pentame-
ters, but we don't take in air like that. . . . How we inhale when we're caught
up in a passion is how our breath-lines come. That's not new. Whitman saw
that. Our breath-lines don't go like 'When I was walking down beside the
sea.' That's not how we take in air. And to force an American poet to breathe
in those forms is stifling. . . . Language [is] a living organism. . . . Metaphors
are alive. When they come into being, they are informed by the politics and
the sociology and the economy of now."[103] In the same talk, Knight stressed
his own artistic origins in the African American "dozens" and "toast" traditions—traditions that, through rap music and through jazz before it, contin-
ually alter the meanings of Mainstreamese. "The 'rap' songs you hear on the
radio nowadays are direct descendants of the 'toasts.' I have heard stanzas
that were lifted—especially of sexual prowess—lifted right out of the toasts."
Knight also credits his first poetic mentor—a wino he sometimes calls Hound
Mouth, but who in the 1987 talk he calls Duty—with teaching him toasts, an
often intensely obscene genre of rhymed narrative poetry. More implicitly
Knight learned from this mentor the importance of keeping poetry tied to oral
culture: "Too great an emphasis on the written word leads to a distance
between poet and audience," Knight told the audience for his talk, "If you
stay too long on the mountain-top, you will miss the development of the language . . . and the people down here will have gone on to something else."[104]

Can Knight's views be reconciled with the view of a mainstream taste-
maker like Harold Bloom? Perhaps. Bloom contends that a poet "is not so
much a man speaking to men as a man rebelling against being spoken to by
a dead man (the precursor [who Bloom concedes can be a compound figure])
outrageously more alive than himself."[105] This can be applied to Knight if one
substitutes, in light of Knight's roots in the toast world, words to the following effect: a poet is not so much a man speaking to men as a man rebelling
against being spoken—almost literally *dictated*—by men who outrageously
have more access to the world's possible futures than he does, and whose
social might consigns him to a "social death"[106] in which he has no rights that
need to be respected and from which most possible futures are inaccessible.

To understand the toast portion of Knight's sensibility, we need not Bloom
but the work of folklorist Bruce Jackson, who contrasts the typical literary-
critical and toast-cultural approaches to assessing poetic achievement as follows: "Most critics consider focus on the creative act ancillary to their main
task—analyzing the product. . . . But for the folklorist, the creative act is part

of the product; each redaction of the text, each re-creation of the event is to some extent controlled or influenced by the situation. And the situation—involving all participants, their physical and psychological relationships to one another and to the material—can be very complex indeed." Jackson suggests that toast protagonists are role models for those—often inmates—who listen to or perform them: "It is just these street roles of badman, pimp, hustler, and junkie described in so many poems that get those jailhouse tellers [their] auditors."[107] These characters model the art of survival and autonomy in hostile surroundings.

Toast protagonists strive to master dangerous environments by any means necessary—including guile, force, disguise, high cunning, physical prowess, or combinations of these things. The world the protagonists live in is a world where, more often than not, all but a few of the possible tomorrows are missing: a world where the protagonist must often cross great gaps in possibility in order to seize a richer bundle of futures—futures that make the present rich, even triumphant. Knight's grasp of this world was such that, in prison, he used the art he learned from Hound Mouth to make his mark before he turned to literary writing.

In "A Nickel Bet," a poem that is not a toast but has a toast subject—gambling—Knight eulogizes an attempt to seize a bundle of futures. His lines advise the bettor to "Be slow" in turning the pages of the newspaper toward the one that reveals, it turns out, that "Again your number did not fall." There is consolation, the poem asserts, in the fact that the mere prospect of victory, all day before the turning of the fateful page, "Made your hope ten feet tall."[108]

The losing bet is a winner because it opens up the shut, even forbidden, world of possibility. And though disappointed, the bettor, Knight asserts, is enriched by possibility—as if possibility were a species of muscle mass added to the bettor's frame; the bettor is enriched and strengthened by the experience of walking, stiltlike, on hopes ten feet tall. Nevertheless the world that opens when the page is turned to reveal the lottery's results is a world where hopefulness is under tremendous pressure.

While Knight's poem applies to anyone who has hurried to place a bet (and not necessarily a money bet, since there are romantic bets too, and career bets, bets of immigrants and explorers—so many sorts of bets that our world is not far removed from the one Borges depicts in "The Lottery in Babylon")—still, the quality of the "DESPERATION" woven into the poem is one especially familiar to street corner men. Only, in their world—if one believes Jackson—hopefulness buckles. At the root of the frequent denigrations of romance that are found in toasts, Jackson argues, is the corpse of hope:

cynicism: "There is a terrific cynicism or resignation to loss in many of the [toasts] that makes me think of Elliot Liebow's comments on futurity in the lives of street corner men he studied." According to Liebow, the street corner man conceives "a future in which everything is uncertain except the ultimate destruction of his hopes and the eventual realization of his fears."[109]

These men, often viewed in advance of any particular action as dangerous by the society around them, are themselves lost in dangerousness, which they try to turn to their advantage like a two-faced coin: Knight opened a 1986 reading at the Library of Congress by reciting two toasts. One is about a "Badman," Runaway Bill, a child and father of dangerousness, who opposes his own iron hand and will to a world of oppression: "I done killed the boss. . . . I'm runaway Bill. . . . old master ain't caught me and he never will." As these phrases suggest, the street corner world of the toasts is a world in opposition, a defiant world, a world of perpetual minirevolution, albeit of revolution that does not aim to overthrow all the powers that be, but to simply make them, for a time, irrelevant.

Making nonfactors of the powers that be—of the boss or slave plantation master from whom Bill escapes if not of the whole slave system—may indeed require the cultivation of dangerousness like Bill's. But the toast characters who are more directly relevant to Knight's own persona are masters of verbal wizardry that in itself structures the thoughts (and therefore the behavior) of others. "It would be difficult to [over]estimate the [importance] of verbal skill, not only in the toasts but in the culture using them," Jackson writes.[110] Verbal wizardry is thus something Knight was oriented toward long before he turned his thoughts to mainstream poetry. Even in toasts about badmen, wit—if only the wit of the performer—is king. The one toast Knight included in his books of poetry is a variation on the famous toast about Shine, a mythical African American who survives the sinking of the *Titanic* by foreseeing the disaster and swimming away. Surviving even as the *Titanic*'s white bosses and wealthy passengers drown, thanks to the strength of his body and will and the superiority of his insight, Shine turns the world upside down, turns the two-faced coins of dangerousness—the dangerousness of the iceberg, of the powerful whites whose wisdom he defies, of the immensity of the ocean, of the ocean's predators—to his advantage. According to Jackson, Shine—whose name is identical with one of the derogatory terms used to refer to African Americans—"combines the ability of the physical hero with the verbal skill of the trickster or pimp [other toast antiheroes]. Shine cracks jokes as he swims away from the sinking ship . . . [and] he ends up safely on dry land in orgies of sex and booze."[111]

As far as bets go, the combination of physical and verbal skill is as close to being a sure thing as is allowed by the sea of dangerousness in which toast tellers and their audiences often lived. It is perhaps not entirely coincidental that the Shine poems often end with orgies, that is, with acts tied to procreation—nature's way of measuring true success: the defeat of dangerousness via the survival of an individual's genes.

In Knight's variation on the Shine toast, which first appeared in print in his second book, *Belly Song and Other Poems* (1973), the tale is framed as a vision of the apocalypse awaiting an America that continues to trample on the rights and the hopes of African Americans. Because some of the backstory of Shine is dropped in Knight's "Dark Prophecy: I Sing of Shine," it is worth quoting a bit of that backstory shared by a number of variants on the toast, so that Knight's subtext will be clear. In one variant, "the sergeant and the captain were havin' some words / when they hit that big iceberg. / Up come Shine from down below, / he . . . say, 'we got nine feet of water over the boiler room floor.'" Shine is ordered below decks, but after emerging a second time and being told everything is under control, he declares, this is "one time you white folks ain't gonna shit on Shine" (184).

In all versions of the poem, the captain's daughter or the daughter of a wealthy white man offers Shine sex and/or marriage in exchange for being saved, and Shine rejects the offer, reminding her in some versions that she would never offer a black man her favors on dry land. Like a financial crisis, the sinking of the ship destroys the value of money and race as storehouses of credit and power. The overall message of the variants on the toast is that Shine's status at the bottom of the hierarchy of the ship of state is an illusion held in place by injustices that the catastrophe sweeps away.

Knight's version of the toast suggests even more overtly than the source poems—and with much more overt rage—that America's ship of state may founder in dangerousness of its own devising. His Shine is "hip enough" to escape the ship while its unhip and pleading passengers and crew drown "With screams on their lips."[112] In Knight's, as in all the Shine poems, the verities of the mainstream white American world—the verities of Protestant virtues that manifest themselves in wealth, in the simultaneous irresistibility and sacred untouchability of white womanhood, and in the godliness and wisdom of preachers—are shown to be shams.

When the ocean begins to swallow the ship, everyone is equally plunged into a dangerousness so deep that all conventions, and all the conventional wisdom and virtues that are supposed to keep risk at bay, are swallowed up, and Shine is shown to be the superior of those who in ordinary circumstances might call him "shine": in Knight's version a preacher calls Shine "nigger" while pleading to be saved in Jesus's name.[113]

Both in its traditional versions and Knight's, the poem is a blasphemously randy and vengeful retelling of the great biblical tales of triumph over temptation—Job's temptation to curse God and die, Lot and his family's to turn back and look at Sodom, Jonah's to flee the gift of prophecy. In the depths of Knight's variant, there is also the strong autobiographical theme of Knight's struggle with various addictions and with urges to break every rule or bond that held him tight. He writes about this struggle overtly in such works as "Welcome Back, Mr. Knight" and "Junky's Song," where he confesses to being involved in a "war, me against my / self / (and THEM against me too.)"[114]

But in its very title, "Dark Prophecy" records another Knight temptation that was critical to his writing—the temptation to divination and prophecy. In sometimes claiming vatic, or prophetic, powers in "Shine" and other works, Knight enters Harold Bloom territory by conforming to one aspect of Bloom's account of poetic strength as something that originates in the battle against annihilation. Using Shelley as his example, Bloom argues that "Shelley understood that [the key poems he struggled to surpass] took divination as their true subject, for the goal of divination is to attain a power that frees one from all influence, but particularly from the influence of an expected death, or necessity for dying. Divination, in this sense, is both a rage and a program, offering desperate intimations of immortality through a proleptic magic that would evade every danger, including nature itself. . . . [The] inherent belief of all strong poets [is] that . . . death is only a failure of the imagination."[115]

In Bloom's formulation, the poet struggles in Promethean isolation in a universe where a strong poem is the great weapon against annihilation— a universe where, aside from death, the greatest danger to an aspiring poet is a precursor who is too powerful for him and drowns out the aspirant's voice and talent. But Knight was struggling against what he saw as an annihilating civilization. As such, Knight's struggle was in some senses more universal than that of the ephebes Bloom wrote about. Why? Because the threat of physical and psychological annihilation against which civilizations (and revolutions against civilizations) are built as bulwarks is always present in Knight's books. Bloom goes so far as to insist that "influence anxiety . . . takes place between poems, and not between persons. . . . All that matters for interpretation is the revisionary relationship between poems, as manifested in tropes, images, diction, syntax, grammar, metric, poetic stance."[116] In making this claim, Bloom excludes not only the motives that move the pens of poets but also the cultures from which the words they write emerge. He excludes the economy, sociology, and the cultural patterns that Knight stressed in his 1987 talk. He excludes, too, the spin a cultural moment gives to particular words. One need only consider the debates and strategic maneuverings in recent decades over and around words such as "gay," "welfare," and "black" to see that poems never reflect, revise, and influence only each other's tropes, techniques, turns of phrase, and tonalities. Words flash through a poet's mind like meteors through a night sky. But before they cross the writer's mind, those words must cross the cultural space in which "gay" ceases to primarily refer to lightheartedness, "welfare" becomes something that some people condemn and use to stigmatize others, and "black" becomes a compliment while "Negro" becomes an insult. Words enter the poet's mind with a certain sociopolitical spin—and, as Knight suggested, an attendant level of tension that can affect breathing and therefore speech and poetic rhythm. The poet can seek to alter the spin with which the words enter his mind by making them more or less provocative. He or she can seek to shock, to make the reader gasp, or to shame, and make the reader sigh. But inevitably the word leaves the poet's mind and appears in his line with a slightly different orientation and spin than it entered with: it leaves prepared to enter a reader's mind innocuously, or in a surprising and breath-changing manner. In the jailhouse letter quoted earlier, Knight showed he sensed this when he wrote, "My / address [to an audience] can only/be created from my/own specific point of departure." The departure point is of course simultaneously psychological, economic, aesthetic, and political. And words launched from it variously combine and emphasize the psychological, economic, aesthetic, and political in their spin. It would be destructive to acknowledge only one dimension.

The anti-black slur "Shine," for example, is dramatically respun in both the traditional folk ballad and in Knight's reworking of it, respun in such a way as to turn the slur and the world it emerges from—a world of unequal dangerousness and of social life built on a foundation of race-based social death—upside down. Shine begins to mean less "socially dead person" and more "star upon which to wish." To the extent that "I Sing of Shine" remains a tall tale, of course, it simplifies—or rather, disguises—the complexities of the inequalities and dangers through which he swims. One must look to Knight's fully original poems to find dangerousness limned in all its complexity.

The actual sea of dangerousness and dangerous temptations (including the temptation to despair) through which many African Americans had to swim, and a likely source of the Manichaean attitude of "Dark Prophecy," is matter-of-factly evoked in "A Poem to Be Recited," the work that immediately follows "Dark Prophecy" in *Belly Song*. "A Poem" offers itself up as a kind of prayer to be said by the unemployed, by those in prisons, by those living in the congealed poverty of crowded inner-city projects, by those drafted to fight, perhaps against their will, in the Vietnam War, by parents of the children of black America, who know their offspring face a higher child mortality rate than do their white counterparts, and by men like Knight himself, who sometimes raged against his own inability to shoulder the responsibilities he chose for himself. Indeed, at the climax of the poem's litany of situations in which it might be recited is a declaration that black American children have to "grow up quickly" and are "ashamed of their fathers." The pressure of dangerousness in its many forms here provokes Knight's urge to use this poem to bless, comfort, and (indirectly) challenge black men. Yet in acknowledging the need for a prayer to recite against endemic risks, Knight's pen touches some of the central dilemmas not only of the African American community but of American literature in general.

Indeed the question of dangerousness is one with which American writers, pundits, and politicians wrestled mightily during the era in which Knight emerged as a poet. The widely read 1968 book *Black Rage,* for instance, offered to explain something that had riveted the wider American public's attention in the wake of riots in Watts and other urban areas: the "black rage" of the volume's title. "The voice of black America has been heard in the explosions of Watts, Newark, and Detroit," the authors, psychiatrists William H. Grier and Price M. Cobbs, declared in their opening paragraph.[117] Senator Fred M. Harris, in his preface to the work, deployed some of the political hyperbole later heard in the report on the White House Conference for a Drug Free America: "The root cause of the black wrath that now threatens to destroy this nation is the unwillingness of white Americans to accept Negroes as fellow human beings," Harris wrote.[118]

Though Harris was pleading for understanding and for the improved conditions that "A Poem to Be Recited" calls for in a different register, his identification of "black wrath" as something that "threatens to destroy this nation" both recapitulates past associations of African Americans (males especially) with dangerousness and anticipates the intensification of these associations that began with the riots and the Black Power movement and that, by the 1980s and 1990s, had reached a fever pitch with the discourses of the war on drugs and the dangers of "inner-city crime." Dangerousness itself became a figurative, and sometimes a literal, prison for many African Americans.

Dangerousness anxiety as a social force, furthermore, also affected people other than African Americans as, increasingly, it took the form of a statistical "new penology" that, the scholar Jonathan Simon noted, "abandons the priority of the individual in penalty" and focuses on "groups, categories, and classes. . . . An important dimension is the priority given to the language of risk [specifically the risk posed by a certain category of offender] in the administration of justice." This new penology, combined with the war on drugs, hit African Americans hard. There was in fact a racial and class component in the pessimism underlying the new penology: "The growth of a permanent poverty class in American cities, often referred to as an 'underclass,' feeds perception that transformational strategies aimed at offenders are both futile and useless," Simon observed.[119] Constructing incorrigible social classes, the new penology reinforced key carceral aspects of American culture as it is experienced by many African Americans. It became yet another building material of the prison Knight felt persons like himself could never escape.

It is therefore worth sketching the psychiatric and criminal justice system discourse of dangerousness that was one of the currents through which Knight and those he wrote about had to swim. Writing in approximately 1985, A. A. Stone noted that during the past two decades—a period, therefore, that began while Knight was still incarcerated—"the question of dangerousness, the clinical and statistical prediction of violent behavior . . . has become the chief battleground in the struggle between law and psychiatry."[120]

The trouble with this battleground is that it remained mined with unexamined stereotypes. Stone noted that the "Blacks who killed whites were much more apt to be sentenced to death than blacks who killed blacks, or whites who killed whites or blacks. . . . [The Supreme Court] has emphasized that judges and juries ought to be guided in their . . . decision to impose the death penalty by certain objective criteria. Among those criteria the Court has found that the likelihood of future violence [dangerousness] is an acceptable objective standard."[121] On the surface, Stone observed, dangerousness seems to be just such "an objective non-race-related criterion"; on the surface it seems that if a forensic psychiatrist identifies someone as a criminal suffering from an antisocial personality disorder, this testimony provides the jury with as objective an example of dangerousness as can be found. But, Stone reasoned, "Given the typical life pattern of urban black men, it is safe to say that a significant percentage of them would meet DSM III criteria for antisocial personality, for example, truancy, repeated sexual intercourse in a casual relationship, thefts, vandalism, delinquency before the age of 15, inability to sustain consistent work behavior, failure to plan ahead, conning others, and illegal occupations after 18. . . . If this thesis is only partly correct, then the diagnosis of antisocial personality, when injected into capital punishment hearings, may restore, under the aegis of clinical psychiatry, the racism that the abstract legal formula was meant to prevent."[122] If even Stone, arguing against racial bias, can list everything from truancy to "illegal occupations

after 18" as part of the "typical life pattern of urban black men"—if Stone
can thereby gloss over the majority of urban black men who, especially prior
to President Reagan's war on drugs, did not fit this "typical pattern"—if even
Stone falls into this trap, then Knight's Manichaean vision in "I Sing of Shine"
is not all bitterness and dread; the water through which Shine swims tastes of
American history.

Indeed American conceptions of dangerousness—whether those conceptions are in psychiatrists' studies, in the heads of a deliberating jury, or in the
recommendation made by a parole board—are part of the sea of risk in which
all African Americans of Knight's generation had to decide just *how* they
would swim. Knight was not engaging in hyperbole so much as painting a
picture of how a standard that is fair in theory becomes unfair in practice
when he took a look at Reagan-era America and decided there is a war on in
America, "And we're killing our sons in America, // In many, many prisons in
America."

CHAPTER 2

Knight in the Aleascape

Once he focused his talents on poetry, Knight's mastery of the art grew quickly. The distance he traveled is clear if one considers one of his earlier, humbler efforts—a verse to Gwendolyn Brooks so heartfelt that it fails as a poem, even as it opens a window onto the budding artist's thought process. First published in *Negro Digest,* "To Gwendolyn Brooks" appears as the penultimate work in Knight's first volume, 1968's *Poems from Prison.* Especially in the context of that volume, it suffers from a self-consciousness and an anxiety of influence that is all the more Bloomian because it marks the nervous entry of an oral poet into the temple of the printing press and the tradition of Western poetry as a whole. In this lyric Knight buried several deep insights and genuine love in a blizzard of clichés that include self-conscious histrionics (three unnecessary "O's"), inverted syntax ("cradle in your bosom us"), and worn tropes like "Daughter of Parnassus" and "Effulgent lover of the Sun." All this testifies to Knight's reading of anthologies and classic volumes. In particular the lines appear to weakly echo the likes of Keats, Milton, Shelley, and perhaps even Lucretius. They testify to a powerful desire to win the admiration of Brooks and her admirers in the Pulitzer Prize–granting world of mainstream (rather than toast) poetry. The anxiety of shouldering a whole tradition is all over the poem, like a nervous rash.

More successful Knight poems and short stories previously appeared in *Negro Digest,* where "To Gwendolyn Brooks" was first published in September 1965. But in the poem to his mentor, Knight was addressing a literary lioness on what he clearly perceived to be her ground.[1] And he made a mistake in the writing this poem that, in a 1977 column published in the *American Poetry Review,* he reported also making in his early prose:

> I first started this column in the Indiana State Prison in the early sixties. I/ was "serving" a 10–25 years sentence for Robbery. And I had/just/been/ assigned to the prison newspaper, *The Lakeshore Outlook,*—as a reporter, columnist, make/up layout man, and token nigger. I worked hard on my first column, . . . using all the "big words" at my command. (Like most people, I/had sensed the power of THE WORD, spoken or written; and I had reasoned, wrongly, that the bigger the word, the bigger the power. And so my first column was/filled with "Whereases," "moreovers," "therefores," and other such bullshit."[2]

In the poem Knight is in some ways even more ambitious, trying to pack in as many "big" tropes as possible. But even though the poem crashes and burns, Knight failed to entirely bury his talent, his quick mind, and his true feelings. One striking metaphor—"soothe our souls with kisses of verse"— shows real invention, and a Keatsian call to the "Effulgent lover of the Sun" to "Forever speak the truth" opens, at least intellectually, a path to Knight's powerful later lyric "The Sun Came."

Another telling contrast between "To Gwendolyn Brooks" and the retrospective, self-mocking column is the latter's incorporation of slash marks that slightly defamiliarize familiar expressions such as "I/ was 'serving' a 10–25 years sentence for Robbery." The slash marks (and of course the quotation marks around "serving") hint at a critique and at least a partial rejection of the incarceration-and-rehabilitation model as Knight experienced it. As the constant presences they became in Knight's mid- and late-career poetry and prose (including his letters)—the slash marks highlight the poet's reluctance to let any declarative statement rest uncontested and uninflected on the page. Indeed Knight uses them not only to break up meanings but also to suggest shifts in vocal intonation and emphasis, so that, at their most effective, the slashes work almost like sharps and flats in music.

In *Poems from Prison,* the slash marks make only one appearance, in "The Idea of Ancestry," a major poem whose origin, as explained by Knight, places it at the center not only of Knight's oeuvre but of his very sense of self:

> The initial creative/ impulses for the poem occurred—and many of the lines were made/up—during one of my many stays in Solitary Confinement, which is generally known as "The Hole." [. . .]
>
> I am being shoved into the Hole. I am stripped naked. . . . I am given a blanket, and the steel door behind me is shut and locked. It is dark and chilly in the Hole. . . . The first/ few/ days . . . I am so filled with anger, fear, and hurt over whatever incident (gambling, marijuana, or the Politics of the Joint) that's caused me to be here, that I do not notice the

smothering. I pace the dark space, do push-ups, masturbate, curse the guards and the gods. Five or six days pass. . . . I begin to slow down, and the smothering starts. . . . I twist and turn on my blanket on the concrete floor, and my mind is like a beehive: I hatch plots, concoct schemes. . . . After being in the Hole for a couple of weeks, not knowing night from day, I begin to lose track of time . . . I become disoriented, out of/ touch/ with myself. . . . So I start re/membering: my grandmothers, grade/school classmates, guys I'd been in the army with, and my Family most of all. . . . I was so disoriented, so desperate to regain a sense of self, of who I was . . . I started re/calling: family, names, faces; I started to mak-ing/up/ lines. . . . Later, back in my cell, I finished the poem.[3]

Even in the context of this riveting description, certain words and phrases stand out. One of them is "re/membering," divided in such a way as to em-phasize Knight's effort to overcome the psychologically dismembering effect of "the Hole." The division of the word, furthermore, sets up a deep reso-nance between memory, the remembering of the dismembered self, the calling out of names and lines and poetry, and the summoning of the storehouse of memories, attachments, and relationships that sustain a self.

"The Idea of Ancestry" itself does not chronicle the psychic disintegration set in motion by solitary confinement. It focuses instead on the "re/calling" of the world in which the self is rooted. That world is partly displayed on the walls of the cell to which Knight is returned after he is let out of the hole. The version of Knight that speaks in the poem feels the change of seasons from summer into fall all the way down in his genes, and says the feeling causes him to "flop" weakly on his bunk bed. He steadies himself by studying the opposite wall, where photographs of the faces of forty-seven relatives are pasted. The genome within him and them fills his mind. But the fact that the faces in the photographs are hundreds of miles away makes him regret having no sons to carry his genes back to their sources among those forty-seven faces—not all of them the faces of living people.

The middle section of the poem recounts a family reunion that the pre-incarceration Knight attends and enjoys for a while but then is pulled away from by the "monkey" of drug lust clawing his brain. The same "monkey," of course, has put him in prison, wrestling, under the gaze of the photographs, with a solitude he fears will become more than carceral—a solitude that threatens to exclude him from what T. S. Eliot calls "the scheme of genera-tion." He responds by attempting to "see through stone," as the prisoner in another of his poems does: that is, he attempts an act of divination. This leads him back to his ninety-three-year-old grandmother's arklike Bible, filled with the birth and death dates of all family members, including information on an

uncle who disappeared as a teenager but continues to be discussed in the family circle and continues to cause family discomfort because he has become a
cipher, an "empty space."

Having reached his grandmother's Bible, in whose pages even the absent
relative is folded, Knight enters apocalyptic space, the space of divination and
rebirth; it is space defamiliarized, not coincidentally, by the poem's intralinear
slash marks—space of the Mississippi landscape sending out "electric messages, galvanizing my genes," summoning him like a salmon whose instincts
summon it "up [its] birthstream." The pre-incarceration Knight, so summoned, finds at first that the love and warmth of his family are almost enough
to break him from his habit. We learn that it is the graves of his grandfathers,
one of whose names he bears, that have called him most strongly—pulling
him outside of ordinary time and space, into an arena, to use Harold Bloom's
term, of the daemonic, of pure potentiality beyond death and limitation.
"When the ancients spoke of daemons," according to Bloom, "they meant
also . . . 'them who for the greatness of mind come near to Gods.'"[4]

Unlike Bloom's poets, Knight, as a poet of the belly, approaches not celes-
tial gods but his grandfathers and their prison-piercing messages. But, of
course, in the end their "electric messages" cannot save him. When his drug
supply runs out, he leaves the family circle in search of a fix and carries the
messages that drew him home only in a feeling of having "almost caught up
with me."

To say one almost caught up with oneself is to say, "I had almost broken
through the walls between me and the self I wish to make stable and permanent." This self is the one able to separate the messages that pierce through
time—the "electric // messages galvanizing my genes"—from the noise of
addiction. This is the self that is driven out of his own body by the addicted
"thief," as Knight calls himself in the eighth line of "The Idea of Ancestry,"
the thief who is as separate as Barabbas from his farmer relatives.

In the cellblock where he composes the poem Knight is twice cut off: cut
off by the drug-driven robbery of Lillian Robertson and cut off again by the
psychological "hole" he lives in as he resists congealing into the prison routine
and becoming simply "thirty thousand five-sixty-two" (the number used to
identify him while he was incarcerated). Knight therefore uses the photographs of family on the wall to reorient himself toward those electric messages, which ultimately signal a way up the "birthstream" out of mortality.
The self that can cross the gap between generations and destinies is the one
Knight wants to call into being and to stabilize with the lines of the poem.

"It seems to me that 'The Idea of Ancestry' belongs to a body of poems
that I have come to call genealogical," he wrote in his 1985 essay, "There

seems to/be/ two (probably more) characteristics that are highlighted in these genealogical poems. The first is Intonation: at some point in the poem, or poems, the re/citing, the re/calling, of the Dead—and the accompanying [poetic] authority—takes place. The past merges with the present, the Dead with the Living. When this occurs, the Leap is made, from the unique to the common, from the I to the We. The breath of the poet and the people come together via the poem, and this common breathing, from deep in the belly, causes a common motion, a common movement, a common Dance."[5] The poet at the center of the dance of his community, his voice resonating up from the belly and literally feeding the audience with the rhythms needed for the dance—this is Knight's self at its most fully realized, the self he summons out of his family's names and faces when he starts to lose himself in the hole.

Surprisingly this re-membered self in some respects resembles the poetic self Bloom describes in *The Anxiety of Influence*. In the course of an argument that compares modern Western poets to Milton's Satan "organizing his chaos" (22), Bloom asks, "Why do men write poems?" He answers, "To rally everything that remains" after the poet (like Satan) realizes "I *was* God [or at least God's right hand], I *was* Man. . . . And I am falling, from myself" (21). Translating Bloom's metaphors, one can say that Knight recalls an occasion when he had the ability to perceive and follow messages that escaped mortal limitation and error and connected him to the part of his ancestors that outlasted death, and that he recalls the messages in a "hole" into which he has fallen. "The Idea of Ancestry" is his effort to organize his chaos by rallying everything that remains. Where Knight as poet separates from Bloom's conceptions is where Bloom himself attempts to impose a limit on poetic activity: for Bloom poetry stops when it ceases to be a struggle for preeminence among poets and becomes a struggle among styles of intervening in or seeking to influence the world and its politics. Bloom cast Satan out from the paradise of poets when Satan "inton[es] the formula: 'Evil be thou my good,' [and] becomes a mere rebel, a childish inverter of conventional moral categories, another wearisome ancestor of student non-students, the perpetual New Left" (22).

This passage is clearly informed by the fact that the first draft of *Anxiety of Influence* was written in the summer of 1967—a summer marked by urban riots, anti–Vietnam War protests, and the rise of the Black Power movement that inspired the Black Arts movement, which in turn cleared the way for Knight's career as a poet. Determined to protect poetry from the upheavals of history that were transforming American sensibility and public discourse—and, therefore, to a greater or lesser degree, mainstream poetic discourse—Bloom came to believe, as he put it in his 1997 preface to *The*

Anxiety of Influence, that "politicizing literary study has destroyed literary study, and may yet destroy learning itself. . . . What we once used to call 'imaginative literature' is indistinguishable from literary influence, and has only an inessential relationship to state power. . . . We need to reassert that high literature is exactly that, an aesthetic achievement, and not state propaganda, even if literature can be used [for propagandistic purposes]."[6]

If one accepts Robert Bly's claim that Knight at his best is as strong a poet as Wallace Stevens—as strong therefore as many of the masters Bloom praised —then Knight's writing demonstrates that there is no need to choose between aesthetic achievement and political engagement. Despite his emphasis on the fragility of all that humans create (including reputations and standards of greatness), Bloom shows that he values above all else a certain kind of stasis. Specifically he values a stability in the paths of influence and transmission of culture that allows norms, reputations, and achievements to be sufficiently fixed to be targeted, misinterpreted, and struggled against by those wishing to make new reputations. To maximize this sort of stability, Bloom excludes all that competes with poetic tradition for a poet's attention.

For instance, for Bloom, the events that set the stage for Dante's writing of the *Comedy*—exile on pain of death by burning if he returned to his native city—are far less important than is the influence and example of Virgil.[7] True, Bloom "unhappily" concedes that individuals are "defined only against" the society in which they live. He concedes, too, that the individual's "agon with the communal inevitably partakes of the conflict between social and economic classes. . . . No critic, not even this one, is a hermetic Prospero working . . . upon an enchanted isle." Bloom even makes a Knight/Giammanco-like point by admitting that "the freedom to be an artist, or a critic, necessarily rises out of social conflict."[8]

Yet Bloom insists that the essence of the aesthetic is as separable from social conflict as a butterfly is from its chrysalis. The essential and purely aesthetic "poet-in-a-poet" is, in Bloom's view, "free of all ideologies." Commenting on John Milton, the author of *Paradise Lost,* Bloom admitted that Milton's art is full of political currents, since he joined "the losing side in [a civil war]" and was "the poet-prophet of [Oliver] Cromwell's revolution."[9] But at the same time he insists that discovering what Milton truly believed is beside the point. In *A Map of Misreading,* he makes his case for the comparative irrelevance of all but the aesthetic by insisting that the question of whether a literary instructor should "teach *Paradise Lost* in preference to Imamu Amiri Baraka" is "self-answering," since the inescapable influence of the classics means that the teacher "will find he is teaching *Paradise Lost,* and the other central classics of the Western literary tradition, whether he is teaching them overtly or not."[10] While it is hard to argue that Baraka is a greater poet than Milton, or that he has shaken off the influence of the Western canon, it is also hard to argue that he is a more *politically engaged* man than Milton, or that the classics are a greater influence on him than are the language, politics, and economics of his own era. In each man, although to different degrees, tradition, economics, politics, and contemporary language politics feed upon one another and prey productively on the poet's mind. By insisting that tradition eclipses the present work a teacher has open in his or her hand, Bloom is insisting on reading with one eye closed. For if one were to teach Baraka's best Black Arts works, to say nothing of "The Idea of Ancestry," identifying the trace elements from Milton and other classics would do little to explain why the poems wield power.

This book nevertheless relies on Bloom in reading some aspects of Knight's work both because of what the one eye Bloom uses makes visible and because pointing out what the closed eye misses helps make the case for the importance of Knight's work. Consider the following assertion from *The Anxiety of Influence:* "Poetic influence . . . always proceeds by a misreading of the prior poet, an act of creative correction that is actually and necessarily a misinterpretation."[11] This is true up to a point, since all poets begin by being moved—transported into verse—by certain poems or poets and by seeking to write up to the level of those poems or poets. But as Knight's own career demonstrates, poetic creation is even more fundamentally a creative attempt to correct (or reinforce) the world in which one lives. "The Idea of Ancestry" seeks to correct the solitary confinement in which Knight literally and figuratively finds himself. That is, the pressure brought to bear upon Knight by the world and by the errors he makes in it is greater than the pressure placed upon him by poets like Gwendolyn Brooks or by the unknown originators of the toasts he told. Poetry is his file for digging through the prison wall. True, it is a tool that can only work if the user puts his stamp on it and makes it his own. And Knight's particular stamp is shaped by more than precursors: it is shaped by heroin lust, imprisonment, personal weakness, intellectual power, ambition (poetic and otherwise), traditions from which he drew inspiration, and family. Did Brooks's verses stir his imagination and, on occasion, freeze it in its tracks? Yes. But for most of his life it was "mad" America that "hurt him into poetry," as Auden said Ireland hurt Yeats. And it is the mad American tradition of toast telling that gave him his first balm.

It is when they connect poetic ambition to the fear of death that Bloom's statements apply equally and without favor or pettiness to Milton, Wallace Stevens, and Knight. Bloom makes this connection best when he writes of divination: "Vico, who identified the origins of poetry with the impulse toward divination (to foretell, but also to become a god by foretelling), implicitly understood (as did Emerson, and Wordsworth) that a poem is written to escape dying."[12] This not only jibes with Knight's statement (printed on the back cover of *Poems from Prison*) that he died in Korea, was resurrected by illegal drugs, died again in prison, and was resurrected there by poetry; it is also consistent with the overriding human effort to foresee and avoid dangers, mortal and otherwise; to calculate risks; to perform rituals and prayers that result in immortality; to annihilate enemies, as the Romans annihilated Carthage, salting its very foundations; to measure or predict the dangerousness of certain persons or groups; and to reform the dangerous with everything from prison terms to rehabilitative programs to chemical castration. Operating between fight and flight and seeking to make both unnecessary, divination is in many ways the characteristic human activity, involving as it does all the senses, the memory, the imagination, and all the latest techniques of calculation, randomization, and control.

"Cell Song," the work that opens *Poems from Prison*, is full of prophetic impulses as well as the urge to resist prophecy. Knight writes of a prison asleep in which he alone, awakened by "Light" slanting into his cell, is able to pace "the red circle" and "twist the space/ with speech." Had Knight been reading about the way gravitation bends and twists space? The fact that he capitalizes "Light" tells us that something like a summons from heaven (or from his Mississippi ancestors) has awakened him and made of the "red circle" a kind of prophet's wilderness. The conclusion of the poem—an unpunctuated, drunken-syntaxed question about whether anything good can come from prison—tells us that the wilderness in question is the wilderness of incarceration—the wilderness that is at its wildest in the hole, but which remains a threat to the psyche anywhere within prison walls. But the earlier lines reveal that something good *is* wrested from the void when the poet "twist[s] the space // with speech."

Yet, as he almost always does, Knight refuses to crown himself with his own vision, warning himself in the second stanza against assuming the role of savior. Still, immediately after issuing this warning, he allows himself to become a kind of god whose words can "shake rain // on the desert." A divining rod—or a prophet—that leads the thirsty to water is not more magical than this. At the opposite end of the poetic spectrum from his "To Gwendolyn Brooks," this poem announces that Knight has the power to bend incarceration to his will, rather than have his will twisted into a prison-issued shape. But it also calls for resistance to the possible corrupting influence of poetic power, lest a new kind of depersonalizing force "come out of prison."

In a weaker because less fully imagined poem called "He Sees through Stone," Knight describes a jailhouse diviner and spiritual savior he clearly admires: a man from whom he wishes to learn new ways of twisting jailhouse time into the time of liberty, a man who in fact taught him "secret rights" in an obscurely remembered "time gone." Divination is among other things the art of uncovering secret paths and connections—something that the man who "sees through stone" is more than capable of doing. Again the escape from prison (signified by seeing through stone) is tied to linking oneself to something more fundamental than the surface life of mortals. But here, too, one senses a certain longing for a father figure on the part of Knight, whose father died while he was in the army. Divination also has to do, of course, with contacting and learning from the dead.

The lesson of a death is the subject of "For P.F.C. Joe Rogers (Killed at Inchon)," one of the few poems in Knight's oeuvre to address directly the Korean War, where the battle of Inchon took place in September 1950, two months before Knight left the military. He writes of night clouds lit by mortars, of a wind "laced with aching cries," and of a moon stained with blood. The evocation of a "wind . . . laced with aching cries" (the most powerful line in the poem) and the echo of Revelation (and perhaps of Yeats) in the line about the blood-stained moon give us a rare glimpse of the war-twisted space from which Knight fled, it seems, into his own medicine bag.

But it is away from the declared battlefield, in a series of four poems devoted to Malcolm X, that Knight grapples most intensely with death and grief. The first of the four, "Portrait of Malcolm," is by far the weakest, more a series of notes (sometimes marvelous notes) for the poems that follow than a "full grown song."[13] But the second poem, "For Malcolm, a Year After," shows marked progress toward mastery of Malcolm X as subject and as, in some ways, poetic precursor. This second poem dispenses with the first's forced and unconvincing assertions of Malcolm X's Moses-like prophet status ("His throat moans // Moses on Sinai") and ascends into the colloquial by including Malcolm X's nickname in his pre–Nation of Islam days ("Red") and finding a means of blending age-old iambic pentameter with rage and grief over the assassination of Malcolm X in the midst of his work to resurrect African American identity: "Adhere to foot and strict iamb," Knight tells himself, and allow the iambic beat to master the raging words that might otherwise "boil and break the dam."

Though this poem is afflicted in places with the same weakness that mars "To Gwendolyn Brooks," it shows Knight struggling to spit out the undigested locutions—to say nothing of the unwelcoming Western tradition that iambic pentameter exemplifies—that gag him, and to replace them with phrases that can represent the meaning of Malcolm's death to Knight himself and to whoever hears or reads his poem. Echoes of what may be Shakespeare's sonnets wrestle within the lines with attacks against the "anglo" he is compelled to write in.

The next Malcolm poem, "It Was a Funky Deal," is the first fully successful one. Tellingly, this is the first of the Malcolm poems in which Knight allowed African American expressions (starting with "it was a funky deal") to enter fully into the poem. What is more, Knight achieves a compression of statement reminiscent of the haiku form—something he used frequently after being taught it (as a means of reducing verbosity) by Gwendolyn Brooks—and successfully ties the red of Malcolm X's beard and the red of his blood into a tourniquet-tight image of red as the "only thing real." If the only thing real as Malcolm X lies dying on the Audubon Ballroom floor is the red of his blood and his beard—and "Red," his old nickname—then what is no longer real is the future that his continued existence would have supported, as a tentpole supports a tent. Oriented toward their own perceptions of a collapsing Malcolm-centered future, supporters for the time being lose touch with what they themselves might have become under his tent.

The next stanza celebrates Knight's favorite power—that of the word—albeit the anti-word of those responsible for Malcolm's death. It opens by quoting the Bible's "in the beginning was the word" as a way of stressing the fact that here anti-word creates the wrong thing: the "deed" of assassination. Judas did the same for "the same Herd," the poem asserts. Just who was in the "Herd" can best be understood by turning to the anthology in which "It Was a Funky Deal" first appeared: the Broadside Press's *For Malcolm: Poems on the Life and the Death of Malcolm X*, which, as a preface, reprinted (from *Negro Digest*) actor-activist Ossie Davis's account of what Malcolm X meant at the time of his death.

America's divided views of Malcolm at the time are plain in Davis's defensive title, "Why I Eulogized Malcolm X." The fallen leader, Davis wrote, violated mid-1960s "common sense [requiring] that Negroes stand back and let the white man speak for us, defend us, and lead us from behind the scene. . . . Malcolm said to hell with that! . . . He scared the hell out of the rest of us, bred as we are to caution, to hypocrisy in the presence of white folks, to the smile that never fades. . . . Malcolm kept snatching our lies away. He kept shouting the painful truth we whites and blacks did not want to hear. . . . It was impossible to remain defensive and apologetic about being a Negro in his presence. . . . I never doubted that Malcolm X, even when he was wrong, was always that rarest thing in the world among us Negroes: a true man."[14] Davis had already noted that whites "do not need anybody to remind them that they are men. We do!"[15]

Though this is an androcentric account of Malcolm X's value, its emphasis on the leader as a model of assertive adulthood, as a wielder of that special brand of consequential speech that is known as "say," highlights what it was about Malcolm that moved and stiffened the spine and mind of Davis and many others, including Knight. "It Was a Funky Deal" concludes with "You rocked too many boats, man. . . . Saw through the jive," and, in articulating this seeing through, "reached the wild guys // Like me."

Truth telling begins with seeing through "the jive"—the obfuscation, false smiles, and all-around hypocrisy to which Davis referred. Seeing through the jive continues with the selection of new role models. In addition to Malcolm X, Knight's concluding stanza names saxophonist Charlie "Bird" Parker (who stands for revolutionary artistry as well as, perhaps, unshakable drug addiction) and "LeRoi" (LeRoi Jones, who was moved to reinvent himself as Amiri Baraka by the assassination of Malcolm X) as people who helped teach Knight how to "pull coats" (communicate what people resist knowing).

By far the finest poem in the Malcolm X series is "The Sun Came." Framed as a response to Gwendolyn Brooks's poem "Truth," "The Sun Came" is "the full grown song" where Knight shook off not only the weaknesses of the previous Malcolm X poems but goes beyond their strengths, surpassing Brooks herself by turning what is a great rhetorical moment in her original poem into a full-fledged vision of the path to African American liberation in Malcolm X's wake. "And if the sun comes/ How shall we greet him?," Brooks asked in lines from "Truth" that Knight made the epigraph of "The Sun Came." Answering Brooks, Knight realized the ambition of the first poem of the Malcolm series—where he links Malcolm with Moses—by making the fallen leader something truly sight giving, the Sun: "The Sun came, Miss Brooks," the poem begins. But it goes on to lament that he and others Malcolm sought to awaken were not equal to the summoning, to Malcolm's "fierce hammering" on the doors of their minds. By including himself, if not exactly in the "herd" he refers to in "It Was a Funky Deal," then at least among the flawed followers who could not rise to the occasion Malcolm X created, Knight infused a tremendous psychological tension into the lines of the poem: tension like that in the mind and limbs of a Jonah fleeing the call to prophecy, the call to risk all he has and knows.

Among the fruitful ambiguities in the poem are those of the word "our" and of the other plural pronoun that appears in the poem—"we." Does "we" extend as far as the members of the Nation of Islam who were convicted of

Malcolm X's murder? Does it extend as far as the white society whose sins against African American life Malcolm X proclaimed, and to which Amiri Baraka assigned the ultimate blame for Malcolm's murder? Or does it include only the "wild ones" who felt the call to "see through the jive"—the misinformation, double-talk, and lies—in which they had to live and think?

The "fierce hammering," however, is a hammering on the doors of cognition, the doors each person closes against certain kinds of information and misinformation—a hammering at the whole pre-Malcolm world to which eyes and thoughts and sense of self had adjusted. Whether intended or not, the image of Malcolm-as-the-Sun parallels Plato's parable of the cave, in which the sun and the realities it reveals are overwhelming and disorienting. The unfinished state of adjustment to its light is conveyed in Knight's second stanza, which mourns that the sun "has bled red" and the world of shadows and night has returned. Again the doors of cognition, half-opened by what Malcolm X had to tell, are swinging shut. Yet the "rays of Red have pierced [so] deep" that it is all but impossible for those whose eyes and brains they touched to accept the shadow world that returns. The grief for what might have been in itself becomes a seed of future change.

In portraying the expansion of the mind beyond the shadow world, Knight testified to the expansion of what might be called the cognitive horizon, the limit of what a person or community can grasp about its own natural or political environment. Before Malcolm, this horizon was the one sealed by the smiles Davis wrote about, the one sealed, in Knight's case, by the unfocused, self-destructive, and wild rebelliousness referred to in the earlier poem. But the rays of "Red"—Malcolm—have shown that there is more possibility than the "wild ones" or anyone else had perceived or attempted to act upon. Malcolm X created a new attitude, a new syntax for existence, through which African American reality could be cognized. One has the sense that, before him, those he reached were living and thinking in a language with only a rudimentary future tense and a constrained present tense. Here it is useful to recall Liebow's observation that the street corner man conceives "a future in which everything is uncertain except the ultimate destruction of his hopes," and to consider Knight's adoptation of Malcolm X's view that all African Americans face the pressures of virtual or actual imprisonment. For what is the expected destruction of hope but the sense that the future is constrained, in effect imprisoned?

With this sense of rising hopelessness, the mind is less able to conceive of and choose among paths to alternative futures. With fewer conceivable futures, and fewer paths even to those that are conceivable, both the present and the future are smaller and dimmer: they are sunless in the sense Knight's poem makes plain. But in the expansion of both the perceptible world and of what can be conceived—an expansion created by the light of Malcolm's fiery speeches—the whole world expands. Even after the fire goes out, the memory of it and what it made visible mean that the darkness "ain't like before."

Nevertheless the fear of having lost too much of what the fire allowed to be glimpsed leads to the fear that he and others mishandled the historical opening Malcolm X provided. But, again, the glimpsed possibilities have in themselves expanded the cognitive horizon—of both Knight and other wild ones and of Ossie Davis and other cautious ones—expanded their sense of what is possible and what can be gambled upon: "we goofed the whole thing. // I think," Knight writes at the end of the poem, adding, "Though ain't no vision visited my cell." The "I think," a characteristic gesture of Knight's, prevents any given vision, however unlimited it might seem, from being accepted as the "Truth" to which Gwendolyn Brooks referred in the verses to which "The Sun Came" responds.

One of the attractive things about Knight's best work is that it illuminates, with a strategically placed "I think" or similar rhetorical gesture, unlooked-for portions of the landscape of possibility: unlooked-for portions of what might more concisely be called the *aleascape*. Just what aleascape refers to can best be outlined by examining a poem in which Knight describes a world of conformity and control that is designed to exclude the unlooked-for, the unplanned, and to exclude the doubt summed up in Knight's "I think."

The two-part lyric in question is called "2 Poems for Black Relocation Centers." The title in itself refers to a place of control and confinement— a black version of the camps to which Japanese Americans were sent during World War II.[16] The relocation camps are in the first instance the military, where Knight had such a traumatizing experience, and in the second instance the streets from which corner toast tellers and others do not expect to escape. Flukum, the protagonist of part 1, is an older relative or family friend of the speaker. His name is obviously allegorical. As a fusion of a rebellious quip— "fuck 'um"—and of an authoritarian command—"flunk 'um," with the added undertone of "flunky"—the name Flukum bespeaks confused purposes and, indeed, cognitive dissonance between the desire to rebel and the desire to obey at all costs that Flukum appears to find unbearable. Seeking "inner and outer order" and a relief from unbearable psychic tension, Flukum joins the army. There he luxuriates in the regulation he finds of every facet of life, thought, and action. He washes away his autonomy like an awful stain, in a bath of instructions on everything from the buttoning of his shirt to the means of killing "the yellow man." Any incipient guilt or sense of sin he feels about killing is "Devilish[ly]" blessed away by "the good Chaplain // (Holy by God and by Congress)."

The tension that drives Flukum into the military is the dissonance of a mind fleeing from any least tap on the locked doors of its cognition. It is the dissonance of a mind fleeing from the choices such taps demand—fleeing into a world of prefabricated decisions. For even with a racially restricted set of possible decisions, the set of possible choices and consequences is large enough and full enough of dangers to strike fear into a Flukum's heart. The reference to the "Devilish" casuistry of the chaplain underscores the anti-Faustian nature of Flukum's bargain. While Faust, Goethe's legendary wisdom-seeker, wagers his soul in an effort to win infinite knowledge and power, Flukum trades his soul for minimum knowledge, minimum perception, and minimum foresight. No amount of knocking from the Malcolms of the world can ever awaken him.

Unfortunately for Flukum, the poem's second stanza makes it plain that the flight from truth-tellers—and the whole world's—"fierce hammering" leads sooner or later to disaster, either for the one who flees or the truth tellers' attempting to add their hammering to that of nature.[17] The protagonist of this second section is a man lying dead in Detroit with lice moving in his beard, a halo around his head, and a white robe partly clothing his body and partly caught on "charred beams and splintered glass." The dead man has red-rimmed blue eyes that are "full of reproach" and a nose that "had lost its arch of triumph." We are told that the man "died outraged," but then "arose out of his own ashes . . . / A faggot in steel boots." To the extent that the term is an antigay slur, Knight's use of the word "faggot" dates him,[18] pinning him and his poem to the historical moment and, perhaps, to the prison culture in which he composed the lyric. But the word tells us that the Christ depicted in the stanza is intended to be an ambiguous figure—at once representative of the culture against which Detroit African Americans rioted in July 1967, and someone who is to some extent co-opted: turned into a tool of that same culture. It is clear that the reproach in his co-opted eyes is directed at the rioters. He died unaware or blind to the fact that the riot was sparked when police tried to arrest those attending a party thrown for two Vietnam veterans at a "blind pig," a sort of post-Prohibition speakeasy.[19] In this context Knight's risen Christ figure becomes an image of redoubled oppression, stomping ignorantly in steel boots. And yet the Christ figure also takes on the characteristics of people down and out on the streets: his beard is alive with lice, his eyes are red-rimmed, his nose is smashed—and like some of those street people, like the prescription-forging Knight who once leapt out of a hospital window, in fact, he rises out of his own ashes.

The two parts of the poem, in short, sketch both the up- and the down-side of certain forms of submission and rebellion. Flukum's throwing away of his own choices in exchange for his version of the peace that passeth understanding is perfectly balanced by the rioter's effort to seize the sort of say over their own destinies that terrifies Flukum. The great irony of the two sections, of course, lies in the fact that neither submission nor rebellion is guaranteed to make life less risky, less vulnerable to the bullet in the chest, to the cognitive dissonance that sometimes attends killing in war, or to the steel boot on the foot of a savior: there is no escape from the implosion of the best-laid plans, no escape from the aleascape, from the human world built on countless bets on this or that future: built, therefore, on the uncertain consequences of those countless bets. There is no escape from the fact that the unpredictable bets themselves, however carefully calculated, are made in an environment full of unforeseeable occurrences—earthquakes, tornadoes, epidemics, and accidents.

In the terminology of the philosopher-scientist Bart Kosko, there is no escape from the fact that everything is fuzzy. That is, nothing our senses touch is 100 percent true, 100 percent where or what it seems to be.[20] "If you can prove a statement 100 percent true, it does not describe the world," in Kosko's view. "Ironic as it sounds, inaccuracy is the central assumption of science. No scientific conjecture or hypothesis or thing is 100 percent accurate. . . . Even if you could squeeze all the fuzz out of statements, you would still face the problem of inductive reasoning, the problem that the next measurement may refute your claim. . . . One day the sun will not rise. . . . Or in the next moment you may turn into a frog or burst into a fiery supernova or collapse into a black hole. You cannot rig nature to prevent it. You can only take the next measurement."[21] Of course, Kosko's examples are hyperbolic. He knows that there was only a vanishingly small probability that a person would suddenly go supernova. But Kosko's hyperbole dramatizes the fact that nothing available to human cognition is "all there," nothing is entirely solid. Everything, to use vocabulary Kosko does not approve of, but which he acknowledges is built into the human way of thinking, is more or less probable.[22] Everything, to use language Kosko entirely disapproves of, has probability—not atoms—as its ultimate building block. That is what the aleascape is: a place made of nothing but probability. In fleeing it, Flukum set himself the task of escaping the universe.

Flukum is the opposite of the gambler in "A Nickel Bet." The gambler behaves as though he knows that a person is best understoood as something indeterminate—as something that the outcome of a wager can diminish or enlarge. He behaves as though he knows that a person is something that exists for an indeterminate length of time, something that—as street corner men know—can be destroyed at any moment by everything from a car crash to a bullet. Such a being has only a limited probability of existing at a future time. And such a being's psyche and lifestyle choices are shaped by this probabilistic aspect of existence—shaped by the fact that he or she is literally made from a chain of probabilities, from the probability of the fusion of parents' egg and sperm to that of contracting a certain fatal ailment.

Probability, after all, is experienced in different ways by different people at different moments. It can be experienced as risk—the sort of thing one buys insurance to protect against. It can be experienced as good fortune. It can be experienced as unfairness or injustice when exposure to high risks are unevenly distributed in a population as a result of policy. (The higher probability that blacks will get the death penalty is an example of this injustice.) Probability, finally, can be experienced as catastrophe by those hurt by hurricanes, tornadoes, and economic disasters not of their own making. Much of human life—from placing bets to joining armies to rioting over a raid on a "blind pig" in a harassed neighborhood—is dedicated to attempting to manage and change probability.

The aleascape—and the necessity and impossibility of managing it—is the ultimate subject of another work from *Poems from Prison*: "The Violent Space (or when your sister sleeps around for money)." The subtitle of the poem—which Knight said in an interview not only does not refer to any of his own sisters but caused him to have a lot of explaining to do to four angry women demanding to know just who he was writing about—emphasizes poverty and lack of options.[23] The opening line adds another element—greed for money and for sex—and perhaps also, on the side of the clients, greed for innocence itself, in as much as the lines make clear that the sister is very young—seventeen, underage—as she and her client "Exchange in greed the ungraceful signs." Seeking to craft some time-and-distance-destroying spell, the poem's speaker, immured far away in his cell, cries out—as he did when she was a child—that she run to escape the "Bugga man."

The "Bugga man" in the poem is danger itself—danger to body and psyche, danger that strips away the innocence of newly formed breasts. In the next stanza, danger takes the form of a painful wasp sting the sister suffered in childhood. But the remembered wasp and its sting, significantly, do not threaten the psyche as, the first stanza suggests, underage prostitution does. What is more, when the wasp stung, the speaker was there to comfort his sister.

But the "Bugga man" threatening her as she trades the "ungraceful signs" embodies a different order of danger. He embodies the danger of becoming less valuable, even in her own eyes, than the "ungraceful signs": the danger of becoming lighter than her own fingerprints on the signs as she loses the weight that real intimacy and love's graces can give a person. To this "Bugga man" reducing intimacies to "thick notes [thrust] between green apple breasts," the Knight persona opposes the poet's divination. The purpose of this divination is to make the space in which the teenager is trapped a little less violent— which is to say, a little more open to better possibilities—not least the possibility that poem making will make the speaker a strong magician whose poem-spell will "drive the demon away." And yet the would-be savior immediately confesses his *own* dependence on ambivalent signs. He admits to his poet's greedy counting of syllables "like Midas gold" and his junkie's cloven-willed inability to commit so fully to the saving divination that he gives up the bad alchemy of boiling of his "tears in a twisted spoon." And yet the poem/ spell is crafted and cast anyway as a last-ditch effort to charge words with power enough to change the balance of risks the seventeen-year-old faces and, thereby, build for her a path across the "nameless void" where, though born potentially as full of grace as the biblical Mary, she "lost [her] name."

As always in his best work, the Knight persona in the poem refuses to overestimate either his own space-twisting power or poetry's, or to underestimate his ability to undermine both with the addiction that has brought prison walls between him and the seventeen-year-old. As in "Cell Song," Knight (or, in "The Violent Space," his persona) is striving to twist space—here "the violent space"—with speech. And—as at the end of "The Sun Came"—he is not sure he can achieve the necessary visionary intensity. In all three poems, he limns the way humans struggle in risk, like flies in amber, and he shows the beauty and nobility of the struggle, and the frailties that can make the struggles fail.

Thus far this chapter has focused on the works from *Poems from Prison* that visit the world *outside* the prison bars behind which Knight wrote. The poems that chronicle the world *within* the bars—many of which Knight reprints in *Black Voices from Prison*—will be the focus of the next chapter. The present one will conclude with a consideration of one of the supreme upsides of the human portion of the aleascape—love, which is so often sparked by chance encounters and so often results in the genetic dice rolling of conception. One of the lyrics in *Poems from Prison* particularly addresses the fate of love in violent spaces. Called, appropriately, "A Love Poem," it celebrates and in itself strengthens a great source of love and nonviolence—communication. The poem's speaker asserts that he does not expect his lover to play Penelope to his Ulysses, since he lacks Ulysses-like might and fearlessness: "I cry and cringe // When the Cyclops peers into my cave." But the Cyclops and the exiling winds can be defeated, the poem suggests, by "Our love [which] is a rock against the wind."

Knight handles the classical references here with ease. He pulls Odysseus's wanderings into his cell by underscoring how he *differs* from the hero. The panoptical eye of the prison system/Cyclops strikes fear in Knight, but his fear makes all the more striking the real hero of the poem—love itself.

Indeed no matter how often he himself failed it, love remained Knight's weapon of choice. "Revolutionaries Live in Houses of Love" is the title of one unpublished poem, dedicated to Hank and Wendy Keene-Sanel, in which Knight celebrates the fact that the couple lives in "a House built of Love, not Fear"—a House that renders obsolete (at least for the duration of the poem) the plan of "Yahweh and Allah and Buddha and Damballa and Brahma . . . and J[e]hovah" as that plan is preached by bêtes noires like Jerry Falwell and Ayatollah Khomeini. "Even Jah, the Father of all/ Patriarchs," Knight wrote, channeling Great Mother thought, "Has become a lie." But the couple, despite "ideological odds and ends . . . blend // In a revolutionary Love" that has the potential to become a door to a new kind of world.[24] Knight himself tasted this new world in another unpublished poem, "'SHE COMES to me' (for Bett Gordon)," where he declares, "I love her. // To my Death. // Which is a whirling and a twirling // And bringing of Breath."[25] Revolutionary love—twirling the poet and all he sees around—is the door to rebirth for self and community, however far community extends. It is a door Knight constantly, desperately sought—and, sometimes, ecstatically found.

CHAPTER 3

Black Voices from Prison

Though less ecstatic than revolutionary love, writing was for Knight another crucial door. Powers argued that "Knight found through writing what he had been searching for through narcotics"—a way to "be himself without violating . . . social restraints." When writing, Powers added, Knight "is functioning, and he likes the feeling." With the growth of his reputation outside prison feeding its growth behind bars, Knight "became aware of his responsibility to his fellow convicts," according to Powell.[1] Knight met some of this responsibility by editing and contributing to—adding his newly minted poetic capital to—*Black Voices from Prison*. When it was first published in Giammanco's Italian translation as *Voci Negre dal Carcere* in 1968, the book became, along with Giammanco's Malcolm X translations and writings, "a frame of reference and inspiration for the Italian Students' Movement in the Sixties," Giammanco recalled in 2011.[2] Yet it appeared in English only two years later, after a determined struggle on Giammanco's part to find a publisher.[3]

Both Knight's preface and Giammanco's introduction to the volume aim to alter readers' frames of reference. Both insist upon a continuity between black life behind bars and life in what Knight dubbed "the larger prison outside"—a larger prison maintained by "a white educational system, a white communications system, a dead white Art, and the white Law."

Knight's sense of things beyond prison walls was informed by the arrival in the penitentiary of young, Black Power–inspired inmates. These inmates "accept—up to a certain point—their own personal responsibilities for being [in prison]," Knight writes, "[but] they no longer accept whitey's definition of their selves. They use a new frame of reference" (9–10).

Writing from a sea and a language away, Giammanco pushed Knight's "larger prison" thesis (itself derived from Malcolm X's), into the realm of absolutes, asserting that white society or

> Suburbia . . . views the ghetto Negro as a threat to that traditional structure of ruling class values which make possible suburban living, the monopoly of degrees from the "right" kind of college, the right kind of jobs. . . .
>
> This traditional psychological structure of the middle class worked as long as the Afro-American was unaware of the international nexus of the mechanisms of exploitation and racism. . . . The Negro fulfilled a precise role, one that symbolized all that the middle class unconsciously detested (particularly in itself . . .). . . . Once the black man realizes . . . that he breaks the law because being black signifies being outside the law . . . the relationship is reversed.
>
> The . . . black man rejects white society's "right" to define him, to teach him to know himself as a black man, to project his future. (22–23)

The struggle for the future is, indeed, the fundamental American struggle—in fact, the fundamental existential struggle, to which all human activity is directly or indirectly targeted. The "traditional psychological structure" to which Giammanco refers depends on the persistence of attitudes and expectations that the coming to life of the socially dead destroys. Giammanco's excitement about Knight stemmed from his sense that Knight is an agent of awareness. Indeed, in his June 1967 letter, Giammanco declares Knight a voice of the wretched of the earth, who could restore meaning to propagandized words and histories, forcing "us, the non-white whites, to do the same and [thereby] help create a new reality."[4] Despite the rhetorical essentialism of Giammanco's "Suburbia" and "ghetto Negro," his emphasis on the struggle for the control of the African American future—and therefore of the destiny of America as a whole—is correct.

Much of the pain in Knight's accounts of incarceration derives from the sense the writings convey of being cut off from the best of all possible worlds, which can be defined as the best of all possible choices among possible futures. A case in point is the poem "For Freckle-Faced Gerald," a chronicle of a youth's confinement in one of the worst possible worlds, which appears in both *Poems from Prison* and *Black Voices*.

Asked about the genesis of the poem, Knight said,

> I was lying in my cell reading one night, when . . . the word came that a young brother had been raped in the prison laundry by some older cons.

. . . I got a little angry. Here was this young brother—only sixteen and in prison. . . . There was a young white boy from Indianapolis who had burglarized some homes and shot some people. He had gotten life, too. When he came to prison, the warden made him houseboy and kept him outside the walls—protected him. But the warden put Gerald back inside the wall because he was just a nigger. I was thinking of all of that. . . . I was trying to express what I saw happening around me and to talk about the subject of oppression. Here we are—black people, oppressed. . . . Women are oppressed. Homosexuals in prison and in the larger society are oppressed. If you're black, a woman, a lesbian and you're in prison, you are oppressed four times. Black men will talk about being free, yet they'll have a woman walking four paces behind them and go "fag hunting." We cannot win our freedom at the expense of anybody. Many blacks—artists, educators, politicians, and other leaders—will say there's nothing to women's liberation or gay liberation. Or they will argue that if we have to become fascists to win our freedom, it's better for us to have the oppressors in jail than for them to have us. But . . . I don't think we can be free that way. I don't think we can dominate the world racially. If you're going to come from a point of view of race, then the Chinese will win since there are more of them than anyone else. . . . Everybody has to be free. I was feeling those things and thinking about Gerald when I wrote the poem.[5]

This is one of Knight's most complete and eloquent statements of the conception of freedom that animates so much of his work. The statement stands as a yardstick against which Knight's own deviations—confessed in brilliant, self-lacerating poems about his addiction—can be measured.

"Freckle-Faced Gerald" itself is a "belly song" version of the statement. It is a tragic allegory in which the Gerald of the title represents those whose freedom—whose ability to choose among possible futures—is crushed for the benefit of others. Gerald is in the middle of puberty. His voice, sixteen years old, has not yet descended into manhood, and neither has his sense of self. He is ignorant even of how to "talk tough."

He is so little experienced in anything connected to sexuality that (in the terms of the poem) he has no role in determining how his sexuality is perceived or expressed, and, as Knight sees it, no experiential momentum to keep the flow of his sexual river from being changed "from south to north." Indeed Gerald's self never matures into anything more than a receptacle for others' lusts. And in the end the "course/ of his river" is not only the course of his sexuality but the course of his choices and the identity that runs through the twists and turns those choices might have carved.

Yusef Komunyakaa suggests, however, that it is not only Gerald's green-ness, but also a certain basic nobility of his character, that leaves him defense-less. In what Knight himself described as the "ride or be ridden" culture of the prison, Gerald refuses to ride. For Komunyakaa, Gerald admirably refuses to follow the rules of "a place where prisoners have to create their own cycle of victims out of situational greed."[6]

But Gerald is not alone in being smothered in concentric cycles of oppres-sion. Knight made the destruction of his will an emblem of the condition even of some who rape him. For while they are responsible for their rapes, they are themselves turned by the cogs of the "larger prison." Their assaults are enabled by restrictions that, to a degree, affect them also: Gerald has no clique to roam with as he did in civilian life, in part because jailhouse rules strip him of protection at every turn. These rules forbid inmates to gather even in groups of three. Groups of four are declared to be conspiracies of "muslims." A gathering of five is a plot to start a riot. Such rules leave Gerald in the posi-tion of prey caged in a "prison/america" designed and run by "wiser and big-ger buzzards" than the ones who make use of him at night. These "bigger buzzards," by maintaining their "prison/america," plot the "loss of his balls . . . years in advance"—like a complicated billiard shot. Worst of all for Knight is Gerald's innocence of the era's rising Malcolm X–inspired black self-asser-tion and confrontational vocabulary. Gerald's "precise speech and innocent grin" deny him the "trust and the [protecting] fists of the young black cats."

At first glance the words "loss of his balls" signify the loss of cliché hetero-sexual manhood and are a weakness in the poem. But in the larger context provided by the rest of the lyric, the words signify the loss of self-determina-tion and the loss of what "balls" evolved to make possible: a connection to an unlimited future, a transcendence of mere mortality. The protective groups that are denied Gerald in particular and the other inmates in general ulti-mately protect one thing above all others: access to the future, which in turn protects access to a stable set of expectations and a stable sense of self.

The stock accusation that groups of four black inmates are obviously "muslims" is due in part to the recognition that the "muslims" are construct-ing a vision of first and last things and all things between—including the human posture in time and time's prisons—of which the prison adminis-tration does not approve. Among the things that helped Knight escape a Gerald-like fate was precisely an alternative vision he constructed in part in exchanges with Muslim inmates.

As Knight told Elizabeth Gordon McKim,

In the mid-sixties, when things were going on outside, things were hap-pening inside. I was listenin' [to] what Malcolm was sayin'. I was reading

Frantz Fanon, Martin Luther King. Baraka. We started doing a lot of organizing. Islam came into the prisons. . . . Earl, the guy that was partners in my crime, he came to prison on another charge. . . . He converted to Islam, and a couple of my other buddies converted to Islam. I'd talk to them. Most of the time I'd be arguin' against any kind of monotheism. . . . [Then came a summons from the warden, who said:] "I hear you been hangin' out with this Muslim cult." I say, "Cult?" . . . I got political. "The United States Supreme Court declared it a valid religion just like anything else." "Well are *you* a Muslim?" "It's none of your business. My religious beliefs are my own." . . . They locked me up. They were already rounding up all the known Muslims. . . . In Segregation where [they put us], we'd get fed. In Solitary you don't. . . . After a couple of days, the brothers started talking. "We don't want no pork . . . [or] food cooked in pork. . . ."

[But pork kept being brought and, in response, Knight and the others went on a hunger strike:] Warden started comin' up every day. // He'd look. // Guys be playin' cards. I'd be readin'. . . . About the third day, I'm so hungry // I ask for a compromise. // I say, "You guys know I ain't Muslim. // I'm just goin' along agreein' with you. // How 'bout me just getting vegetables without the meat?" // They say, "Naw, Man, just hang." // About the fourth day, I was hallucinatin'. // I saw Elijah Mohammed [the founder of the Nation of Islam and the mentor of Malcolm X] // I saw Malcolm . . . Finally, on the sixth day, // they brought the trays up // with no meat. // And the ol' Protestant chaplain came by // and told us it was a pork free diet // and that's when I told them // "Bring me some Meat!" . . . After a while, the warden pushed Islam, because they knew these guys didn't gamble, fuck with homosexuality, they didn't drink, they didn't fight. In fact they were model prisoners. . . . That was a turning point for me, and that's when I began to develop social and political consciousness.[7]

The six days of the strike helped revise Knight's interpretation of reality, helped change the man who leapt from a second-story hospital window for the sake of cocaine into the man who changed his outrage at Gerald's fate into a portrait of the whole whirlpool of injustice that sucks Gerald down.

In *Black Voices*, "Freckle-Faced Gerald" is followed immediately by an essay, "The Innocents," which includes a portrait of an inmate who sounds very much like a model for Gerald. This inmate, Donald Peck, is innocent of the rape and kidnapping for which he is serving a life sentence. Knight's portrait of him dates to 1967, but the destruction of Peck's possible futures began in 1947, when he returned from the U.S. Navy with an honorable discharge. The year, Knight wrote, was "a turbulent" one in which white young men came home from World War II and "hurled themselves into the 'rat race,' making up for lost time and money," but black veterans like Peck came home to the same partial social death that they had left. Many, Knight wrote, became "disenchanted, disillusioned, unemployed and confused," and "a few of them in their pain had turned to the two new things that were then sweeping the avenues: heroin and be-bop. Many more of them turned to whiskey, wine and violence" (87).

Peck's disaster began when he joined a group of five other men for a night on the town. While driving, the men were insulted by racial epithets hurled by the driver of another car. They gave chase until a policeman in a patrol car ordered them "to get [their] black asses off Illinois Street." "It is safe to say that such an incident is an ordinary and minor one in the life of most black men in the United States," Knight remarked, but "still . . . they acted in one of the ways usual to a large number of black men when they are caught in a vortex of fear-hate-policemen-emasculating racism: they drove away and got drunker."[8] It is to this sense of emasculation that Malcolm X and the Nation of Islam offered alternatives. It is of this same sense of emasculation that Peck becomes the embodiment. Knight's identification of the midpoint on the scale of emasculation—driving away and getting drunker—is not insignificant in light of the poet's own decades-long struggle with various addictions.

Peck himself, "a novice drinker," soon passed out. But the seasoned drinkers he was with somehow broke a taboo of the era by bringing a white woman into the car. In his interviews with the men, Knight was unable to determine whether what ensued was rape. The one certainty is that Peck did not participate. As for the other men, even "now, twenty years later," Knight wrote, "one senses ambivalence. On the one hand there is the shame, the sorrow and the guilt; on the other hand, there is an odd kind of self-esteem, a statement of haughtiness that belies the shame, if not the sorrow and guilt [about what they did]" (100). Knight went on to speculate that, in bringing the woman into the car and doing whatever they did, the four acted on the sense that their "manhood [had been] . . . threatened with immediate extinction: [As] in war, when soldiers . . . after the battle, with the song of death still singing in their brains . . . ravish the women of the vanquished. . . . [These men seemed to feel that one response to] soul-crushing racism [was to] somehow, rightly or wrongly, redeem and reassert themselves as men" (100).

Knight was careful not to excuse the assault that may have occurred. Instead, in a manner that some readers will no doubt find offensive, he lifts it out of the realm of American stereotypes and places it in the almost cosmic context of the impulse to survive and to be filled with the assurance of survival in the face of death—an impulse that, in his account, is bound up in the sexual violence of men saturated with war's threat of "immediate extinction."

This threat, in Knight's account, functions like the stings that Elias Canetti says pile up in the psyches of those who are saturated with commands. The archetype of such a person is the soldier "who lives in a permanent state of expectation of commands." Canetti theorizes that, in a soldier, these stings commands leave behind "must accumulate to a monstrous degree. Everything he does is in response to a command. . . . All his spontaneous impulses are suppressed. He swallows order after order, whatever he feels about it. . . . Each command he carries out . . . leaves a sting behind in him."[9] While this sting concept is too metaphorical to pass scientific muster, it is nonetheless a sharp insight into the psychology of frustration, repression, guilt, and fear. Stings are not unlike especially concentrated versions of Jung's complexes— "psychic fragments which have split off owing to traumatic . . . influences or certain incompatible tendencies."[10] In Knight's story of black men battling for their masculinity, the stinging commands are those of the racial hierarchy demanding that black men accept partial social death.

These racial commands are built into the American meanings of "black" and "white"[11] and, to a "monstrous degree," into the men Knight writes about. Canetti believed that if the same command is "pitilessly" repeated from different sources, then "the sting loses its clear outline and develops into a monster which endangers life. It grows until . . . its host . . . can never forget and carries it around, seeking any opportunity to get rid of it."[12] Might a genre of commands—a constant sequence of reminders that one is tainted with social death—similarly endanger, if not life itself, then one's sense of being alive? Canetti believed that the sting of a given order can be gotten rid of only by ejecting the sting in an equal and opposite command. Of course there is no such symmetry between the violence of rape (or at least the violence of sexual taboo breaking) and the violence of enforced social inferiority, and this lack of symmetry is reflected in the "shame, sorrow and guilt" some of the participants feel twenty years later. The expulsion of at least some small proportion of the commands that sting them toward Gerald-like social death— however the expulsion was accomplished—accounts for the "odd kind of self-esteem" that, Knight discovered, coexists with the shame and guilt.

As for the life sentences they received, Knight reported that "newspapers and radios screamed of 'lawlessness and crime in the streets'"—"citizens' committees were formed," and "ambitious detectives and similarly motivated young deputy prosecutors made inflammatory and incriminating statements to the press." In this atmosphere the six men (including Peck) were pressured to plead guilty to kidnapping and rape in exchange for a sentence of two to twenty-one years. And prosecutors—"bigger buzzards"—would agree to no deal that let Peck go free. "They wouldn't let us tell the whole truth, man," one of the other men told Knight. "If we told them that Peck had nothing to do with it, we'd all get life, they said" (104). The fact that the woman herself testified that Peck had not been involved in what happened made no difference.

In prison Peck was "passed . . . around like a beach ball for sex" (106). The incarcerated passed on some of their stings to him, adding to the stings of the injustice he had suffered. (For what command is more severe than the command to yield up one's lifetime?) Knight reported that Peck's "spirit has been broken. From 1963 to this date [1967] he has not even bothered to petition to appear before the annual Clemency Board."

In his preface to *Black Voices,* Knight was less sympathetic to Peck than he was in "The Innocents"—and far less sympathetic than he was to the Peck-like Gerald in "Freckle-Faced Gerald"—in part because his focus in the preface is not Peck in particular but correctional culture as a whole. Peck, Knight insisted in the preface, "has accepted the 'sanctity and dignity' of the racist Law—and has been programmed into near nonexistence." Peck, stung and stung and paralyzed by stings, has, in other words, failed to develop any of the "social and political consciousness" that Knight's experience with Muslims created in him. Peck becomes an emblem, then, of correctional culture at its most effective—stinging free will and self-determination into nonexistence.

Immediately after his prefatory comment on Peck, Knight quoted from his own "To Make a Poem in Prison"—an account of how hard it is to write poetry in prison: of how hard the struggle is to disentangle creativity and self-determination from the efforts of those who run penitentiaries and "the larger prison outside" to "hold the black inmates' minds in chains." And yet self-pity, and even pity for others, can blur the poet's vision and is "not for the poet." Still, somehow "poems must be primed," despite the fact that jail squeezes away the lucid sadness that inspires song, allowing "Not even a beautiful rage rage" or a burst of laughter or, of course, not love.

Ingeniously in these lines, Knight both catalogs things that snuff out poetic inspiration and defines, by summoning their ghosts into the lines, all that "primes" poetry and other efforts to keep the spirit from being paralyzed by stings: sadness untainted by annihilating despair, rage that does not shut down understanding but that actually opens the eyes and is therefore "beautiful," laughter that introduces joy into joyless places, and, above all, love. To make a poem, then, out of the unpromising materials of the prison—the elements of incarceration that, to vary Art Powers's words, rub prisoners' faces in their apparent insignificance—those materials must be somehow transmuted under the pressure of the poet's spirit, like sand transmuted into reflecting glass.

One of Knight's tools of transmutation is irony, very much on display in his poem "The Warden Said to Me the Other Day." Knight introduced this lyric in a 1986 Library of Congress reading by saying, "It's a fact that in prison in the springtime the escape rate goes up. When the flowers [open] and the birds start singing the young guys start running off. And this warden I had evidently didn't understand biology. So he was upset." Spring as the archetypal time of rebirth and generation is the opposite of prison and the suspended animation it induces. But there is more to the story than this basic opposition, as the brief text of Knight's poem makes clear:

> The warden said to me the other day
> (innocently, I think), "Say, etheridge,
> why come the black boys don't run off
> like the white boys do?"
>
> I lowered my jaw and scratched my head
> And said (innocently, I think), "Well, suh,
> I ain't for sure, but I reckon it's cause
> We ain't got no wheres to run to."

The "larger prison outside" appears here to cancel out spring and its possibilities of regeneration. The Brer Rabbit/minstrel show argot of the of the poem ("Well, suh // . . . we ain't got no wheres to run to") suggests that there is an impassable gap in communication between Knight and the warden. What makes it impassable is the difficulty of conveying, up through the hierarchical gap between prisoner and warden, and up through the racial, cultural, and ideological gaps between white authority figure and incarcerated (but politically and sociologically awakened) prisoner, the fact of the different concentrations of stings in the psyches of the white and black prisoners.

The warden of the Indiana State Prison for the bulk of the time Knight was there—and therefore the warden who is probably being referred to in the poem—was Ward Lane. Known among inmates as "Cool Tom," "Big Tom," and "Old Stone Face," Lane was variously "cursed, praised, feared, respected, smacked [on one occasion], and worshipped" by them.[13] Mike Misenheimer, who reported on "Cool Tom" in An Eye for an Eye, compared Lane very favorably with the previous and subsequent wardens, and blames the lingering inhumanity of the Indiana State Prison on politicians who refused to heed Lane's call for greater support for his rehabilitative efforts.

In the annual report he submitted for the 1962–63 fiscal year, Lane noted that, since the beginning of his tenure at the maximum security prison in January 1961, he had worked to clean up the public image of the institution and to improve its operation. He noted that a "Debating Club, Dale Carnegie Alumni Club, Fish Club, Stamp Club, and an Occupational Therapy Program to provide for inmates to make leathercraft, needlework, weaving, beadwork, and art work in quarters have all been initiated to occupy spare time." Furthermore the inmates "are now permitted to mail out 10 letters per month instead of the 6 previously allowed and visiting is permitted 7 days per week instead of 5." Both morale and discipline, Lane added, had been improved by "firm but fair and extended treatment programs in conjunction with the new employee training programs. Consequently, the incidence rate of inmate violence has been markedly reduced." Lane provided a chart showing that in his two and a half years as warden, threats to prison officers had fallen from 22 to 4, attacks on officers had dropped from 18 to 3, and fights among inmates had dropped from 102 to 84. The "treatment" program at the prison, according to one of the last documents prepared under the warden who preceded Lane, included elementary school education, especially for the 58 percent of black inmates judged to be functionally illiterate.[14] Lane added that, under him, for "the first time, Negroes are employed in Custody and clerical positions. . . . Currently there are a total of 8 colored people working here and there are no colored applicants for employment . . . at present." In a prison that employed some 28 heads of departments and had some 2,400 prisoners as of 1960, 8 is a small number. Lane's representation of it as a sort of breakthrough suggests that, at best, he had little understanding of the civil rights movement and the other forces, at work even in 1963, that changed "colored" into "black," and midwifed Knight's political and artistic awakening.

In comments like those he made on the origin of "For Freckle-Faced Gerald," Knight suggested that Lane's was a mere veneer of gentility—a public-relations glaze over a harsh, sometimes brutal reality. And Misenheimer, without mentioning Lane directly, confirmed some of Knight's suspicions about Lane, adding a class element to the racial one that was Knight's focus and citing what seems to be the same protected prisoner that Knight refers to:

During my ten years in this prison, I have seen only one youngster protected by the administration when he first entered. . . . This sixteen-year-old, whom we will call David, was kept in the Admission and Orientation section of the prison for almost a year. . . . By [the time he was placed in the general population] . . . the "wolves" had gotten the administration's message of "hands off!" . . . He got this protection—but why him and not others who came in as young?

David came from a middle-class family. . . . [His parents were] concerned enough to come here and talk to the warden before David even arrived. . . . Unfortunately, most young cons' parents are neither intelligent nor middle class. (171–72)

In "Hard Rock Returns to Prison from the Hospital for the Criminal Insane," the work that is perhaps Knight's most profound—in the sense that it touches the depths of all his great themes and connects them to major currents in American life—the poet shows the full brutality of the Indiana State Prison, proclaiming that though Hard Rock is known for taking "no shit" from anyone, his scarred and battered head and face show the price of indomitability. Indeed the poem turns on the "WORD" that doctors have transformed Hard Rock: "Cut out part of his brain, and shot electricity // Through the rest." The "WORD" is biblical in its significance, precisely because Hard Rock has become such a symbol of inmate invincibility that what is at stake in the battle between him and the prison authorities is ultimately not only his prison prestige but the legitimacy of the prison hierarchy and of the American justice system.

This is why when the "WORD" about what has been done to him circulates in advance of his return, the other inmates wait nervously. When he arrives in handcuffs and chains, they watch him with the same consternation with which they might look into a mirror after having lost a savage bar fight. For, as the next stanza makes plain, Hard Rock is more than the inmates' champion. He is the seed of a budding and defiant "inmate culture."[15] This is why, as they wait to see how Hard Rock will behave, Knight and the other inmates recite among themselves sagas of his exploits—including his record-breaking endurance of solitary confinement and the "jewel of a myth" that he poisoned a prison guard with "syphilitic spit." Viewed as criminally insane by the prison authorities, Hard Rock for the inmates is a Promethean rebel, a walking incarnation of the unstoppable self-determination they long for. Despite his possibly syphilitic bite, for them his violence is not "criminally insane" but, instead, an expression of an Old Testament eye-for-an-eye justice that is equal in ferocity to that of the prison authorities. Hard Rock is "crazy" from the inmates' points of view only because he fights against overwhelming odds and, as it turns out, against the ultimate in choice- and future-killing force.

In Komunyakaa's view Hard Rock is "misused by his fraternity of black victims," since he is allowed and, indeed, subtly pushed to sacrifice himself in a war they are careful not to fight.[16] They learn what he has lost when a "hillbilly" spits a race-based insult at him with impunity, a guard humiliates him and is answered with an uncomprehending grin, and it takes Hard Rock three minutes to recall his own first name. Witnessing all this, the inmates turn away, beaten, cut off from vicariously doing all they "dreamed of doing" but dared to do only through Hard Rock, and scarred again, "across their backs," by the whip of an enslaving fear. Hard Rock the person has been blotted out, and, with him, an incipient inmate culture. From the point of view of the authorities, this is a good thing—in line with "firm but fair" treatment programs aimed at reducing violence. For Knight it was an abiding source of trauma. Hard Rock "was really seven or eight guys I know who had shock treatment. But it was only one guy I had in mind. Yes, it actually happened,"[17] Shock treatments are not mentioned in Lane's annual report, and their use may have ended before or during his term as warden. In any case Lane's silence—or ignorance—is part of a major gap between his and Knight's—to say nothing of Hard Rock's—conceptions of the future. Although "Lane forbade brutality," according to Misenheimer, and although he worked to change the reputation the prison had when he assumed office as the worst "maximum security prison in the United States,"[18] he had little help in improving conditions: he "begged the legislature for funds and facilities but was ignored."[19]

The programs Lane was able to support surely helped Knight's birth as a poet. But they did little to relieve the psychic burn Knight received from the seven or eight examples of shock therapy that he was familiar with.

In a letter written to a younger inmate who called some of the older prisoners Uncle Toms without knowing what those men had faced, Knight explained that in earlier days, prisoners "didn't have the protection of this sham atmosphere of genteel liberality [created by Lane]. They sent troublemakers to the nuthouse, and burnt their heads to a crisp with shock treatments." Whether as a medic, prescription forger, or poet, Knight's life and his access to such futures as he could conceive depended upon his wits. "I am not like you," he told the editor of *Callaloo* after he was released from prison. "I don't have academic credentials. I did not finish high school. I live by poeting. . . . Sometimes people attach me to universities. If I don't poet, then I am a thief because that's what I was doing before I was poeting. I don't know anything else to do but hustle or poet." Both hustling and "poeting" require intense intellectual activity—something obviously disabled by the "treatment" given to Hard Rock.

The poem about Hard Rock is, again, perhaps Knight's most profound because, along with works like Anthony Burgess's *A Clockwork Orange,* it touches upon one of the fundamental issues in Western society: the point of contact between individual free will and public authority—namely, the consent of the governed, whether the governed are in prison or "free." The reaction of the other inmates to Hard Rock's annihilation as a free being—the fact, too, that a single guard succeeds in intimidating them all by humiliating him—makes it clear that not just Hard Rock's legend but the alternative universe of freedom to which the legend is the door are at stake in the poem.

One of the prisoners who may have been a model for Hard Rock is J. W. "Icewater" Prewitt, who, Knight reported, was innocent of the crime for which he was incarcerated and driven to a brutal rebelliousness by his situation: "In the Indianapolis County Jail of 1961, a young man—unless [he] was extremely unattractive—had two choices: to ride or be ridden. Prewitt chose to ride" (109). Prewitt insists on "acting up" during his trial; he becomes ever more defiant as he is squeezed in the coils of a court system complete with coached witnesses, biased rulings, and an inevitable conviction (112). In other words, he becomes more and more like Hard Rock. "If he keeps in his same groove," Knight concluded, "he is likely to wind up in the mental institution. There, they will attach little electrodes to his head and blot out his brain." The fear of falling victim to psychosurgery or some nonsurgical but equivalent mind control (such as Stockholm syndrome) is naked here. It runs like a subterranean current through much of Knight's poetry and prose.

For instance in a letter that was later published in the *American Poetry Review*, Knight wrote of the hot light that Michel Foucault called panopticism—a prison system's effort to remake inmates by subjecting them to constant surveillance and regimentation. The letter was a response to the one (quoted earlier) from the younger inmate who called Knight "Dear Brother Tom" and demanded to know "just who . . . you [are] speaking TO" in your newspaper essays. Knight replied by explaining just who he wass writing *around*: "Of course, you/ know that one says a poem or writes a column here in prison with the warden's eyeballs hovering/ over one's left shoulder, and with the Commissioner of Corrections' eyeballs glaring only a few inches above the warden's, and finally with the Governor's eyes hanging like twin bulbs from the whole prison. Of course, you've heard stories of the entire *Lakeshore Outlook* staff/ being thrown in the hole? . . . So, lil b'rer, the main/ thang that keeps me from speaking to and for myself [is] FEAR." Again the fear of having one's mind shaped or destroyed—the fear of having one's re-memberings of oneself undone by the hole or even harsher outside measures—is a major theme in both *Poems from Prison* and *Black Voices*. And Knight was not alone in feeling the point of authority's sting touching his brain.

The Kaimowitz Case and the True Meaning of Psychosurgery

The scariness of that sting was dramatized a few years after Knight was released from prison by the landmark case of *Kaimowitz v. Department of Mental Health of the State of Michigan*. Because the case makes explicit many of the undercurrents in works as diverse as "Hard Rock" and "The Warden Said to Me the Other Day," a detour into its details will be useful here. The origins of the Kaimowitz case date back to 1967, when, in a letter to the *Journal of the American Medical Association* (*JAMA*), Drs. Vernon H. Mark, W. H. Sweet, and F. R. Ervin argued that there was a possible overlooked cause of urban riots like the ones in Detroit and Newark that rocked the United States that year. Pointing to rioters who allegedly engaged in arson, sniping, and physical assault, the doctors noted evidence from "several sources" that "brain dysfunction related to a focal lesion plays a significant role in the violent and assaultive behavior of thoroughly studied patients."[20] Furthermore, they claimed, "individuals with electroencephalographic abnormalities in the temporal region have been found to have a much greater frequency of behavioral abnormalities (such as poor impulse control, assaultiveness and psychosis) than is present in people with normal brain wave patterns."

The doctors went on to cite research supporting their conclusions, including a study of "delinquent psychopaths tested in a medical center for federal prisoners in the United States [who] had a high frequency of abnormal brain wave patterns." What percentage of murders and attempted murders during the riots, the doctors wondered, were done without a motive? The three called for studies that would "pinpoint, diagnose and treat those people with low violence thresholds." Perhaps because they did not have access to accurate figures when they wrote, or perhaps because it did not occur to them to look for violent propensities in minds other than those of the rioters, the doctors make no mention of the fact that, in the 1967 riot in Detroit, for instance, almost 80 percent of the fatalities were African Americans shot by police and National Guardsmen for "alleged looting, sniping, and curfew violations." Helen Hall, a white woman, was shot by guardsmen who believed they had detected a sniper. One white man was killed by rioters he tried to drive away from his shop with a baseball bat. A twenty-three-year-old white man was killed after carrying a mop to the roof of his building and being mistaken by National Guardsmen for a sniper. A twenty-three-year-old white woman was killed by what may have been a sniper's bullet. Two black young men died in a burning store that it is speculated they were looting. Three unarmed black teenagers who were partying in a hotel room with two white young ladies were killed by National Guardsmen and policemen who burst into the room looking for a sniper. The young women were beaten.[21] All of these deaths are tragic, but those that were not accidents seem to have sociopolitical rather than biological causes.

The three doctors did concede that the "urgent needs of underprivileged urban centers for jobs, education and better housing should not be minimized." But they promote their own research agenda by locating the hottest spark of the urban fires in the brains of malfunctioning persons, asking, if "slum conditions alone determined and initiated riots, why are the vast majority of slum dwellers able to resist the temptations of unrestrained violence?"

Here the doctors overlook the socioeconomic and intellectual ecology of the riots in order to focus on brain physiology. Proof that intellectual ecology was more important than brain physiology can be found in the counter-example of riots of whites determined to attack blacks—the dominant form of American race riots prior to the 1960s. Those whites acted to preserve their preferred sociocultural and intellectual ecology—one in which no African Americans were present as neighbors or equals. As Joseph Boskin noted in a 1969 essay, "With the exception of the Harlem riots of 1935 and 1943 . . . the riots of the past two centuries were initiated by Caucasians and were motivated by racist attitudes. . . . The most intense violence occurred when minority groups attempted to change residential patterns or when a number of Caucasians defined the situation as one in which such an attempt was being made."[22]

Intellectual and emotional ecology was also a dominant factor in the riots of 1967. Riots in Newark and Detroit in particular were sparked in part by plans for "urban renewal" that promised to bulldoze sections of the African American community where housing was already so scarce that blacks were paying, on average, higher rents for worse housing than their white counterparts, all while earning lower average salaries. "In both cities the shortage of housing was further exacerbated by 'urban renewal' projects," Max Herman wrote. "In Detroit, entire neighborhoods were bulldozed to make way for freeways that linked the city and [suburbs to which whites fled after failing to prevent blacks from moving into their urban neighborhoods]. Nor surprisingly, the neighborhoods that met their fate in such manner were predominantly black. . . . In Newark, 'urban renewal' or 'Negro removal' as it was referred to by local residents, would play an equally important role in fomenting rebellion."[23] When one adds to urban renewal the overcrowding caused by de facto segregation and disproportionate joblessness in which discrimination played a role, it is clear that these ecologies quickly became ecologies of frustration.

Nevertheless the champions of psychosurgery had good reason to look forward to the success of their projects. For they had not only what appeared from some angles to be inexorable scientific logic on their side; they also had a well worked-out legal argument underpinned by laws built on ill-defined medical-legal terms such as "criminal insane," "defective delinquent," and "sexual psychopath." (Commenting on the state of affairs at Connecticut's Bridgewater State Hospital as of 1963, Dr. A. Louis McGarry noted that the "state hospital . . . sometimes referred to as the hospital for the criminal insane is, like similar institutions in the larger states, the end of the line for men felt to be both mentally ill and criminal (or at least accused of criminal offenses). To quote the statute, hospitalization at Bridgewater is to be reserved for the mentally ill person who has 'been a criminal or is of vicious tendency.' Men who are unmanageable in the state hospitals or state prisons are sent to Bridgewater. The institution is administered and staffed by the Department of Corrections and is, in fact, a prison."[24]

The fact that an accusation or a perceived "vicious tendency" could land a person at Bridgewater suggests that the widespread alarm that followed the eventual public discussion of the three physicians' *JAMA* letter was on the mark—in spite of disclaimers issued by the three doctors in the wake of condemnations of their speculations.

Both the doctors and their critics wrote and spoke during the prolonged period of national crisis marked by events like the Detroit riot. That his fears about the prison system and about the culture that sustains it were not mere epiphenomena of Knight's own experiences, perspectives, and mistakes is illustrated by the attack on total institutions (functional parallels of Foucault's panoptic ones) launched by Gabriel Kaimowitz in the winter of 1972–73, when he sued to stop a psychosurgery experiment inspired by the work of Mark and his associates. Kaimowitz argued that, although the experiment, conceived of and headed by Dr. Ernst Rodin, had been approved and funded by the state of Michigan, it was "not science." Eager to try a technique advertised by Vernon H. Mark and Frank R. Ervin in their book *Violence and the Brain*—a technique that allegedly could burn uncontrollable aggression out of brains found to be abnormal—Rodin and his colleagues at the Lafayette Clinic in Detroit had begun efforts to recruit potential subjects for their experiment. The first person who met their criteria and who signed the informed-consent form they designed was Louis Smith, who had been committed to Ionia State Hospital as a "criminal sexual psychopath" eighteen years earlier, when he was himself eighteen years old. Smith had been accused of killing and then raping a student nurse at a psychiatric hospital to which he had been sent. Believing it to be illegitimate, Kaimowitz zeroed in on the informed-consent document that Smith, who was known as John Doe during the legal proceedings that followed, had signed.

In January 1973 Kaimowitz filed a petition and complaint with the circuit court in Wayne County, Michigan, demanding that the pending psychosurgery be canceled. More specifically Kaimowitz insisted that the researchers, who planned to probe Smith's brain with small wires and destroy any offending small abnormality with electric current, "be enjoined from using state funds to conduct a study . . . involving the use of means which have permanent effects, when the subjects of such study are not in a position to voluntarily consent to participation in such experiments."

The question of why, despite the fact that he had signed a consent form expressing the hope that the experimental trial he was about to undergo would help him control his aggression, Smith could be seen as having *not* consented was at the heart of the legal proceedings that followed. In the historic ruling in favor of Kaimowitz that it issued on July 10, 1973, the court explained why. "To be legally adequate," the court stated, "a subject's informed consent must be competent, knowing and voluntary." Relying on sources that included the Nuremberg Code (handed down by the tribunal that tried Nazi war criminals), the court argued that an "involuntarily detained mental patient . . . must be so situated as to be able to exercise free power of choice without any element of force, fraud, deceit, duress, overreaching, or other ulterior form of restraint or coercion. . . . Although an involuntarily detained mental patient may have a sufficient I.Q. to intellectually comprehend his circumstances . . . the very nature of his incarceration diminishes the capacity to consent to psychosurgery. . . . [This is in part because in] the routine of institutional life, most decisions are made for patients. For example, John Doe testified how extraordinary it was for him to be approached by Dr. Yudashkin [Rodin's boss] about the possible submission to psychosurgery." Like a hostage with Stockholm syndrome, the involuntarily institutionalized person identifies those with power over him as the source of his possible comforts, well-being, or even survival. This gives suggestions made by such a person a special authority. Kaimowitz appeared to be driven, in this action and others, by a determination to undermine such illegitimate authority posing as something liberating and just.

In his essay "My Case against Psychosurgery," he asserted that "in the hands of the state, one does not choose even when to live or to die." For example, "the state is troubled when a . . . condemned murderer like Gary Gilmore attempts to take his own life before a designated time of execution. The state will decide, not the person who has forfeited choice."[25] Kaimowitz, who has litigated against everything from the warehousing of children (who might merely be unruly) in state hospitals to educational policies that, he argued, disadvantage speakers of Black English (called African American

Vernacular English by linguists), has made a rambunctious career out of res-
urrecting choice when he believes it has been, or is in the process of being,
unjustly diminished. A danger his 1973 case called attention to—and that he
specifically cited—is that of what sociologist Erving Goffman called the "total
institution": the sort of institution where "the inmate's life is penetrated by
constant sanctioning interaction . . . especially during the initial periods of
stay before the inmate accepts the regulations unthinkingly."[26]

The diminishment of one person's capacity, whether brought on by psychosurgery as in Hard Rock's case or by a total institution as in Louis Smith's
case, is unfortunately sometimes made the condition of the expansion of
another's—as the diminishment and even the destruction of Hard Rock was
necessary for the expansion of the prison authorities' power. Both Kaimowitz
with the 1973 case and related actions and Knight with "Hard Rock" and
related works strove to tip society's scales in the direction of enhancement
rather than diminishment of individual capacity.[27] Both experienced success.
Kaimowitz created a legal landmark, and Louis Smith, Kaimowitz reports,
gained a new understanding of and confidence in himself once he was released
to live freely. And Knight's life was of course transformed first by the words
of Malcolm X and then by his own words. Yet the forces of diminishment
never sleep.

No one, of course, was more aware of this than Knight. In his powerful
1967 short story "On the Next Train South,"[28a] Knight painted an Icarus-like
flight away from diminishment. His protagonist, T.G., defies the Mississippi
culture into which he (like Knight) was born—a culture summed up in the
assertion by an ex-girlfriend of T.G.'s that "when the white folks call, us niggers gotta come." T.G. beats up the local sheriff and then escapes an all-
but-certain lynching by fleeing to Chicago. But in Chicago, T.G.—a Hard
Rock–like character with precursors among the protagonists of Richard
Wright's *Uncle Tom's Children* and *Native Son*—clashes with and kills a
policeman and is sent to his own death in the electric chair. T.G.'s destruction
by his own efforts to free himself shows us, from yet another angle, the Scylla
and Charybdis—subservience or revolt—that Knight struggled to think and
write—and sometimes, unfortunately, drink and drug—his way clear of.

A Puzzle of a Poem

The question of whether there is a wise middle path between Scylla and
Charybdis is one of the subjects of a prose poem that is one of the most puzzling presences in Knight's oeuvre. The poem is puzzling because, although it
appears under Knight's name in a later collection, in *Black Voices from Prison*
it appears under the name Joe Martinez in the section of the book devoted to

writings by inmates other than Knight. Is it a poem that so captured Knight's sense of an important aspect of his reality that he simply appropriated it? Is it a piece that he did so much to help bring to the page that he felt as if it was really his? Did Knight come to see it as a toast that could be freely retold? In 1980, during a reading at the public library in Scranton, Pennsylvania, Knight explained that Martinez was an older inmate who spent twenty-five years in various prisons and died shortly after being finally released.[28b] Martinez compared the ministrations of the criminal justice system to those of an incompetent doctor, and apparently boiled his quarter century of mendicant incarceration down into Knight's "favorite anecdote." The anecdote-turned-poem appears under the title "Rehabilitation and Treatment" in *Black Voices from Prison* and, slightly revised, under the title "Rehabilitation and Treatment in the Prisons of America" in *The Essential Etheridge Knight* sixteen years later. The poem reads very much like a literary version of a game-theory forecast of a constrained set of futures. It begins as an inmate, seeking counseling for "personal problems," walks through the main door of the prison administration building and finds before him new doors labeled Parole, Counselor, Chaplain, Doctor, Teacher, Correction, and Therapist. He picks the door labeled Correction, only to walk through and confront two new doors, labeled Custody and Treatment. Opting for Treatment, he goes through its door and encounters doors labeled Juvenile and Adult. After choosing here, he is delivered to two new doors—Previous Offender and First Offender. His pick here brings him to a choice between doors labeled Democrat and Republican: "He was a democrat; and so he hurried through that door and ran smack into two *more* doors: Black and White. He was black, so he rushed—ran—through that door—and fell nine stories to the street."[29] Though unlit by the Promethean fires of "Hard Rock," this poem captures the dangers of interactions with Stockholm-style authority—which can be defined for present purposes as authority that causes those in its grip to work against their own best interests—in a similarly unmistakable way. Specifically it transmutes, into a Kafkaesque allegory, the ultimate downside of the sort of adaptation required of all who wish to function in an organization—even an organization that falls well short of Goffman's "total institution."

As Herbert Simon has observed, someone cannot "live for months or years in a particular position in an organization, exposed to some streams of communication, shielded from others, without the most profound effects upon what he knows, believes, attends to, hopes, wishes, emphasizes, fears and proposes."[30] The structure through which the inmate passes to his death in "Rehabilitation and Treatment" is an elaborate trap that, as the inmate moves through it, has, for him, the appearance and feel of an organization as

Simon defines it: "The term *organization* refers to the complex pattern of communication and relationships in a group of human beings. This pattern provides each member of the group much of the information and many of the assumptions, goals, and attitudes that enter into his decisions, and provides him also with a set of stable and comprehensible expectations as to what the other members of the group are doing and how they will react to what he says and does."[31] In the poem the fatal mistake that the inmate makes happens at the very beginning, when he unquestioningly accepts the patterns of communication in which he is ensnared, and accepts the idea that his "personal problems" are among the true concerns of those behind the door marked "Correction." Going through the doors that follow, it never occurs to the inmate that the process of "correction" is actually a sorting mechanism meant to identify those who think "black"—those who *run* through the "Black" door and thereby signify their desire to accept the organizing norms promulgated by the Black Power and Black Pride movement. Clearly the new black norms are antithetical to those of the prison administrators. For the administrators the norms are noise interfering with the signals they wish the inmates to receive—as the inmate learns in his last moment of life. The life-and-death weight carried by mere words on doors is closely linked here to Knight's idea of keeping the doors behind or before which one lives slightly open—of keeping the entire structure of meaning in which one lives slightly open, even if one must force it open.

Jean-Paul Sartre, whose book *What Is Literature?* directly influenced Knight's thinking, argued that a work of art is a work that inspires human freedom and is therefore always a little dangerous—always a threat to organizations as closed as the one described in "Rehabilitation and Treatment." Writing about the status of the work of art in what he calls "bourgeois society"—his French equivalent of Knight's "prison/America"[32]—Sartre asserted,

> Bourgeois art . . . would forbid itself . . . to probe the human heart too deeply for fear of finding disorder in it. Its public feared nothing so much as talent, that gay and menacing madness which uncovers the disturbing roots of things by unforeseeable words and which, by repeated appeals to freedom, stirs the still more disturbing roots of men. . . . Thus, [the bourgeois] conceived human progress as a vast movement of assimilation. . . . At the end of this immense digestive process, thought would find its unification and society its total integration. . . . [The bourgeois] regarded his fellow-men as marionettes, and if he wished to acquire some knowledge of their emotions and character, it was because it seemed to him that each passion was a wire that could be pulled. . . . All they wanted was to be provided with infallible recipes for winning over and dominating.[33]

The inmate in "Rehabilitation" has his wires expertly pulled—in spite of the fact that he is in a society that offers him only an assimilation into an intolerable social death. He is drawn out, as in a conversation that is unwisely entered into. He is in fact made to fall victim to his own cognitive and experiential limits—limits symbolized by the doors he chooses among and then ignorantly passes through.

Whether he was author, collaborator, or appropriator of "Rehabilitation and Treatment," Knight wanted the poem in his "essential" oeuvre because it so unequivocally expresses another of his major themes: that of the need to fight against unnatural cognitive and experiential limits and, where possible, to push one's perceptions and knowledge beyond them. This is something Knight clearly did in his evolution from addict to major poet—an evolution that continued, albeit fitfully, after he was paroled in 1968.

CHAPTER 4

Belly Song and Other Poems

In a letter that serves as the preface and, in effect, the opening poem of his second solo book, *Belly Song and Other Poems,* Knight tells Sonia Sanchez about what it was like for him to go, on November 7, 1968, before the parole board in hopes of being released. "Yeah, well, I made it. Parole," he writes. "Each day we move closer, Lady." Knight then backtracks to describe being summoned to the "Guard's Hall"—the bottom of "a large 'T,' with the administration building at the top."

As he continues, Knight enters the territory allegorized in "Rehabilitation and Treatment":

> In order to get to the Parole Board Room from the bottom of the "T"—one has to go thru four locked doors to reach the top, then he turns right and goes down a long corridor and knocks (lightly) on a big brown door. . . . From the "Hot Seat" on my right I could see the outside world thru the glass of two locked doors. . . . At last, the guy before me, a gray [a white person], came out of the corridor. He had made it. The buzzer sounded. I got up and went down the corridor. . . .
>
> The parole board is made up of five men: three ofays [whites], one super/black anglo saxon, and another black who . . . is Chairman of the Board. . . . They shuffle some papers and study me; I tremble inside and study them—especially the super/black anglo saxon. Then the Chairman takes me thru the paces, and I respond with the proper "yessirs" in the proper tone, like a well trained thoroughbred. It is clear from the first couple of questions that I'm going to be given parole, but the ritual has to be played out. The pins have to be stuck in, until I bleed. I bleed.[1]

This game of display and resistance—so covert as only to be a posture of the neurons—is something of which Knight shows himself here to be a past master. But he shows his wariness of being diminished by the game with his use of the term "Black Anglo Saxon"—defined in a *Negro Digest* essay as a black person who tries to "throw off the smothering blanket of social inferiority" by severing ties to black life and becoming as "white" as possible. Such people succeed only in achieving "what sociologists call a 'looking glass self'" that must be endlessly erased in order to approach an unreachable whiteness.[2] When Knight checked the mirror, of course, he wished to identify and erase traces of looking-glass selfhood. Just what sort of self he would have to become in the looking glass of Sanchez's eyes is another question—the answer to which he is not sure he can find: "A few more weeks and you'll be stepping/ off that plane, scared as hell . . . and I'll be standing there waiting for you, scared as hell."

Knight goes on to comment on the more strictly professional complexities of the life he was about to enter: "Dudley said a Donald Hall wanted to use some of my poems in an anthology? According to Dudley, Donald Hall wrote to LeRoi [Jones, later Amiri Baraka] for some poems too. And LeRoi said, No. I can [understand that]. That lil cat is the Boss Black Poet and if he's going to contribute his name and poems to white anthologies, he might as well marry a white girl and move to Sweden. . . . His refusal has to be seen as both personal and symbolic—in his case both are probably the same. On the other hand—at this point—I see very little wrong with lesser (in terms of reputation) poets allowing their poems to appear in ofay/mixed anthologies. Because you can bet, wherever whitey is (including anthology readers) there'll be some brainwashed brothers, and perhaps the Black poems will pierce their red, white, and blue brains."[3]

The freedom into which Knight was about to step resembled a flooding river, with powerful Black Aesthetic currents reflected in both the relationship between him and Sanchez (two rising stars of the movement) and in the "No" LeRoi Jones said to Donald Hall; but the flooding was also reflected in sociopolitical currents that included the backlash against African American demands for equality (reflected in the assassination later that same year of Martin Luther King Jr. and in the Republican Party's race baiting "southern" electoral strategy); in, unfortunately, the rising currents of Knight's suddenly freed drug cravings; and in the continuing currents of prison authority that cling to any parolee's life.

The typical parolee has "literally forgotten what the outside world is like, is disoriented, unable to cope with the simplest aspects of everyday living—ordering something at a hot dog stand, producing the right change for a bus ride, even crossing a busy street," Jessica Mitford wrote in her book *Kind and Usual Punishment*. Parole status itself prolongs the disorientation, since the parolee is "deemed to have lost all rights" and "is in a state of 'civil death'"—the twin of social death. His freedom is therefore "infected from the outset with an arbitrariness and unpredictability."[4]

Arbitrariness is pinned to the parolee by the contract he or she signs with the parole board, Mitford wrote. This contract commits the parolee "to abide by numerous arbitrarily imposed conditions" set by the parole officer, "in whom is vested the right to enter and search the parolee's house at any time without warning or warrant. . . . The parolee sees the contract as a delicately-triggered trap."[5]

While there is no evidence that Knight suffered setbacks because of any specific action of a parole agent, the fact that Sanchez needed Department of Corrections permission to seek a marriage license for herself and Knight, and the fact of the extra' risk infused into his days by the nature of parole as Mitford described it, could only have added to the stresses of a new marriage and a sudden career as a poet in demand on both the LeRoi Jones/Black Arts side of the poetry world, and on the mainstream/Donald Hall side. Haki R. Madhubuti believes that "in the final analysis, [Knight] was not ready [for his new life]. . . . It was naïve . . . to think that he could reenter the population without serious reeducation, economic support, professional counsel, and drug rehabilitation."[6]

Both the expected ecstasies of freedom and the deep and never-fully-expressible despair, frustration, anger, and fear that were part of his prison experience are quietly acknowledged and addressed in a November 1968 letter that Sanchez wrote to him while he was still behind bars. She assures him in the letter that he is a "beautiful/ blk/ man" able to endure all that might destroy him and who *must* survive "to tell the world abt itself." The state of mind Sanchez seeks to soothe here is captured in the assurances that Knight can endure all that would destroy him, and her insistence that it is incumbent upon him "to tell the world abt itself."

And yet, despite attaining both freedom and marriage to Sanchez, Knight's lack of preparation for the world of 1968—together with the stings left in him by jailhouse commands—seemed to have left him infused with a kind of post-traumatic stress, which, in turn, as Madhubuti observed, made the marriage to Sanchez "a nightmare [that] ended within a year."[7] Although according to Giammanco, Knight and Sanchez wowed audiences during a visit to Italy that Giammanco arranged,[8] back in America Knight fell back upon toast-world personas characterized by a "hustler-pimp mindset which included heavy drug usage."⁹ (It is not insignificant here that Knight's first artistic role model was the "wino" Hound Mouth.)

"I've asked myself a thousand times how I could get hooked again—after having lived in this kind of hell before," Knight wrote in an April 1970 letter to Dudley Randall. "On the surface it would seem that I'm some kinda nut, but I am not. Maybe I stayed in prison too long; maybe I didn't really survive like some of the strong ones; maybe the damage done to my insides are irreparable. I came out of prison naïve as far as the [African American freedom] movement is concerned. I was (still am) ready to give up my life if necessary for my people. I was committed, totally. And, man, I found a whole lot of people bullshitting. That really blew my mind. For some reason I could [not] accept/ adjust to that. I also think I got married too soon. After living/ looking out/ for myself alone for eight years I found it difficult to adjust to a married/ family/ situation. The two problems plus a few minor hang/ ups caused me to revert to my old way of solving problems: the needle. . . . I stopped writing almost altogether. (I couldn't be dishonest enough to write for Black people while living such an unblack life.) . . . I frankly do not see how [Sonia] endured as long as she did."¹⁰

Looking back on the last moments of the marriage in a 1998 interview, Sanchez commented on the overlap of those moments with the emergence of her celebration of sisterhood: "The female students [in a course on the black woman she was teaching] were driving me insane, always coming in for conferences. They needed help being Black women on a White campus. . . . I tried to write to those young sisters about what it was to love themselves. I wrote *We a BaddDDD People* that year. Etheridge tore up the finished manuscript for this book because he was not writing. When I found myself on the floor, trying to piece together this book, I knew it was time to leave."¹¹ Here the love Knight looked forward to through prison bars is literally ripped to pieces by the same thirst for poetic primacy he expressed in his prison letter, when he suggested that he could be considered a lesser poet than LeRoi Jones *only* because his reputation was smaller, and not because his talent was less. The profound respect for women and other "others" he expressed in his commentary on "For Freckle-Faced Gerald," as well as the profound love for Sanchez he expressed in his April 1970 letter and elsewhere, is torn up here too—temporarily. Friendship between Knight and Sanchez was restored, and she joined the vigil in his apartment when he lay dying in 1991.

Belly Song (1973) is, significantly, dedicated not to Sanchez (Knight's by-then ex-wife) but to his mother and to his then "woman, Mary Ellen McAnally." The book chronicles all Knight's postprison flights, falls, and heartbreaks, self-inflicted or otherwise. It opens hopefully with "Genesis," a poem of regeneration, in which the poem itself is said to have a "snake shape" and said to have the possibility of drawing blood from the heels of Eve and Adam. Adam and Eve here, in light of all that happened between the marriage to Sanchez and the dedication to McAnally, may well be Sanchez and Knight, marrying in the mouth of the black revolution, and eager to send world-changing words out from that mouth, but made to bleed by the fang-sharp mismatch between Knight's ambition, addiction, and his "rehabilitation and treatment" anxieties. The poem itself is focused more on rebirth than on wounds, however, and concludes with a call for its addressee to split the speaker's skin open with love as powerful and perdurable as "the rock // of Moses." The poem represents the healthier half of Knight, the part that is not the dybbuk for some drug, the part that can be forced out of its old skin by love and loving, the part that can tap love as Moses tapped the rock that then gushed water for Israelites dying of thirst in the Desert of Zin.

Asking for his skin to be split by the rock of love, Knight is asking for the rock of his lesser self, his snake-bitten addict self, to be split by a rock from which a miraculous love can spring. The last two lines, however, declaring that Knight's poems "love you," introduce a twist, changing the poem itself into the rock from which love might gush if the love in the poem and love in the reader are fruitful and multiply together. Such multiplication promises to heal the broken Eden of Eve and Adam—whether Eve and Adam are Knight and Sanchez, or Knight and McAnally, or Knight and the wider audience that "Genesis" might inspire.

The poem that immediately follows "Genesis" is a portrait of Knight himself destroying Eden—a portrait of Knight out of control—Knight in his old addict's skin, solving problems, as he says in his April 1970 letter, with the needle rather than with his love of himself, Sanchez, or the cause of black liberation. Called "Another Poem for Me (after recovering from an o.d. [over-dose])," the poem asks, "what now dumb nigger damn near dead"? The inter-rogation continues with Knight asking himself whether he has what it takes to be what he should be, rather than "what white/ America wants you to be"—a lost soul "crawling from nickel bag to nickel bag." The poem con-cludes with Knight exhorting himself to "be black"—to be, in the poem's vocabulary, a source of empowerment for both self and community, "black" like the brother holding him as he thrashes in withdrawal, "black" like the lover at his bedside summoning him back, "black" like the mother "praying to a white/ jesus to save her black boy."

Knight strikes himself with this poem as Moses strikes the rock. The water he wants to bring from the rock of his own heart is a rehabilitative love strong enough to answer that of those who, in the overdose in question, saved him from the self that is not what it should or can be. As a transmutation into poetry of the thoughts expressed in the April 1970 letter, the poem captures Knight's angry bewilderment at himself. But, eschewing self-pity, it leaves out the speculation that "maybe the damage done [by prison] to my insides is irreparable." It also leaves out Knight's postprison disillusionment with those who undermined the Black Freedom movement from within.

In fact, in his bitterest charge he all but accuses himself of having become (temporarily) one such person: the self white America allegedly wants; the self, powerless as freckle-faced Gerald, whose whole substance can fit in a needle tip and in the criminal law. Imploring himself to be "black," Knight is imploring himself to be self-determined rather than drug-determined, imploring himself to ride the crest of self-love and community building of the civil rights and Black Power eras. At the same time, the lines about his mother underscore his doubts about a source her strength: her "white/ jesus" separates Knight from the "black" autonomy he seeks, even as the love she founds on "jesus"—who for her, as the slash mark suggests, is just Jesus, and not "white"—helps pull him back from the brink.

Knight turned his questioning eye on the Black Power movement itself in a lyric to Huey P. Newton that is simply called "Huey." In 1966 Newton cofounded the Black Panther Party for Self Defense, a grassroots organization whose founding principles included the idea that "white America is an organized imperialist force for holding black people in colonial bondage."[12] For Newton and the Panthers the tip of the white imperial spear was the police force patrolling black communities such as Newton's native Oakland, California. Eldridge Cleaver, who became the Panther minister of information in 1967, called the Oakland Police Department "notorious, repressive, racist and brutal" in a 1968 open letter to then-governor Ronald Reagan. "This gestapo force," Cleaver told Reagan, "openly and flagrantly terrorizes the black people of Oakland."[13]

By the time Cleaver wrote this letter, Newton was facing trial on murder charges brought in the wake of a clash with policemen who pulled him and a friend he was driving with over in the wee hours of October 28, 1967. In what followed, Newton was shot in the stomach and two officers were wounded, one fatally. Newton's trial the following year became the center of a national ideological uproar, with supporters both black and white demanding that Newton be freed. On the other side of the debate, the head of the FBI, J. Edgar Hoover, labeled the Panthers a threat to the security of the United States and launched a covert program to destroy them. Newton was convicted of voluntary manslaughter in 1968 and given a two- to fifteen-year sentence. After his conviction was reversed upon appeal, he was tried again twice, in proceedings that resulted in hung juries. In 1971 prosecutors dropped all charges and Newton, who at that point had spent almost three years in prison, was released into an environment where both his authority and Panther unity were increasingly undermined by FBI activity.[14] According to Peniel E. Joseph, "a stream of imaginative FBI measures, conspired to poison a [Newton-Cleaver] relationship forged in mutual admiration. Less than six months after Newton's release from jail, an FBI memo emphasized his deteriorating psychological state, taking pains to note that he appeared 'on the brink of a mental collapse' before suggesting a stepped-up disinformation campaign."[15]

Though he could not have known the details of the FBI covert efforts when he wrote "Huey," Knight had a clear path of extrapolation from the public campaign against the Panthers that resulted in a "growing list of Panther cases in which the prosecution . . . failed to win a conviction,"[16] and in violent deaths like that of Fred Hampton (the Chicago leader of the Panthers), during a nighttime raid on his apartment. The latter, together with a similarly violent Los Angeles police raid, for the first time "brought cries of sympathy from moderate black leaders who once shied away from any identification with the Panthers."[17]

Knight's poem accepts Newton's self-definition as a revolutionary and seems to accept the view (expressed by a preschism Eldridge Cleaver) that "Huey P. Newton is the baddest motherfucker ever to set foot inside of history. . . . For four hundred years black people have been wanting to do exactly what Huey Newton [has done], that is, to stand up in front of the most deadly tentacle of the white racist power structure, and to defy that deadly tentacle, and to tell that tentacle that . . . if he is moved against, he will retaliate in kind."[18] With this sort of romantic assessment of Newton serving as a backdrop, Knight welcomes Newton back from prison—"the House of many Slams"—to "These mean bricks," and declares that the common people now have a "prince."

Newton as "prince" and agent of his own and other African Americans' agency is here a kind of second coming of Malcolm X. He is a Hard Rock with a real chance of changing America, of removing the "sword buried in the heart of [black] people,"[19] to quote words Cleaver wrote about the Panthers' intentions in Oakland, but which apply to the entire civil rights and Black Power struggle.

The "mean bricks" of the streets to which Newton returns represent not only the "bricks" patrolled by the Oakland Police Department and the bricks of the buildings raided by the police and FBI but also the bricks on which Knight himself was struggling to get his own footing. Prison, the "House of Many Slams," and the means by which he and other African Americans might escape it in all its forms, was still very much on Knight's mind, as the poem that immediately follows "Huey" shows. The poem, called "On the Yard," catapults the parolee author of *Belly Song* back behind bars, into the presence of a "young" and "beautiful fascist" who demands to know why Knight is not "*doing* something." Knight reports in the lines that follow that he stays up all night writing in an effort to prove that writing is a way of doing something. But the "beautiful fascist" remains unconvinced, and Knight admits to being himself not "completely" sure that the five thousand words he produces during the sleepless night are, after all, a kind of action. Read after the Newton poem, this admission shows a poet struggling to resolve the complexities of what Sartre calls *engagement*.

Though Sartre excludes poets from his formulations,[20] the following account he gives of the engaged writer applies, like a second skin, to the Knight who writes not only five thousand words of prose, but also a response poem, to his "beautiful fascist": the Knight who also, even as he worries that he is not doing enough, refuses to plead guilty to the fascist's charge of inaction: "To speak is to act; anything which one names is already no longer quite the same. . . . With every word I utter, I involve myself a little more in the world, and by the same token I emerge from it a little more, since I go beyond it toward the future. . . . It is therefore permissible to ask [the prose writer] this second question: '. . . What change do you want to bring into the world by disclosure?' The 'engaged' writer knows that words are action."[21] Sartre is writing here in the immediate post–World War II era, with memories of the Nazi occupation and the French resistance (and resistance writing) fresh in the minds of his readers. Sartre anticipates some of what Knight and other black writers engaged with years later when he wrote that "from within oppression itself we depicted to the oppressed collectivity of which we were a part its anger and its hopes."[22] The parallel with those writing from within racial oppression is one Sartre himself draws several times by pointing to similarities between African American resistance and occupied French resistance. Specifically Sartre uses Richard Wright as an illustration of the way in which the writer's public and the situation in which it finds itself structures the nature of the writer's engagement.

For Sartre, there is a strong parallel between the position of an author like Wright and the position of one of Sartre's own precursors—Jean-Jacques Rousseau: "The appeal which the writer addressed to his bourgeois public was, whether he meant it or not, an incitement to revolt. . . . The condition of Rousseau was much like that of Richard Wright's writing for both enlightened negroes and whites. Before the nobility [Rousseau] bore witness and at the same time was inviting his fellow commoners to become conscious of themselves." Moving forward in time and its parallels, it is hard not to think that Knight must have seen precursors of his own options in Sartre's account not only of Rousseau, but, more urgently, in resistance writers' wartime work of dissecting Nazi propaganda and racial mythology: "Against the vague and synthetic notions which were crammed into us day and night, Europe, race, the Jew . . . we had to awaken the old spirit of analysis which alone was capable of tearing them to pieces."[23a]

How to convey all this to the "beautiful fascist," whose mind is clearly made up, and who does not believe that five thousand or any number of the sorts of words Knight wrote under the eye of the prison authorities constitute an action? Of course Knight's calling the man a fascist, however beautiful, in itself speaks volumes and might serve those following in the steps of Knight's criticizer by disclosing the choices his rigidity closes off—by disclosing, in fact, a spectrum of possibilities that even includes the one Knight places at the end of the poem—the possibility that there is justice in the accusation of the "beautiful fascist": that Knight's five-thousand word night changes nothing.

The Knight who, on parole, might have thought guiltily back to the accusation was the drug-prone one—the one who rendered himself incapable of living up to Sartre's rules of engagement. This Knight, who leaves himself open to the fascist's contempt, is on full display in "Feeling Fucked Up," another poem about losing Sonia Sanchez fed up with Knight's addiction and addict ways. Sure there is no power in the universe that will bring her back, Knight loses his faith in the whole universe and utters one of the great rants in poetry.[23b] He begins by casting aside icon after icon of late 1960s and early-1970s artisitic and political engagement. "Fuck Coltrane," he writes, and not only him, but Marx, Mao and Castro on the left, Nixon on the right, and beyond them and all the earth itself, the Virgin Mary, God, and Jesus in their heaven. Even Malcolm X, the original tongue of Black Power, is shown the door, along with the cosmos itself: "Fuck . . . the whole motherfucking thing."

This tantrum suggests that revolution as Knight conceives it rests on eliminating disruptions in the information-rich interweaving of lives that is summed up by the word "love." With the interweaving of his and Sanchez's lives ripped apart, all the elements of their interwoven universe become meaningless. All the choices they would have made together between, for instance, Marx and Mao, or democracy and communism, or even Jesus and Malcolm X—all these choices seem to Knight suddenly not worth making. Even the substances he chose at times in preference to Sanchez herself—"smack" (heroin), in particular—seem not worth touching. The pain expressed by Knight's dispensing with essentially the whole world, and the Whitman-like eloquence of the dispensing, make this one of the standout poems in *Belly Song*.

Out of the despair over the end of the Sanchez relationship emerges, on the next page of *Belly Song,* a poem celebrating the relationship with the woman who became Knight's second wife—Mary Ellen McAnally. The McAnally poem is devoid of political references, and it expresses simply the joy of arrival, the joy of a shipwrecked man washed up on shore. McAnally is like fertile "warm black earth" dribbling from the fingers, Knight writes.

Politics returns and is, in fact, the entire subject of the next lyric, "On Watching Politicians Perform at Martin Luther King's Funeral." Knight does not name any particular politicians in the poem, but there were certainly many degrees of sincere grief and sincere opportunism and performance among the many who attended or sought to attend the funeral. According to *Time,* "60 U.S. Congressmen . . . attended the funeral," more than there were seats for in the Ebenezer Baptist Church where the funeral took place and where King's father was pastor.[24]

Luminaries who made it into the church included Jacqueline Kennedy, then–vice president Hubert Humphrey, Richard Nixon, and, from the other end of the political spectrum, Stokely Carmichael. The coffin King lay in was carried after the service in a mule-drawn sharecropper's wagon followed by his family and close associates. But behind them came "the politicians aspiring to the presidency—Vice President Humphrey, Senators Robert Kennedy and Eugene McCarthy, and former Vice President Richard Nixon."[25] Politics, then, were decidedly in play—and not only politics of which Dr. King would have approved. (In the last year of his life, King expressed a preference for "either Kennedy or McCarthy as the 1968 Democratic nominee, and Governor Nelson Rockefeller of New York to carry the Republican standard. He was definitely opposed to Richard Nixon.")[26]

This distasteful (albeit inevitable) mixture of ambition, political expediency, and real mourning is Knight's target: "Hypocrites shed tears // like shiny snake skins," he writes, remaking the snakeskin image from "Genesis." The skins here are not a symbol of regeneration but of the recycling of a hypocrisy that neutralizes the revolutionary changes King sought to make. At least within the compass of this poem, the "stacked deck" that Knight refers to in one line—a deck that King died to make fair—remains stacked, and by the very people who pretend to mourn him.

Yet in the very setting down of this despairing message, in the striking originality of the idea of snakeskin tears, Knight answers Sartre's questions: "What aspect of the world do you want to disclose? What change do you want to bring into the world by disclosure?" The snakeskin tears disclose the loss, at his very funeral, of the promised land that King, on the night before he was shot, spoke of glimpsing. The change disclosure calls for is the ending of the cycle of hypocrisy. The question of how to bring this change about has to do with tactics, tools, alliances, and the "belly," and is a key theme of the rest of *Belly Song*. The title lyric, without directly addressing politics, addresses the healing of hypocrisy in Knight and in America.

The poem is dedicated to the "Daytop Family," in a clear reference to the Daytop, Inc., organization of Seymour, Connecticut. Knight entered Daytop as part of a sentencing agreement following his arrest and trial—during a stint as a poet in residence at the University of Hartford—for heroin possession. According to the *Hartford Courant*, Knight was arrested in late 1970 and, after his trial, was put on probation on condition that he enter Daytop. (He was saved from a harsh sentence by the intercession of Anthony S. Keller, then executive director of the Connecticut Commission on the Arts, who testified that Knight was a "pre-eminent writer.")[27] Daytop was described as a "humanizing community" that viewed drug addiction as a symptom rather than the cause of the problems of an "immature person" by its then director George Tocci, in an April 23, 1971, letter addressed to "Broadside Press." In boilerplate language that is the opposite of the language Knight crafts in "Belly Song," Tocci explained that Daytop's staff of ex-addicts took a tough-love approach to rehabilitating drug abusers.[28]

"Belly Song" does not address either addiction or recovery in direct detail. Instead, it focuses on the love and the courage—the *belly*—needed to fight past addiction and toward recovery, which for Knight is something that cannot be achieved alone. The poem begins with Knight declaring his love for a "you" who has made something of the inner emotional and experiential sea that can drown a person. The poet then dives into the "belly," into a sea of feelings he distinguishes into feather feelings, feelings of bone, and feelings made of stone. It is not clear whom Knight addresses as "you." It may be Mary McAnally, with whom he remained in contact while at Daytop and whom he visited after decamping from the facility in November 1971. But it is also possible that Knight is addressing a member of the "Daytop Family"— someone who by fighting addiction has "made something // out of the sea // that nearly swallowed you." Or he might be addressing his whole support system, including McAnally and the "Daytop family." What is clear is that he plumbs the depths where the conscious self meets all that shapes it and its actions. He enters depths the intellect cannot reach and where one sees, if at all, by the mercurial light of feelings that, when touched by action, turn to stone, or to bone, or to feather. The plunge into depths lit only by flickering feelings that can suddenly change to stone is, Knight has suggested, a dangerous thing. "It hurts to be aware in this country," he told *Callaloo*,[29] And yet poetry depends on the maximization of awareness: "To make a poem or to preach a sermon or to create in any sense, you have to become extremely aware."[30] Poetry making and therefore awareness in prison—and at the time of *Belly Song*'s publication Knight still believed that "in all the real senses I am still in prison"—mean connecting one's nerves to "a very painful reality": it means plumbing the bitterness of the "belly."[31] As Knight explained in a 1985 interview, "I think my primary thrust or mission is to tell as clearly as possible what it is that I feel and think about my world and my relationship with my world—other people and myself and nature and with the gods, as I see them. As Baraka [says], 'The duty of a poet is to say as exactly as possible what it is he or she means.' Because what you're dealing with is so intangible. It's why we have to speak in similes and parables and metaphors. You can't speak in the language of the technocrat."[32]

To plumb the belly and to speak exactly enough to map it in words, Knight must strive to sense not only what the self represses or fails to consciously process, but also what other people, nature (including one's own biology), and the gods do not say. When one considers what Knight sought to sense, and then to capture in words that could reach other people's depths, one realizes that there is no deeper sea than the "belly," and one realizes that Knight's is a Jonah's journey. Hence his joy at finding—in the first section of the poem—another person surfacing from feeling's depths, and his determination, in the next section, where he turns the poem into a kind of dirge, to take on the priestly tasks of public mourning and public blessing:

> This poem/ is/
> a death/ chant
> and a grave/ stone
> and a prayer for the dead:
> > for young Jackie Robinson.
> . . . .
> [who moved] thru the blood and mud and shit of Vietnam
> . . . .
> thru the blood and mud and dope of America

"Young Jackie Robinson" led a life that strangely paralleled Knight's. The son of the barrier-breaking baseball legend Jackie Robinson, Robinson Jr. entered the armed forces at the tender age of seventeen, after running away from home and out of the shadow of his legendary father. Robinson Jr. later said that, fighting in Vietnam at eighteen, he became ever more "confused about manhood, responsibility, and a lot of other things."[33] By the time he returned to the United States in 1967, he was badly addicted, having been initiated into the use of everything from marijuana to opium to pills he obtained from army medics. While acknowledging his own errors, Robinson Jr. blamed the army too, saying, "I was helped by a very insensitive organization to get further and further down the road to destroying myself."[34] In a Knight-like moment, he adds that war itself, with the necessity it imposed of coping with an "extraordinary amount of fear," helped open the door to addiction.

Despite the resources his family was capable of providing for him, Robinson Jr., back in the United States, followed a road similar to the one Knight had stumbled down earlier, becoming "heavily involved in all types of drugs," and dipping into "about every type of crime that you could get into, in order to support [his] habit."[35] When, inevitably, Robinson Jr. was arrested and convicted, he was given the same choice that Knight would be given in 1971: go to jail or go to Daytop.

Daytop seems to have broken addiction's grip on Robinson Jr. But Daytop staff warned his father that relapse was always possible and suggested that "one of the most successful ways a former addict can keep himself cured is through deep involvement in helping others who are fighting addiction."[36] Did Knight's citizenship in the parallel world of poetry prevent him from continuing to focus on defeating addiction? Did it give him an excuse not to? Perhaps. But it also allowed him to choose to focus on the goal of all his poetry: contributing to the fruitfulness and multiplication of freedom that would chafe at even the tough love of Daytop, and contributing, more constructively, to the fruitfulness and multiplication of communication and what it enables— community. The blessing he sends to the departed Jackie Robinson Jr.—who was killed in a car accident—is not only a heartfelt act of mourning but also part of that aspect of community weaving that involves the selection of heroes who can serve as ethical paragons.

Knight next shifts the focus of *Belly Song* directly to the force behind the tough Daytop regimen: love, the feather emotion that promises flight above a world of troubles:

> this poem/ is/ a silver feather
> . . . .
> . . . for Sheryl and David—and
> their first/ kiss by the river . . .
> . . . .
> . . . [for] love/ rhythms—and LIFE.
> for Karen J. and James D. and Ronald M. and David P.
>   who have not felt
> the sun of their eighteenth summer.

Love, the great repairer of generations, growing like Whitman's grass from the tops of graves, and growing up also in young hearts, is captured here in its first moments ("the first/ kiss by the river"), in its lasting rhythms ("LIFE"), and in its future possibilities in the lives of those who have "not felt // the sun of their eighteenth summer." But love itself, of course, is riddled with chance— from the sperm that reaches the egg at a certain hour in the body of a woman of a certain status and health, to the twists of addiction and error that might cause future lovers to meet at a place like Daytop, to the ripping away of Jackie Robinson Jr. from his family by a car crash on a road he had probably driven without incident many times before. Knight turns to himself and his troubled history with love's chances in the third section of "Belly Song":

> this poem/ is/ for me
> and my woman
> and the yesterdays
> when she opened
> to me like a flower
> but I fell on her
> like a stone

Knight here settles accounts with his own conscience, confessing with the honesty that he believed poetry required and that the Daytop community believed recovery demanded. The evocation of what appears to be his behavior during his marriage to Sanchez provides the poem's most shocking and powerful moment—the abrupt transition from the sexual opening of the flower to the brutal fall of the stone. In the poem's final section, Knight repeats the opening declaration of love. But he adds a reference to the fact that he is in his fortieth year and has arrived at a "House of Feelings" and a "Singing Sea." This suggests that mourning and confession have led to a rebirth of his heart and of both his moral and poetic powers: a rebirth, in short, of his ability to contain and share love.

Knight's joy and apparently achieved stability continue in the following poem, "Green Grass and Yellow Balloons," which celebrates his discovery of a tiny poet—Alexandra Keller (probably a relative, perhaps the daughter, of the Anthony Keller who testified on Knight's behalf). Alexandra lives in a world not haunted by drug addiction or other demons. In the course of the poem, Knight underscores the transformative power of language, of words like lures that draw possible futures: reciting a poem she has composed for Knight, Alexandra creates an Alice in Wonderland–like reversal of the rules of time and causality and makes the sea that almost drowns Knight in "Belly Song" a sea of renewal:

softly you sang
your words warming me
and the sea rose in me
and your song sent me spinning
. . . .
and suddenly
I was 4 and you were 40

Returned to the age of four, Knight is drawn, like a thread out of a needle's eye, out of his years of addiction and incarceration, out of even the full awareness of racial inequality, out of the age of forty, which, as he informs readers earlier in *Belly Song,* is only four years short of the age at which his father died—"Peaked out," in the words of the doctor who examined him. Knight, with various overdoses on his résumé, suddenly finds that an age that must have weighed on his mind has receded from him by forty years—and all because of a four-year-old whose age, added to his, equals his own father's final age. He escapes, in other words, all that destroyed his father and that is in the process of destroying him. And he escapes because of an "open sesame" pronounced by pure innocence unmarked by the world Knight found it so difficult to live in.

His escape does not last though. He soon recalls that "demons stalk/ this land // that smash // people and poets // whether 4 or 40," But on the whole he remains confident in the tot's potential to eventually produce words that lure better futures into ordinary time: "your words [will] // be eagles // that rise . . . to soar // above this . . . froze and frigid land // and we // who walk in new ways // will hear you . . . and sing too // of green grass. and yellow balloons."

Just what sort of "new ways" Knight has in mind here is clarified by the thematic twin of "Green Grass and Yellow Balloons"—a poem called "One Day We Shall All Go Back" whose tone and inspiration is dramatically different, but whose Moses-hungering-for-the-promised-land subject is identical:

One day we shall all go back—
We shall all go back (down home
To the brown hills and red gullies (down home
Where the blood of our fathers
Has fed the black earth . . .
. . . .
We shall surely all go back (down home
and the southland will tremble to our marching feet (down home

The structural ingenuity of this poem is its most remarkable feature. The repetitions of "down home" in open parenthesis give the poem a mazelike structure that cancels each definitive statement of home's standout features, or of how home will be reached, or of what the consequences of reaching it might be, while simultaneously keeping the prospect of home ever present. Structured thus, the poem conveys the sense that its author is trying various doors leading to alternative instances of the future variously tainted by the past. The attractive "brown hills and gullies," where a new life might be built, have been watered by "the blood of our fathers" feeding the black earth. Not surprisingly the third stanza of the poem speaks of vengeance. But the poem's structure keeps the grief and anger the lines express from narrowing into dead-end "sloganeering."[37] The structure, in fact, keeps the concluding section inconclusive. Even as it arrives, the last open-ended "down home" suggests alternative possibilities perched in the very prophecy the poem tries to make. The "cold northlands . . . of frozen hearts" that the poem references at one point are clearly spiritual conditions to be escaped by returning—or creating home by summoning it into words. But having spied the promised land, the poem cannot tell how to reach it. It ends up not so much asking the reader for help as luring the reader into the maze its own structure creates, as if to say, "This problem cannot be solved without you."

The meaning of "home" and the immensity of the problem of finding it is further explored in "The Bones of My Father." As the title suggests, Knight's father—or rather Knight's struggle with the ghost of his father—dominates this lyric:

> There are no dry bones
> here in this valley. The skull
> of my father grins
> at the Mississippi moon
> from the bottom
> of the Tallahatchie,
> the bones of my father
> are buried in the mud
> of these creeks and brooks that twist
> and flow their secrets to the sea.

The key image in these lines is that of "dry bones"—an image that makes the following passage from Ezekiel 37, in which God places the prophet Ezekiel in a valley full of bones, the loom upon which the poem is woven:

> Then [the Lord] said to me, "Prophesy to these bones and say to them,
> ". . . [The Lord] will make breath enter you, and you will come to life. . . ."
> So I prophesied [and] . . . there was a noise, a rattling sound, and the
> bones came together, bone to bone . . . and tendons and flesh appeared on

them and skin covered them. . . . Then he said to me, "Prophesy to the breath," . . . So I prophesied . . . and breath entered them: they came to life and stood up on their feet—a vast army.[38]

For the Knight who felt robbed of breath in the Hole, this passage must have meant much. When he writes, there are "no dry bones // here in this valley," he is indicating that there is little prospect in Mississippi, and in the sphere of his poetic talent, for a reclothing of his father's or any other bones or a refilling of his father's lungs. There is little prospect of reversing either death itself or social death. The image of the father's skull grinning up from the bottom of the river is the image of a Shine who does not make it across the waters—the image, too, of all that Knight must overcome to escape the violent noise of Mississippi history and to hear, if not the voice of God, then the voice of his own inspiration speaking future-opening words.

The poem takes a positive turn, therefore, when Knight hears the wind singing and the sun speaking of the dry bones of his father. But in the next two sections of the poem, the world he lives in overwhelms his efforts to summon an Ezekiel-like miracle—to make the wind and sun transmit breath and life into the Mississippi mud and the bones of his prematurely lost father. Instead Knight transmits a twentieth-century version of the message God wants Ezekiel to deliver to Israel when the deity tells the prophet, "Son of man, these bones are the whole house of Israel. They say, 'Our bones are dried up and our hope is gone: we are cut off.' Therefore prophesy and say to them: 'This is what the Sovereign Lord says: O my people, I am going to open your graves and bring you up from them.'"[39]

Knight, following in the footsteps of ancestors who created the corpus of African American spirituals, makes the African American community the house of Israel that is "cut off." In the process, he makes the bones of his father represent "the whole house of Israel"—all of African America and, beyond that, all of miracle-needing America, of whatever race: the poem joins together black junkies in Harlem who "Nod on the stoops of tenements // And dream // Of the dry bones of my father" with "young white longhairs who flee // their homes . . . and sing songs of brotherhood // and no more wars" and, thereby, search "for // my father's bones."

The "house of Israel" that is to be brought up from the grave here is clearly the America of its leaders' best promises: the America that does not shatter communities like the ones in which addicts sit on the steps deeply stung and on the nod. More idealistically, the poem's vison is of an America that not only does not prosecute wars like the one in Vietnam (much condemned by "white longhairs") but finds a way to put enough flesh on the bones of brotherhood to make war unnecessary.

"The Bones of My Father" is ultimately about America's need for an infusion of bone-clothing idealism—which really is a kind of faith—and about
denials of, and flight from, that need:

> There are no dry bones
> here, my brothers. We hide from the sun.
> No more do we take the long straight strides.
> Our steps have been shaped by the cages
> that kept us. We glide sideways
> like crabs across the sand.

Written after the arrest that led to his commitment to Daytop, these lines
expand like ripples out of what appears to be a moment of profound self-
doubt. Crucially the self-doubt here arises out of a suspicion of having had
one's free will removed and replaced by something alien: "Our steps have
been shaped by the cages // that kept us," cages like the Connecticut jail in
which Knight was held after his late 1970 arrest and, of course, the cages of
his previous incarcerations. Striving to move forward through space, time and
possibility, he fears he has lost his self-determination (his "long straight
strides") and has been possessed by a manner of movement that has no connection to the progress forward to freedom that he desires: "We glide side-
ways // like crabs across the sand." The poem ends where it began, with an
evocation of the father's skull at the bottom of the Tallahatchie—wet and, as
it were, drowned in history and in the contingencies that wrenched the father
out of the world and beyond Knight's powers of communication.

Knight's effort to find a mode of thought that, if it will not resolve all his
contradictions, or dry the bones of his father, will at least allow him to master
and harmonize those contradictions, like notes in a chord, is further displayed
in the second section of "Untitled 1," which follows "Green Grass and Yellow
Balloons,"and addresses "Third World Guerrillas, urban or otherwise." The
guerrillas, as the poem describes them, are men "who move in mountains" and
are therefore "the first to see the sun"—unlike "we" in "the valleys" who
"live in shadows."

To fully unlock this imagery, we need a key Knight provides in the letter
that opens Belly Song. There, in a passage on revolutionary struggle, he tells
Sanchez about coming across "a book, edited by Breitman: Trotsky on Black
Nationalism and Self Determination, which cleared up some of the confusion
in my mind that Brother Anderson had created with his piece in the latest
Negro Digest. Hell, I knew there was no contradiction between the Black
Nation Concept and Revolutionary Nationalism. Trotsky spells it out clearly—
clear enough at least to satisfy me at this point."[40]

This passage is a map of the conceptual issues Knight was struggling to resolve in his effort to build the sort of freedom he wished to occupy (and write from) outside of jail. The *Negro Digest* essay he refers to is "The Fragmented Movement," a critique of the Black Freedom movement and the philosophical dead ends that the essay's author, S. E. Anderson, believed the movement must avoid. Anderson successively dismissed incarnations of the following dead ends: (1) "The Integrationist" who "believes that he actually can participate in the decision-making processes of 'his' country";[41] (2) the "The City-States-man" who attempts to build "quasi-autonomous [black] city-states" within "the American politico-economic structure"; and (3) the advocate of "Back to Africa-ism" who is in fact demanding "withdrawing one's forces from the belly and brain of the [globally powerful] enemy."

The revolution Anderson endorses begins with a revolution in the analysis of reality. He calls for snatching serious "black terminology" out of the mouths of "integrationists, separatists and pseudo-revolutionaries (the black fascists)." Anderson, a poet himself, brings his argument directly into Knight's bailiwick when he writes: "The Black Morality's vitality lies in its ability to define . . . and refine our liberation struggle. It is the Black Aesthetic becoming ethical. . . . More than that, it is the Brother or Sister who asserts that to be a Revolutionary is to be for life."

As chronicled in "Belly Song" and many other poems, Knight struggled to find a way to be a revolutionary for life. (As late as 1990, he condemns himself for a period of "coking away my money" and vows to "live a revolution[ary] and artistic life" and to "dedicate my feeling and my life to the freeing of oppressed people everywhere.")[42] In the letter to Sanchez, he is clearly both inspired by Anderson and troubled by Anderson's dogmatism. There is a kind of rhetorical question addressed to Sanchez in Knight's careful turning to Trotsky—the sort of white thinker Anderson would probably have excluded on racial grounds—for his proof that one could be both a revolutionary and the builder of a black nation.

Thus, from Anderson's spinning of the roulette wheel of dead ends, Knight appears to extract a problem that he himself had written about in a Michigan City letter dated October 6, 1968: the problem of seeing and controlling the image of oneself in one's own mind. Addressing the inmate he informs about the unapologetically brutal pre–Warden Lane era, Knight writes, "You asked me once if it is possible not to love one's self. Yes, if one has no sense of, no concept of self, in a positive sense, then he could not possibly love himself, now could he?" The ethical dimension of the ability to define oneself—to "make up" oneself as Knight said he made up poems—becomes clear as Knight continues: "It is true that understanding is one of the things that

moves one towards freedom. But again, before one can understand his situation, the nature of his existence under oppression, he must first understand
that he exists. . . . Do you remember Malcolm telling about this house nigger
that identified with the slavemaster to such an extent that when the slave master's house caught on fire, the slave said, 'Massa, *our* house is on fire?' Do you
think that slave had any awareness of himself or his situation?"[43] One sees
here that in both his prose and many of his best poems, Knight was engaged
in an epic—and he hoped exemplary—battle for understanding beyond any
trace of the Stockholm syndrome.

The Malcolm X speech he refers to is a 1964 jeremiad, "The Ballot or the
Bullet," that features, in addition to the "house Negro" theory, an account of
guerrilla warfare that seems to have influenced Knight's writing of "Untitled
2." Specifically Malcolm X asserted in the speech, "It takes heart to be a guerrilla warrior because you're on your own. . . . Just as guerrilla warfare is pre-
vailing in Asia and in parts of Africa and in parts of Latin America, you've
got to be mighty naïve, or you've got to play the black man cheap, if you don't
think some day he's going to wake up and find that it's got to be the ballot or
the bullet."[44] Malcolm X is calling here not for immediate guerrilla warfare
but for the assumption of the guerrilla's heart and resourcefulness. His speech
raises the specter of guerrilla war itself as a last resort and as a threat—as the
bullet to be chambered if the ballot is denied.

In "Third World Guerrillas," a section of "Untitled 2," the Knight persona aspires to the guerrilla's heart and resourcefulness—and the guerrilla's
optimism in the face of seemingly overwhelming odds. For those guerrillas in
the mountains are not only the first to see the sun rise, they are also the "last
to see it leave." Meanwhile, in the valley the poem's speaker and others
like him adapt to "Early night that hides the slender self." The "slender self"
here is almost literally a shade, saturated with its own civil death. The "early
night" that makes it invisible to itself is the reality of civil death—the reality
of lacking voting power, of choices that cannot be made by a self that has
grown too thin: a self that is too little realized, too empty of self-understand-
ing and conviction to act upon and influence the world. By contrast, the men
on the mountains have the power to live in illumination, in a state of maximum cognition ("first to see the sun,/ And last to see it leave") and maximum
ability to move with confidence, avoiding dead ends, toward the ends of life.

Though Knight does not include himself among those who stalk the
mountaintops, his valley perspective allows for the painting, in "Untitled 1"
and other poems we encounter toward the end of "Belly Song," of paradoxi-
cally illuminating accounts of his own and others' darkness. A case in point
is "This Poem Is For," a mini-jeremiad Knight directs at the New York City

made infamous by the 1964 murder, in front of a reported thirty-eight witnesses, of Kitty Genovese. The poem makes all eight million people in New
York into passive bystanders watching "A Sister or Brother (Black or White
or Yellow or Red)" being assaulted, and concludes with a sharp message to
them: "I pee/ on thee." This New York is devoid of empathy and altruism. It
is a place that lacks the imagination and courage for such things—a place
with a stopped heart that must be shocked back to life—in this case by a poem
able to "pee" on a city. Interestingly "This Poem Is For" is not a condemnation but, like "Dark Prophecy: I Sing of Shine," a warning. And what it warns
against is a catastrophic failure of communication with self and others: a catastrophic breakdown of the feedback loop that connects sense impressions
with cognition and decision making and then connects decisions with actions
and the responses they provoke. Here there is only disassociation—of "Black"
from "White" from "Yellow" from "Red" from "male" from "female." Of
course, by calling attention to this atomization, the poem attempts to create
linkages—attempts to jump-start a feedback loop that, if it ever grows powerful enough, might confirm Knight's notion that "understanding stems from
love, is in fact a component of love":[45] that is, understanding, like poetry,
starts in the belly, in feelings that are everyone's by birth and that merely need
to be stirred, as feelings are stirred, by powerful signs such as a poet might
make.

Unfortunately signs strong enough to push understanding to its limits are
not often accessible to those who live in society's valleys—who live, in fact, in
places like the New York City where Kitty Genovese was murdered. One of
the great lessons of Belly Song is that it is almost impossible to escape the valley of the shadow of death. And worse, for Knight as for so many others, it
was difficult to avoid "copping out"—shirking responsibility—and thereby
contributing to the breakdown of empathy, love, and understanding. In the
poem "Cop-out Session," Knight casts the same cold eye upon himself that he
casts upon New York, and thereby picks up, at the other end of the book,
where "Another Poem for Me" left off:

> I done shot dope, been to jail, swilled
> wine, ripped off sisters, passed bad checks,
> changed my name, howled at the moon,
> wrote poems . . .
> . . . .
> I been confused, fucked up, scared, phony
> and jive
> to a whole/ lot of people.

The list of emotional states ("confused, fucked up, scared, phony") explains but does not excuse the actions enumerated in the first three lines—actions that, the fourth line suggests, are the dead ends Knight avoids when he is able to tie love and understanding together in poetry and life. But Knight does not allow his readers to be mere voyeurs. He ends the poem by asking, in effect, haven't you been somehow guilty of shirking duty? The question brings the reader up short because the emotional states Knight lists are, as he knew, universal. The reader cannot flatly deny ever having been "confused, fucked up," etc. with respect to some, if not "a whole lot of people." One needn't have attempted to destroy a Sonia Sanchez manuscript to admit to this.

Immediately following, as it does, "This Poem Is For," "Cop-out Session" confirms the feminist insight that the political is sometimes personal— whether the political takes the form of neighbors who "cop out" as a Kitty Genovese cries for help, or the wealthy who never notice Shine and others working below decks until their *Titanic* is sinking. In universalizing his own "cop-out" after assuming "full responsibility," as the erring politicians like to say, Knight, in fact, does *not* "cop out." Instead he lights his self-digust like a wick and makes the poem illuminate perhaps unexamined portions of the reader's psyche.

Strikingly, Knight signs this and the other five final poems in *Belly Song* with a revised name—Etheridge Knight Soa. "Soa" appears to signify "Servant of Allah" or "Sword of Allah," and to acknowledge a new source of strength for Knight—the Nation of Islam and its leader, Elijah Muhammad. Recall that a Knight hero, Malcolm X, came to prominence as a spokesman for Muhammad's idiosyncratic fusion of Islam, black supremacy, and science fiction. Malcolm X broke from the Nation after discovering evidence of corruption on Elijah Muhammad's part. But Knight includes "the Honorable Elijah Muhammed (Peace and Blessings of Allah be upon Him)" as one of those who "helped me to be and grow" in the acknowledgment pages of his 1980 solo volume *Born of a Woman*. Although, by the time Knight had his encounter with Muslim inmates in prison, Elijah Muhammad was usually referred to as the "Messenger of Allah," he designates himself in some of his earlier writings as a "Servant of Allah." The Prophet Mohammed himself insists on the designation in passages such as the following: "Do not exaggerate in praising me as the Christians did to (Jesus) the son of Mary, for I am only a servant, so say [he is] the servant of Allah and his Messenger."[46] The popular Islamic name Abdullah in fact means "servant" (*abd*) of Allah.

Knight, without going so far as to take an Arabic name (as did one of his role models, Amiri Baraka), revises his identity by adding "Soa." This revision—or at least the intention behind it—is illuminated by the following account of what is meant by "servant of Allah": "The Islamic conception of freedom requires that mankind should be subject to none but Allah. . . . Man has carved out so many deities in the secular sphere—nation, color, race, economic class. . . . Islam aims at . . . restoring dignity and freedom to the masses by making them subject to none but Allah."[47] Navigating his way through the American intellectual minefield, with its explosive conceptions of nation, color, race, politics, and aesthetics, Knight needed sometimes to lean on Elijah Muhammad's counterconceptions. Thus, while he never became a member of Muhammad's Nation of Islam, and while he took what appealed to him in the teachings of "the Messenger" and passed over what did not in silence, still the Knight who felt he had died more than once must have been electrified by Muhammad declarations such as the following: "We believe in the resurrection of the dead—not in physical resurrection—but in mental resurrection."[48] That Knight's name with the "Soa" added serves as the final line of four of the six poems that end *Belly Song* signifies the staking of a claim on Knight's part to dignity and freedom, and a mind reborn. Even if one translates "Soa" as "Sword of Allah" (and in one haiku, Knight urged then presidential candidate Jesse Jackson to "grab the Sword of Allah"),[49] it is clear that Knight is seeking to construct a persona he hopes will be sharp enough to cut through incomprehensions, social deaths, and "cop outs" of every stripe.

This freeing function of "Soa" is clearest in one of those final six, "The Last Poem (that'll be coming at you thisaway)"—actually *Belly Song*'s penultimate poem. Here Knight expresses the suspicion that "WE"—he himself, and apparently all the other would-be seers—have been "Bullshitting," regardless of philosophy or political program, all of them except "the Messenger, of course." But, opening a door through which every wisp of dogmatism escapes, Knight ends the poem by holding out the possibility that he might be wrong in his suspicion (and perhaps also in his confidence in the Messenger) by twice writing the M-word:

> Maybe—just maybe . . .
> Poet.
> —Etheridge Knight Soa

This lyric's basic theme is familiar from "Another Poem for Me," "This Poem Is For," and "Untitled 1." It is the same "cop-out" theme, the theme of betrayal that begins with the shirking of responsibility and empathy and ends unexpectedly in a shirking of the basics of being human. Holding up Elijah Muhammad as a likely exception to the shirking acknowledges the astounding, Malcolm X–creating boldness of "the Messenger," who announced in his

book *Message to the Blackman* (hailed by Knight in 1968 as "the most important" African American publication)[50] that "the worst kind of crime has been
committed against us [black people], for we were robbed of our desire to even
want to think and do for ourselves."[51] White America, Muhammad asserted,
is an "Arch deceiver," depriving blacks of "justice even at the bar of justice."[52]
This aspect of Elijah Muhammad's message—like the declaration of faith in
the resurrection of the mentally dead—must have struck a deep chord with
Knight. Muhammad clearly functioned at crucial times (such as during the
hunger strike in which Knight participated) as a welcome anti-warden.

While there is no evidence that Knight agreed for any length of time with
Elijah Muhammad's demand for complete separation of blacks and whites or
for a separate country for blacks, the poet clearly agreed not only with the
charge of the denial of justice at the bar of justice but probably also experienced the thrill that supporters of Malcolm X are said to have felt: the thrill
of encountering a black man willing and able to ruthlessly catalog the sins of
the American power structure and have it hear him.

On the other hand, the inclusion of "Black White Yellow or Red" in the
list of "Sister[s] and Brother[s]" being at once called on the carpet and offered
mutual protection in "This Poem Is For" makes it clear that even "Etheridge
Knight Soa" does not agree with Elijah Muhammad's demand for absolute
separation of "black" (which for Muhammad included all nonwhite races)
and "white." Ultimately what Knight seemed to value most was the Messenger's effort to—and partial success in—relentlessly exposing the net of decep-
tions and self-deceptions to which African Americans, Americans, and, finally,
humankind are susceptible. And Knight was likely drawn, too, to the demand
for self-love that was probably the most fundamental aspect of Muhammad's
teaching: "One of the gravest handicaps among the so-called Negroes is that
there is no love for self. . . . This . . . is the root cause of hate . . . disunity, dis-
agreement, quarreling, betraying, stool pigeons and fighting and killing one
another."[53] In lines like *"The children of Blk america have sad eyes"* and
"The children of Blk America are ashamed of their fathers," Knight showed
his sympathy with sentiments like Muhammad's, since the sadness and shame
of the children suggest a dysfunctional bond with fathers whose broken self-
love tears families apart.

But again Knight—whose early boosters of course included Donald Hall
and Robert Bly—also sought to follow love's currents farther and deeper than
race or even family ties could reach, and he refused—first in his personal life
and then in his published work—to accept Elijah Muhammad's prohibition of
interracial relationships. The most telling example of this effort to follow love
wherever it might lead can be found in the revision of the poem "For Mary

Ellen McAnally" between its appearance in *Belly Song* and its reprinting in *Born of a Woman*. In the earlier version the title functions as the first line, and the second and third lines, which start the poem proper, are "Who is // a perfect poem." In *Born of a Woman*, Knight, insisting as always on total honesty with his audience, began the poem proper thus:

> Who is a white / woman / and
> a perfect poem

The slash marks—which separate "woman" from the "white" that the Messenger links to the "Arch deceiver"—are crucial to the revision, since they both acknowledge race and separate it and its public meaning from the woman Knight loved.

The overlap of the relationship with McAnally and the longing for reconciliation with Sonia Sanchez,[54] however, and the fact that the Manichaean vision of Elijah Muhammad cohabited with Knight's own evolving conception of a world without fundamental separation between "Black or White or Yellow or Red" suggest that, even without the complicating factor of Knight's continuing susceptibility to drug use, the Knight-McAnally relationship was doomed to be a rocky one. Ultimately only invention and art—as well as affection—could resolve Knight's tension and contradictions, if only temporarily. Such invention, such binding of clashing notes into a surprising chord, does happen in one of the Soa-signed final lyrics of *Belly Song,* "A Love Poem" (to McAnally):

> And Mary/ is/ on the High/ Way
> Coming to me/ thru the rain
> . . . .
> And.
> We are Singing.

This poem, dated September 1, 1972, a little over a year after "Belly Song," celebrates at least a period of full recovery for Knight. He is here is fully harmonized with himself and his beloved—regardless of the social and psychological dissonances signified by the rain she is traveling though. Thus harmonized, Knight and his beloved are indeed "Singing." Though it is not the very last poem in *Belly Song,* this lyric signifies a temporary triumph over all the "cop-outs" and disasters represented elsewhere in the volume. It is emblematic, too, of Knight's view that poetry, while being realistic, should always be "ultimately . . . celebratory."[55] All obstacles, in other words, can be overcome, if only in the chanting of the poem.

As Knight expressed it in the title and refrain of a poem that appeared in a number of the journal *Nimrod* of which McAnally was a prime mover, it is imperative "To Keep on Keeping On." Opening with an image of "The Sun" (probably Malcolm X, and the expansion of consciousness he represented for Knight) having set in the "West/ urn world" ("urn" signifying a post-Malcolm immurement in civil death), the poem shines its light on the inside of the urn. Specifically it alludes to government overreaching that burst like a sore in the Watergate scandal. Past Watergate, Knight and those he speaks for and with (the poem is subtitled "after the fashion of Alice Walker and Denise Levertov")[56] press on; they press on past the memory of blows struck by men hell-bent on "knocking niggers and women . . . to / their knees." But pressing on is no picnic. It requires Knight and his fellow writers to will themselves, even with fingers trembling, to lift "the speaking pen"[57] and let its truths—starting with those about the writer—pour out.

CHAPTER 5

Born of a Woman: New and Selected Poems

By the time *Born of a Woman: New and Selected Poems* was published in 1980, the Knight-McAnally marriage, caught between trembling and speaking, had collapsed, and Knight was in the midst of a new relationship with Charlene Blackburn. Knight appears to have struggled in these years like an escape artist striving to throw off chains, straitjackets, and lead weights while hung upside down in water. The impact of his struggle on some of those closest to him is clear in the Mary McAnally "Family Chronology."

During the period in which *Born of a Woman* was composed and in the period immediately after what should have been its triumphant appearance, Knight did tremendous damage to himself and others, for reasons that are not entirely explicable. Poetry seems to have remained the most orderly aspect of Knight's life, and the least destructive of his lifelines.

Indeed *Born of a Woman* begins with acknowledgments to many of the people who had helped Knight keep body and soul together after his exit from prison. Those thanked include Gwendolyn Brooks, Belzora Knight Taylor (Knight's mother, the obvious first referent of the phrase "born of a woman"), Haki Madhubuti, Mary McAnally, Anthony Keller, Andrea Keller, Sonia Sanchez, Donald Hall, Galway Kinnell, Dudley Randall, and "charlene blackburn, my third wife." All three of the wives appear in the volume in either reprinted or new poems. Major themes of the book include birth, spiritual for the most part but also, in one poem, physical—and all that threatens birth.

The first section of *Born of a Woman* consists mostly of lyrics from *Poems from Prison,* but "Inside-Out," the title of the book's opening section, quietly introduces the birth theme—as well as the theme of emergence from prison: the very first poem in the section ("Genesis" serves as a preface to the volume

316

100

as a whole) is "Hard Rock"—a chronicle, of course, of an antibirth: of a permanent walling up of any possibility of psychological or spiritual rebirth, or any sort of emergence from prison.

Coming after the concluding call in "Genesis" to split the speaker's skin with love's rock, "Hard Rock" here becomes emblematic of the reversal of Moses's miracle: the drying up of the future rather than its gushing forth. The poems in the remaining seventeen pages of the first section follow the roller coaster pattern of Knight's own life, offering everything from the tragedy of "Freckle-Faced Gerald" to the tongue-in-cheek self-praise of a haiku celebrating the poet's ability to make the seventeen-syllable concoction "swing" like jazz. Knight the poet is indeed the Knight who is not powerless to be born or to nurture others' births. He is the Knight capable of making language—and therefore communication and communion and their self-strengthening feed back into themselves—swing, in the jazz sense of attaining irresistibly joyous forward momentum.

The next section of the book, entitled "Outside-In," mixes reprinted and some new poems that aim mainly to move from the skin of relationships and the self into the heart of love and its malfunctions. In the four-line poem that opens the section, Knight compares a lover to a light lingering on a lake—light, it seems, that remains on in the belly after the whole relationship has set like the evening sun. This image of the afterlife of love is followed, though, by "The Violent Space" and its sketch of the loveless exchanges of prostitution defeating the love of a would-be rescuer who is incarcerated.

Joy reasserts itself two poems later in "The Stretching of the Belly." Dedicated to Charlene Blackburn, this poem celebrates a pregnancy that resulted in the birth of Knight's only biological son. It begins with a verbal close-up of stretch marks:

> Marks / of the mother are
> Your / self
> Stretching
> Reaching
> For life
> For love

The stretching of the belly here becomes a symbol of the transforming effects of motherhood. The stretch marks—which, the consoling tone of the opening suggests, may cause the expectant mother to mourn for her prepregnancy figure—introduce into sociopolitical time an alternative time of generation. This time, with its alternative paths to the future, interrupts history and interrupts conventional notions of beauty and, indeed conventional ways of thinking in general. Such interruptions are signified in the lines immediately following, where Knight strives to reinvent the word "markings":

> Markings are / not to / be mocked
> Markings are medicants
> Markings / are / signs
> Along the hi / way

The key line in this passage is "Markings are medicants": Markings, in more familiar usages, are medicines, antidotes, correctives that, in the case of the stretch marks depicted in the poem, signify the onrush of new life. Though they may appear unsightly at first, the markings also force a change of perspective, almost a change of interpretive systems that changes one system's ugliness to beauty. In the new system the markings are medicants that heal the mind that dwells upon them.

What the markings do not do, however, is make forgetting possible. Thus, in the poem's third stanza, Knight contrasts ordinary scars with the harbingers of birth.

> Scars are / not
> Markings scars do / not / come from the stars
> Or the moon. Scars come from wars
> From war / men who plunge
> Like a bayonet into the gut
> Or like a blackjack against the skull

If in the first stanza the markings seem to have been made by the touch of the sacred, Knight emphasizes here that the sacred that touches human life can not be separated from the things of the earth—cannot be separated from "fury and mire of human veins," in Yeats's great phrase. The war scars, and the fury and mire they come from and cause, are clearly not only those of the battlefield but also those made by men like the one who sexually assaulted and killed Kitty Genovese: "men who plunge // Like a bayonet into the gut." The man who strikes like "a blackjack against the skull" is, tragically, not entirely separable from the Knight who in "Belly Song" falls upon his flowering beloved like a stone. Knight appears, in fact, to be once more striving to harmonize the notes of his selves into a stable chord. At the same time, he is making a larger statement about the world that helped to shatter him into those often discordant selves—the world of white-supremacist Mississippi and of the Korean War, the world that scarred both his face and his soul.

In the final stanza of the poem, Knight works hard to strike a chord that will include both his scarred and jangling self and the song that Blackburn's pregnancy is singing:

> Scars are stripes of slavery
> Like my back
> Not your belly
> Which / is bright
> And bringing forth

A rich chord indeed resonates here. But it is a chord cut through by slash marks, that fall in the poem like dissonances—slash marks that function in the poem as indicators of the limits of lovers' attempts to become one, even as their oneness is commemorated by the child they make together. The slash marks also separate the "poeting" Knight and his scars from Blackburns's markings—just as an unintended screech of feedback can separate a listener from music. Blackburn is the one who brings forth a song that does not end when mouths or books are closed. She thus functions in the poem as both muse and role model. She even functions, to a degree, as liberator, turning scars like those that stopped Hard Rock's mind and that, metaphorically, scarred Knight's back, into what stretch marks foretell: the future-filled wrinkles of newborn skin.

Another role model Knight brings into *Born of a Woman* is Eric Dolphy, one of jazz's great improvisers. A Dolphy improvisation, which tends to expand and alter perceptions of time the way fireworks alter perceptions of the three dimensions of air, cannot be captured on the single, two-dimensional page that Knight's "For Eric Dolphy" occupies. Knowing this, Knight merely gestures in the direction of Dolphy's rhythmical and harmonic complexities. He focuses instead on the emotion he discovers at the core of Dolphy's flute work—an emotion not unlike the one that is made flesh in Charlene Blackburn's belly. Dolphy's flute, Knight writes, spins "Love // Thru / out // The universe." This is how Knight begins—cutting "Through" to "Thru" to add Dolphy-esque vocal inflections to his lines—and to evoke his own speaking voice. For poetry does not live in books, Knight insisted, but in the poet's voice physically touching listeners by vibrating bones in their inner ears.[1]

"For Eric Dolphy" goes on to compare the love in Dolphy's music to that of a sister

> Who never expressed LOVE
> In words (like the white folks always   d
> She would sit in the corner   o

```
And cry                        i

Everytime                      n

I                              g

Got a whippin
```

Writing the word "doing" perpendicular to itself and parallel to the main body of his poem adds a Dolphy-like twist to the lyric. The superiority of deeds to hollow words are thereby emphasized—but, slyly, by the formal performative of the vertical "doing"—a formal performative that makes visible the contrast between the idealistic words and discriminatory deeds of the "white folks." Just what Knight is up to here is clear if one recalls that, as defined by the philosopher J. L. Austin, a "performative" is an utterance—"I pronounce you man and wife," for instance, or "open sesame"—that is also an action: saying it makes it so.[2] A "formal" performative, then, would occur when writing something—like "STOP" on a red octagon or the perpendicular "doing" in Knight's poem—makes it so. By standing white folks' "doing" on its ear, Knight, at least in the context of the poem, separates the real from the fake. Offhandedly in these lines, love and empathy are celebrated as potential cures for hypocrisy and abuse. Quiet tears become as powerful and performative as a faith healer's laying of hands on the body of a believer. But in art, the love and empathy signified by the sister's tears can be communicated only when combined with the virtuosity and creative power of an Eric Dolphy—a shy man who at parties reportedly liked to sit in a corner practicing. On stage, matters were different: improvising with others, Dolphy spun mighty collective messages.

As if acknowledging this, Knight reprints "A Love Poem" immediately after "For Eric Dolphy" and thereby evokes the mutual improvisation of a great love—love like "a rock against the wind." But the rock begins to crack in the very next poem, a new one called "From the Moment (or, Right / at / —The Time)," which focuses on the moment when love and lovemaking stop being joyful improvisations and become desperate calculations, desperate attempts to program time, character, and unscriptable communication: "Right / at / the time she began to count— // To compute, her comings. . . . The world was void, void, void." A probably deeper source of discomfort is the focus of the next stanza, where the woman declares, "'Marriage is not a union— // It / is / a 50–50 proposition"—and again makes the world "void, void, void."

To some extent this latter voiding of the world is what Knight himself would call a "cop-out" on his part—a refusal of the compromises of true mutuality, a denial of the disappointments that rise like smoke from the sparks and fires of any true love. Read with Mary McAnally's chronology in mind, it is above all a refusal of spousal responsibilities. But at the same time that it is a "cop-out," it is an honest expression of Knight's desire for an impossible oneness with his beloved—an endless harmonic integration of moods and habits.

As Wynton Marsalis has noted in a discussion of the paradox of great jazz artists who threaten and destroy their own talent with drug abuse, the performing musician on stage (and in the Knight context, the lover in a transcendent act of lovemaking) is in a world without flaw: "when you're playing music—jazz—you could lose track of time. . . . The world that you're in is perfect."[3] But this perfect world bursts bubblelike as soon as the music ends—as soon as, in the Knight context, the lover is jolted out of orgasmic bliss. Marsalis argued that it is then, as the perfect world fades from the synapses, that the musician becomes susceptible to drugs and other fool's paradises: "When you have that kind of extreme relationship to the world that's around you, it's very difficult not to need stimulation. . . . But that dope is always there for you. And the dope is going make you maintain that high [achieved while playing]." Did Knight, then, crave paradise too much, in and out of relationships, in and out of the states of extreme receptivity and in-the-hole vulnerability that allowed him to write works like "The Idea of Ancestry"? There is no way of knowing, but the speaker in "From the Moment" clearly does fall away from his dream of a more perfect union into "void, void, void." The gap between a man seeking a perfect world, shot through with incalculable happiness, and a partner insisting (as no doubt McAnally and others did) that he live at least part-time in the world of calculation—this gap is so great that it can, indeed, only be described as a void. The poem concludes thus:

> And the children of / our / love
> Will turn to / pillars / of salt—
> If we don't walk the same walk—
> And talk the same talk
> 'Bout being free. and thee. and me.

Here the origin of Knight's hunger for perfection (or that of the very Knight-like speaker of the poem) is shown to lie in his desire for freedom. And who can say how deep the hunger for freedom became in a highly sensitive man who had been incarcerated, spent time in the "hole," had his psyche marked by the vicariously experienced electricity pumped into the brains of prisoners like Hard Rock, and left prison only to enter the larger enclosure of parole and the still larger enclosure of the psychic (and sometimes physical) race war between advocates of Black Power and defenders of the old American racial hierarchy? It may be that Knight suffered from a never diagnosed and never cured form of posttraumatic stress disorder that made him fear permanent enclosures of any kind—even the permanent enclosure of a beloved's arms.

Bliss, in any event, bursts in the next three poems—two of them about lost or departing love, the third the aptly titled "Feeling Fucked Up." The poem that follows them—"Three Songs"—steps away from personal relationships and moves back into the exploration of social dysfunction. Although the love theme persists in the epigraph from Guitar Slim ("I was so in love I was miserable"), "Slim's Song," the bluesy toast that is the first and strongest of the poem's three sections, pivots quickly to the social. Slim voices the usual bluesman's lament about losing "the best girl // I ever had," but then he provides reasons that open the deepest mysteries of humans, those political animals:

> Of course it didn't last long.
> Not after the coconut was opened.
> No milk. No milk.
> Just bubble, bubble
> Toil and trouble.
>
> We call and call:
> It wasn't me.
> Me neither—

In these lines, Knight brings a kind of collective anomie into focus: he shows a society suffering from the opposite of solidarity, a society incapable of producing the kind of moment made famous in the movie *Spartacus* when each slave in a crowd of slaves responds to a demand to know who the rebel slave Spartacus is by stepping forward to declare, "I am Spartacus."

In Knight's poem the chorus is "wasn't me. // Me neither." Community falls apart, with results predicted in the previous stanza's allusion to *Macbeth*: "No milk. No milk. // Just bubble, bubble. // Toil and trouble." Though the immediate reference is to coconut milk, the evocation of the witches' rhymes in *Macbeth* ("For a charm of powerful trouble, // Like a hell-broth boil and bubble. . . . Double, double, toil and trouble") changes the coconut milk into something more sinister.[4]

The toil and trouble Knight sets down before his reader is, in the context of Lady Macbeth's famous prayer to be unsexed and filled with "gall" and "direst cruelty," shown to be the toil and trouble that result from "direst cruelty" and defiance of human norms. The Slim of "Slim's Song" ends up being closer in his message to the Shine of the *Titanic* toast than he is to Guitar Slim.

The second of the "Three Songs," referring to a tornado from which people must be taught to flee and a well whose water is tainted with a sickness, expands on the theme of toil and trouble. The concluding lyric, "Healing Song," points the way toward healing by pointing toward, not a bubbling cauldron, but a better sort of heat—a heat that gives off light: "the fire is bright // in the hearts of the people." This fire has the potential to burn away anomie, irresponsibility, cruelty, and gall. But it has only potential, which the poet alone cannot bring into being. Knight asserts as much when he writes, "It all seems so simple // so I'll tell you where to look // not what to see." Unlike the version of Knight that speaks in "From the Moment," the speaker here acknowledges and even depends on the plurality of points of view that is the prerequisite of real social communication and, alas, of social discord. The witch's brew of anomic forces alluded to in the first of the "Three Songs" appears victorious at the end of the poem, where Knights writes, "And always the white streets // and ladies departing. Ladies // departing."

The overall sense of the three songs is that they are three probings of possible ways to move forward through a fog of dangerousness that includes risks to individuals like Slim (whose heart gets broken in the first stanza), risks to communities (risks like the tornado people must be warned against in the second song), and risks to the cohesion of a people. The brief poem that follows "Three Songs" is another kind of probe—a probe of a potential ally's sincerity. This poem, "For Dan Berrigan," addresses the Roman Catholic priest, poet, and anti–Vietnam War activist who was sent to jail in August 1970 for helping to burn more than 370 draft files. In a diary he wrote while on the run, before finally being caught, tried, and jailed, Berrigan critiques, among many other things, the Black Power movement. Since it appears to be this aspect of Berrigan's thinking that Knight's short poem responds to, it will be useful to consider a Berrigan critique of an Eldridge Cleaver critique of Martin Luther King Jr. Key to Berrigan's argument is a condemnation of either/or reasoning. He endorses the "modesty required in order to include opposition as an element of integration. Even such an opposite as a tyrant who makes the revolution possible." With the possibility of prison hanging over him he adds, "The prison makes the free man." Then he turns his attention to Cleaver:

> It was right and just for Cleaver to go slow on Martin King. . . . Cleaver has more courtesy and sense [than some black revolutionaries]; the sense at least to take it easy on a good man. He sees something that can't be easily touched. . . .
>
> . . . Martin heard other voices, he was after a long race and goal. No one should allow the "revolutionaries" to make a nigger of him, in contempt.

The question they still have to deal with, before the people, is: what is a revolutionary anyway?

   . . . What do a few men draw on, to live and die less unwell than most men? Cleaver is haunted by this, in his better moments. He is wise to go slow.

Berrigan, quite prophetically as it turns out, goes on to observe that "religion has a bad taste in [Cleaver's] mouth, even while his attitudes are in the main, religious. It is by now a cliché to say, religion is part of the problem. It is another thing to say it cannot be part of the solution." He adds:

> Rage is indispensable to the new precipitate; so is compassion. Cleaver, but also Martin King. . . . It is to the credit of men like Cleaver, Malcolm X, King, that they knew it. . . . Self defense: a keystone of the Panther struggle. . . . King went unarmed; in a sense he invited personal disasters. The Panthers accuse him of even more folly than that. A kind of ideological retardation of black people, keeping the truth about their lives from them, about the monstrous character of the forces they must deal with. Cleaver calls it something like the "plantation mind." Unjust, an oversimplification if there ever was one. . . . Who is to say that such hope . . . does not actually create a new face in the enemy? . . . There is a cruel lesson here for revolutionaries. . . . Concentration on the sights of a gun inevitably contracts the bore of the mind. How does one keep the mind open to the full range of action possible to its powers?[5]

This last question is very much like the ones Knight asks throughout his poetry, in many ways. The wrestling with the choice between King's nonviolent direct action and the Black Panther advocacy of violent self-defense as well as the question, "What is a revolutionary anyway?" are all—differently worded—also part of Knight's dialogue with himself. But Knight lacks Berrigan's confidence that the hope King embodied might "actually create a new face in the enemy." The sharpest parting of the ways between Knight's perspective and Berrigan's, however, is no doubt marked by Berrigan's claim that "The prison makes a free man." Knight's poem for Berrigan addresses this parting of their perspectives:

> I don't know about you, whiteman all dressed in black.
> . . . .
> Maybe you see it all, whiteman, or maybe you blind.

The double repetition of the epithet "whiteman," which tolls like an especially loud bell in a four-line poem, underscores all that Knight believes Berrigan fails to grasp about the black experience. Berrigan pronouncing on strategies for black liberation "dress[es himself] in black" psychologically, just as he dresses his body in black as a priest. But merely dressing in black does not give him access to the constriction of paths to the future that is the basis of the experience of dangerousness that Knight (and most other African Americans of his generation and economic background) lived with. Once he went to prison, Berrigan wrote a volume of poems and a diary about his experience. Both of these books were published, thereby thrusting Berrigan into Knight's arena of prison testimony and poetry. Did Knight believe, perhaps, that Berrigan—who entered prison as something of a celebrity and therefore (despite the suffering chronicled in his writings) did not have to fight his way up from the bottom of the pecking order—had not fully earned the right to write on behalf of people like the character commemorated in poems such as Berrigan's "One Prisoner Was Driven Mad: Let This Be a Lesson"? Knight, apparently, is not sure and, as he always does at his best, he leaves the door open to contending possibilities: "Maybe you see it all, whiteman, or maybe you blind."

Knight continues to probe philosophical, aesthetic, strategic, and generational possibilities in "Indiana Haiku—2," a five-part piece that includes, under the title "Indianapolis War Memorial," an ominous snapshot of boys playing on monumentalized weapons and dreaming already of battle and bloodshed. The message here is a quieter and more universally directed warning than the one we read in "Dark Prophecy: I Sing of Shine," but it is if anything even more pointed in its call for readers and those they might influence to exit the camp of those who "know not what they do."

A similar issue is raised unexpectedly in a poem, "For Langston Hughes," that follows the haiku sequence and first appeared in *Poems from Prison*:

> Another weaver of black dreams has gone
> we sat in June Bug's pad with the shades drawn
> and the air thick with holy smoke. . . .
>
> . . . .
>
> But, TG and I went out and swung on some white cats.
> now I don't think the Mythmaker meant for us to do *that*
> but we didn't know what else to do.

The contrast between the grief at the beginning of the poem and the violence and confusion at the end testifies to the importance of Hughes's dream-weaving and culture-making poems. Hughes's message survives in, and gradually redirects the mind, helping the older Knight concede: "I don't think the Mythmaker meant for us to do that . . ." Knight explained during his 1980 reading at the Scranton Public Library that he and his friends went out to knock heads after playing Billie Holiday's performance of "Strange Fruit"—a song about lynched Black people hanging from poplar trees whose lyrics, Knight was later (incorrectly) informed were by Langston Hughes. So when news of Hughes's death reached Knight in Michigan City in 1967, Knight is taken back to the hour when he and his friends played "Strange Fruit" and allowed themselves to be overcome by something too little removed from the infection the boys in the haiku catch when they touch "War." The events chronicled in this Hughes lyric testify to the difficulty of keeping the mind open in spite of realities that are sure to bruise it and to push it in the direction of Berrigan's "concentration on the sights of a gun [that] . . . contracts the bore of the mind."

Knight as a mature poet, but a deeply wounded and conflicted man, became himself the Hughes whose loss he mourned in a species of poem—the relapse poem—that is his poignant addition to the American canon of great subjects. The masterpiece of this group of masterpieces is "Welcome Back, Mr. Knight, Love of My Life," which immediately follows "For Langston Hughes" in *Born of a Woman*. In this poem Knight once more struggles to craft lines prehensile and powerful enough to pull his addiction up by the roots.

Given the fact that this struggle never ended for him, it is worth taking a moment, before we proceed to "Welcome Back, Mr. Knight" itself, to consider what drug addiction entails. A source of authoritative statements on the subject to which Knight had access while he was in prison was 1967's *The Challenge of Crime in a Free Society: A Report by the President's Commission on Law Enforcement and Administration of Justice*. Knight quotes a portion of this text that is devoted to the subject of plea bargaining in *Black Voices from Prison*. In another portion—which it is hard to imagine that Knight did not read—the commission noted that there is "no settled definition of addiction."[6] But it wrote that possible sources of addiction include drug-induced rewiring of susceptible parts of the nervous system, or "psychic dependence," manifested by strong craving. Ultimately the commission characterized the impact of drugs as probabilistic: "The effect of any drug depends on many variables, not the least of which are the mood and expectation of the taker. Drug effects are therefore best expressed in terms of probable outcomes" (212). Highly relevant to Knight's case, and to the all-pervading "DESPERA-TION" he refers to in one poem, is the commission's account of a heroin high: "Euphoria is an effect often associated with heroin, often reflecting the relief a particular individual gets from chronic anxiety."[7]

A sort of confirmation of Knight's perception of himself as someone struggling against an irrationally punitive justice system is the following remark by the commissioners: "It would appear that heroin is outlawed because of its special attractiveness to addicts and because it serves no known medical purpose not served as well by other drugs" (213). Living with and, as it were, *in* an irrational system is of course itself a source of anxiety; but since it is not always a source of addiction, one must ask, why was Knight never able to shake off the drug dependence "monkey"?

The question may not be answerable. One expert on addiction, Avram Goldstein, acknowledges "our profound ignorance of the brain mechanisms of relapse. Even after prolonged abstinence, an ex-addict may inexplicably revert to drug use. This behavior is often accompanied by conscious craving. . . . [Perhaps] that conscious craving is simply a state that accompanies an independent and automatic unconscious compulsion . . . provoked by stored memories of hedonic satisfaction. In experiments with former cocaine addicts, craving has been provoked by conditioned cues—for example, video scenes associated with former drug use."[8] It appears that drug addiction is, in Knight's terminology, stored in the belly—in the very nexus of craving, desire, and will—perhaps in the very matrix of hurt, resistance, receptivity, and hope into which poetic inspiration must descend.

"One kind of addict," Goldstein asserts" is a risk-taker, a sensation seeker, a nonconformist . . . readily influenced by nonconforming peers."[9] This is also a definition of one kind of poet, someone with the "guts" to refuse to accept the injustices and irrationalities of his or her environment. The "belly" of the addict, however—and the poet too—lies not in the actual "gut" but in the neurotransmitters that the nervous system uses to communicate with itself and the body. Addictive drugs succeed by mimicking or blocking the action of naturally occurring neurotransmitters.

Goldstein cites a passage from *The Odyssey* as an exemplification of the effects of the actions of some of Knight's favored drugs—the opiates, including heroin: "Into the bowl in which their wine was mixed, she slipped a drug that had the power of robbing grief and anger of their sting and banishing all painful memories. No one who swallowed this dissolved in wine could shed a single tear that day, even for the death of his mother and father, or if they put his brother or his own son to the sword and he were there to see it done."[10]

This state of euphoria via the banishment from the "belly" of all cares, but also of all caring—of all wounds, but also of all guilt and responsibility— makes plausible both the love Knight expressed for, for instance, Mary McAnally, and his ability to forge her checks and pawn almost all the possessions in their apartment, in all likelihood in order to purchase drugs. It also explains why the banished memories, the exiled cares, and the locked-away guilt could come rushing back, like his own spirit possessing him, and move his pen to write "Welcome Back, Mr. Knight: Love of My Life," where, apparently addressing himself, he demands to know:

How's your drinking problem?—your thinking
Problem? You / are / pickling
Your liver—
. . . .
How's your dope
Problem? . . .
. . . .
How's your lying and cheating and
Staying out all / night long problem?
. . . .
How's your ex-convict problem?—your John Birch
Problem?—your preacher problem?—your . . .
. . . sitting in your / chair, saying
How racist and sexist they / will / forever / be
Problem?—How's your Daniel Moynihan
Problem?—your crime in the streets, runaway
Daddy, Black men with dark shades
And bulging crotches problem?
How's your nixon-agnew—j. edgar hoover
Problem?—you still paranoid? Still schizoid?—
Still scared shitless?
How's your bullet-thru-the-brain problem?—or
A needle-in-your-arm problem?

Here all Knight's betrayals of his own ideals and of other people escape whatever drug or psychological defenses had been blocking them. In making the poem, Knight seeks to forge them into an antidote to his own weaknesses, into a verbal equivalent of naloxone, which, Goldstein reports, neutralizes most effects of drugs: "Nothing in medical practice is quite so dramatic as a naloxone injection in the emergency room," Goldstein writes. "A person is carried in, barely breathing, blue, and moribund; instantly after naloxone, the patient takes a deep breath, sits up, and wants to go home" (28). Knight wants his poem to act in a similar manner on all his many but interrelated problems.

Most of these problems appear to be symptoms of more fundamental ones. And the most fundamental are addressed in the questions, "How's your nixon-agnew—j. edgar hoover // Problem—you still paranoid? Still schizoid?— // Still scared shitless?" As has already been indicated, Knight's addiction as a whole is rooted in panic—in being "scared shitless" before the wounds of the Korean battlefield that it was his responsibility to tend. But this state of disorienting panic—the sort of panic one feels when one wishes to flee a place, only to discover that one is chained to its floor (panic no doubt swallowed and stored in the belly while Knight strove to perform his medic's function) is kept alive in civilian life by the maneuverings of the likes of J. Edgar Hoover, the FBI head who had his agents infiltrate and undermine would-be liberation organizations like the Black Panther Party. Richard M. Nixon, too, was viewed with antipathy by many in Knight's generation who accused Nixon of race baiting for his "southern" electoral strategy, blamed him for his Vietnam War policy, and named him, on the basis of tactics that earned him the nickname of "Tricky Dick," an exploiter's exploiter. With the nation's Hoovers and Nixons serving as wardens of the "larger prison," the impulse to paranoia is understandable but, as Knight recognizes here, ultimately destructive of the balance of the "belly"—ultimately destructive of empathy and other links between self and other.

"Schizoid" appears to refer to the popular understanding of schizophrenia as something characterized by split or even multiple personalities. The Knight alone at his desk, writing works like "Welcome Back, Mr. Knight," and the Knight gripped by drug or alcohol cravings—the problem Knight—certainly functioned as two different people.

Knight the poet and prose writer is the one equipped to combat—rather than to reinforce—the misrepresentations of persons like himself that are summed up in his reference to his "Daniel Moynihan problem." The reference here is probably to the famous (for many, infamous) 1965 "Moynihan Report," whose official title is *The Negro Family: The Case for National Action*. This report created a firestorm, earning the liberal Moynihan accusations of racism. This was in part because, the year after the passage of the 1964 Civil Rights Act—an event driven by Martin Luther King Jr.'s demand for recognition of the "somebodiness" of African Americans—the report announced that poor urban blacks were caught in a dangerous "tangle of pathology" that emasculated black males and left black families and futures in ruins. Moynihan traced the tangle all the way to slavery and cited in support of his argument the since severely criticized "Sambo" theory of Stanley M. Elkins. Elkins argued that slavery, like internment in Nazi concentration camps, implanted in its victims the most severe version of the Stockholm syndrome conceivable: both slavery and concentration camps "were closed systems, with little chance of manumission, emphasis on survival, and a single omnipresent authority. The profound personality change created by Nazi internment . . . was toward childishness and total acceptance of the SS guards as father-figures—a syndrome strikingly similar to the 'Sambo' caricature of the Southern slave."[11] Elkins's critics pointed out that, among other things, the Sambo thesis overlooks the slaves' ability to organize pockets of freedom within the peculiar institution, and to sometimes plot and succeed in escapes from that institution.

Moynihan, accepting the Elkins thesis, emphasized the continued emasculating effects of postslavery institutions such as Jim Crow: he argues that it is the "very essence of the male animal, from the bantam rooster to the four star general, . . . to strut. . . . [But the] 'sassy nigger [. . .]' was lynched." In America's patriarchal culture, even after African Americans migrated from the South to the North, Moynihan argued, an emasculating environment led to matriarchy, broken homes, and "pathology": "In every index of family pathology—divorce, separation, and desertion, female family head, children in broken homes, and illegitimacy—the contrast between the urban and rural environment for Negro families is unmistakable." Moynihan concluded, "It is by destroying the Negro family under slavery that white America broke the will of the Negro people. Although that will has reasserted itself in our time, it is a resurgence doomed to frustration unless the viability of the Negro family is restored."[12]

Moynihan was probably on firmer ground in identifying, as a source of "social disorganization" in poor urban neighborhoods, the "fundamental, overwhelming fact . . . that *Negro unemployment,* with the exception of a few years during World War II and the Korean War, has continued at disaster levels for 35 years. . . . In 1963, a prosperous year, 29.2 percent of all Negro men in the labor force were unemployed at some time during the year."[13]

In any case, when Knight refers to his "Daniel Moynihan problem," he is referring to an extremely complex tangle not of pathologies but of historical, political, and psychological struggles, outcomes, and potentials. He is referring primarily, and with derision, to the widely condemned thesis of communal pathology rooted in the damage done to the African American male. But he is also referring to the personal problems he condemns in himself—problems that make him a person touched by pathology, make him what, as he writes in "Another Poem for Me," "white/ america wants you to be"—namely, a "crime in the streets, runaway // Daddy, Black [man] with dark shades" and a bulging crotch. The "Moynihan problem" is thus a synecdoche for Knight's whole postprison struggle to shake off his addict's "crawling from nickel bag to nickel bag" and become an autonomous maker of visions and possible futures, "black // and blooming in the night," as he writes in "Another Poem for Me."

Knight's greatest disappointment in his addict self is clear from the second half of the title of "Welcome Back, Mr. Knight": "Love of My Life." To be the love of one's own life, after all, is to fail in creating the communion and communication that were at the heart of Knight's aesthetics and, clearly, his erotics. The bitterness of his "schizoid" existence appears to have inspired suicidal thoughts—his "bullet-thru-the-brain problem"—and the serial quasi suicides of the overdoses caused by his "needle-in-your-arm problem."

Was a sort of suicidal despair over the split in his free will, then, one of the reasons for his many falls through the floor of his domestic and professional lives, into the pit of addiction? The penultimate line of "Welcome Back" zeroes in on the Gordian knot Knight could never untie, asking "[how's] your heart problem—your belly / problem?" Here the poet is asking, in effect, "How have I come to be so tied up in knots; how has my existence become so painfully knotted that one effort to untie it produces a poem, another effort produces an overdose, a third produces a beautiful visit with family, a fourth produces another marriage, and a fifth produces a divorce?"

In a fascinating essay on addiction that he published while incarcerated in Michigan City, Knight suggests that the knots in his being are philosophical ones: "The key to the solution of the 'drug problem' is hidden, I think, in Philosophy; that is, the study and proper application of the process governing thought, out of which comes a particular conduct." The "process governing thought" is a more abstract and less gritty designation of what Knight later preferred to call "the belly." It is a process that includes all the governors of the mind—from neurotransmitters to the drugs that mimic them, and from the social-scientific philosophies that guide law and politics to the insurgent self-conceptions (like those embodied in the Black Aesthetic) that challenge dominant socioeconomic models and stereotypes, from the sort of self-mastery demanded at Daytop to the bittersweet belly laughs called up by a well-told toast. Knight focuses in his essay on the context of all these things—the environment:

> Biology and History teach us that man is in constant clash with his environment. Elementary Psychology teaches us that the basic mechanism of life is response to stimulus; and response is composed of thinking, feeling and acting. . . . Now it has been said that "man is the sum total of his experiences." However, the whole truth, it seems to me, is that man is the sum total of his *interpretation* of his experiences. Because, from one's interpretation of felt instincts and of impressions received from the external world comes his attitude or outlook. (By attitude and/ or outlook I mean the total expression of the individual, i.e., his experiences, his tastes, sensitivity, wishes, beliefs,—his general philosophy of life.) And, from this outlook comes his particular conduct. In the case of the narcotics addict, his processes of thought, his interpretation of the clash between his felt

instincts and his environment is incorrect; so, only with a logical philosophy can he fashion an order, however restless, in his person, and a har-
mony, no matter how uneasy, with the existing society.[14]

Perhaps one reason why Knight later emphasized the belly is that the "logical
philosophy" he advocates here never came to him in a form strong enough to
overcome his appetites and, more important, "the clash between his instincts
and the environment."

The struggle to interpret this clash—and to undo it like a knot—is clearly
among the sources of both his poetry and his prose: exhaustion with the effort
to interpret and act upon interpretation may be a factor in his relapses. Certainly a source of continued frustration for Knight was the difficulty of arriv-
ing at an interpretation of his environment that would not leave him in the
Shine-like position of choosing between remaining on the *Titanic* and diving
into uncharted dangerousness in an effort to swim away from the false promises of its passengers. If the addict errs in this context, it is in part because narcotics muddle the choice between sinking ship and scary sea. But if the addict
errs, it is also because he turns away from the world beyond the self—turns
in fact to the mimic world of opiates playing ruses on the brain—and turns
thereby away from communication.

In the struggle to interpret drug dependence, Knight's essay "Addiction:
A Philosophical Problem" turns strongly in the direction of communication.
It addresses—on behalf of the class of addicts—authorities within and
beyond the prison and includes insights that might enlighten the Avram
Goldsteins of the world: "I further submit that narcotics addiction is not a
symptom of insecurity, immaturity, criminality, etc., all of which are effects
of rather than the cause of narcotics addiction. Narcotics addiction is, more
correctly, the symptom of a most unusual outlook. Which, in the main, is
very similar to oriental fatalism, in that the addict has tried to reduce the
conflict between his inner and outer worlds by simply equating all values, all
things, to an absolute zero."[15]

This "absolute zero" appears to be achieved by adding the false positive
of narcotic joy and peace of mind to the actual negatives of, say, check forging, jail time, and fractured families. Knight then suggests that the outlook of
authorities who jail addicts is no less a pursuit of an absolute zero than is the
addict's own: "attitudes cannot be legislated out of existence. Just as most
people would risk jail or even death for their religion or family or country—
whatever offers them soul-satisfaction, so does an addict risk jail and death.
Witness: harsher laws—even the death penalty in some instances—have
already been enacted, but there has been no decrease in narcotics addiction.

An addict may be locked up for months or even years without narcotics, but once he has returned to the anxiety producing, psychically painful world, he, by his thought processes (unless they have been changed), arrives at his previously held method to ease soul pain: 'get a fix.'"

Consistent with the essay's focus on logic, addiction emerges here as an illusory solution to an essentially strategic problem. Knight, as the essay continues, argues that "the addict's 'will power,' or, rather, his lack of it is . . . meaningless. Because, will power, it seems to me, is the energy one directs toward obtaining that which he deems necessary to his existence as a being." The addict's strategic error is to aim his will at the wrong target. But in the simple act of aiming the will, the addict is the same as everyone else: "One man turns his will toward the accumulation of riches because his interpretation of life's struggles so dictates; another man sacrifices his life defending his family or country because without them he has no psychic satisfaction, and so, no sense of being." The addict's fundamental battle is that of everyone trying to make a noise loud enough to bring from the world an echo of his existence. His hit of heroin is a hit of being, which he probably knows is illusory. He is, in fact, in the position Sartre sums up in the following words: "Convinced of being impossible [and a black prisoner wishing to arrive at a correct interpretation of the clash between himself and environment that would eliminate that clash is in an impossible position], he aims at giving existence, in the teeth of the evidence, to the impossibility which he is."[16]

A major source of the addict's lapses, in this context, is the fading of the "hit" of being and the unmasking of the absence of whatever the "hit" was a substitute for—love or art, racial or national pride, praise or even, in the end, the previous hit. Knight stresses the need to rewire the addict's sensibilities: to make the addict aim his will at a properly reinterpreted reality rather than at the mimic universe driven through the tip of a needle.

"One squad of contemporary, worldly, 'hip' philosophers [existentialists?] could reap a golden harvest in the field of narcotics addiction," he concludes in a section of his essay labeled "The Cure," "because the whole picture of life would be treated rather than aspects of it. Sociology, economics, ethics, and the like may be the chipped and cracked stones in the Temple of Living, but Philosophy is the mortar."[17]

Treating "the whole picture of life," in part by representing it from a strong and, he hopes, highly communicable point of view, is a major part of Knight's work as a poet and teacher—as his demand to know if Francy Stoller was a "valid woman" shows. An interpretation of the world—or, rather, a style of interpreting it—that spreads from mind to mind like wildfire or like some strong immunity to alienation and psychic implosion—this is the ulti-mate goal of Knight's writing. Recall that in the preface to *Belly Song,* he describes poets as people who meddle with the status quo and thereby join a crowd of good and evil meddlers ranging from Jesus to Hitler and including more ordinary folk like social workers and the Watergate burglars. The poet meddles out of loving concern, Knight asserts, to provoke or help sustain liberating reinterpretations of reality. Calling attention in the preface to some of the small changes he has made in previously published poems, Knight explains that after his poems' various births in "prison, and outta prison. In poolhalls, college campuses, street corners, churches, and city parks," and after his readings around the United States, "I became aware (sometimes was made aware)" that some of the phrases or words he had used were "perpetu-ating the racism and sexism that is inherent in our language."[18] Loving con-cern, then, involves re-visioning both one's own language and the milieu and the minds with which the language meddles.

"For instance," Knight writes, "an 'English' teacher at Bucks County Community College . . . pointed out . . . that the line 'And we waited and watched, like Indians at a corral'—from 'Hard Rock Returns'—contained a racist phrase. And she was right. And so I changed 'like Indians at a corral' to 'like a herd of sheep.' . . . The authority, the authenticity, the integrity of the poet's voice is 'grounded' in the WORD as connotation, as evocation, as imagination (hence: image), and to perpetuate a lie, an evil, whether through omission or commission is to commit artistic and / or actual suicide. . . . I see the Art of Poetry as the logos ('In the beginning was the WORD') as a TRINITY: The Poet, The Poem, and the People. When the three come together, the com-munion, the communication, the Art happens."[19] The stakes Knight specifies here are high indeed. For what he requires of himself is not only poetry but a kind of priestly care of the Word that calls a new, revised, and re-visioned community into being: a community able to craft a better idiom and therefore a better form of communication and communion in partnership with the poet. This is a vision that demands far more of the poet than the creation of an art object to be recognized by connoisseurs like Harold Bloom. Along with all of the other pressures on Knight, this conception of poetry is another. Insisting on it no doubt led to many of his poetic triumphs—but it surely contributed to the occasional episodes of writer's block like the one that led to his eruption of jealousy against Sonia Sanchez's manuscript.

What might be called the "burdens of the office" that he assigned himself are clearest in "A Poem for Galway Kinnell," which appears in the last of *Born of a Woman*'s three sections. A famed poet, Kinnell was one of Knight's great postprison friends and supporters. Knight's poem to him converses with

Kinnell's poem, "Brother of My Heart," itself dedicated to Knight. Knight will not return "among us" and allow his "cried-out face" to laugh, Kinnell laments in the poem. He then implores Knight to leverage hurt into song that is all the truer because it arises from, and survives, heartbreak and weeping.[20]

Knight's address to Kinnell takes the form of a letter by an expanded Knight persona—"Imamu [Spiritual Leader] Etheridge Knight Soa," a name that appears on the page like an invocation of a more potent self, a self capable of using its voice to knit together those the poem refers to as "THE PEOPLES." Playing like a pensive jazzman on the letter form, even before approaching "THE PEOPLES," Knight sets down first the date of his writing and then his location in space, history, and the mutual matrix of his own and Kinnell's imagery:

> Saturday, April 26, 1973
> Jefferson, Missouri 65101
> (500 yards, as the crow flies,
> from where I am writing you
> this letter, lies the Missouri
> State Prison—it lies, the prison,
> like an overfed bear alongside
> the raging missouri river–
> the pale prison, out of which,
> sonny liston, with clenched fist,
> fought his way, out of which,
> james earl ray ripped his way
> into the hearts of us all . . .)

The comparison of the prison to an overfed bear evokes Kinnell's best-known poem, "The Bear," where a shamanlike Kinnell stalks a bear dying for days and nights and finds it as the bear breathes its last breath, and tears the animal "down his whole length // and open[s] him and climb[s] in // and close[s] him up after me, against the wind." The shaman does all this only to awaken at end of the poem to announce that the bear which sheltered and fed the speaker earlier in the lyric is inspiration itself and poetry itself: "that sticky infusion, that rank flavor of blood, that // poetry, by which I lived."

Since prison is sometimes referred to, by Knight and others, as "the belly of the beast"—a belly from which Knight was never confident that he had fully emerged—the comparison of the state prison to an overfed bear reverses the shamanistic transcendence of Kinnell's description, and makes the bear something that devours the human and the humane, and threatens to spill poetry's blood. Sonny Liston, the boxer who rose to the heavyweight

championship after leaving the Missouri state prison but died under myste-
rious circumstances, and James Earl Ray, the small-time criminal who assassinated Martin Luther King after escaping from the Missouri prison
system—these men represent opposite, though tragically unequal, products of
America's carceral culture. In ripping "his way // into the hearts of us all,"
in fact, James Earl Ray adds his assassin's bullet to the forces of "prison/
america"—weakening the trinities convened by King's words and diminishing
life and poetry, rather than preserving life and poetry as the bear's body does
in Kinnell's poem.

The letter proper begins as follows:

> Dear galway,
> > it is flooding here, in missouri,
> the lowlands are all under water . . .
> . . . .
> our president, of late of watergate,
> is spozed to fly above the flooded areas
> and estimate how much damage has been done
> to THE PEOPLES . . .
>
> dear galway
> > it is lonely here, and sometimes,
> THE PEOPLES can be a bitch

The first stanza fuses the damage done by the flood with the damage done by
the Watergate burglary (carried out by associates of the Nixon administration
in an effort to find compromising information about Nixon's opponents) and
the further damage done by the Nixon administration's efforts to cover up its
ties to the burglary. It fuses, in other words, the property and human losses
caused by the flood with the damage done to the free will of "THE PEOPLES"
by the breaking of the rules of democracy entailed in the burglary at the
Watergate hotel and the subsequent cover up. And it makes Nixon's flyover
into just another trick played upon "THE PEOPLES."

The second stanza addresses the fact that "THE PEOPLES" do not necessarily make the connections that Knight makes, and that enacting the word-poet-
audience "TRINITY" with them can be difficult or impossible—"a bitch." In
line with this despairing insight, Knight writes in later stanzas,

> Dear galway,
> > OUR SONGS OF LOVE are still
> murmurs among these melodies of madness . . .
> dear galway, and what the fuck are the irish doing /

and when the IRA sends JUST ONE, just one soldier
to fight with say the American Indians, then I'll believe them . . .

dear galway,
        the river is rising here, and I am
scared and lonely . . .

The "melodies of madness" include not only the noises of the Watergate
break-in but also the "red madness" Knight refers to in another lyric in *Born
of a Woman*—"Comes Now the Red Madness"—about Richard Nixon's
prolongation and selective escalation (into Cambodia) of the Vietnam War,
and Nixon's call for "law and order" crackdowns on antiwar protests and
Detroit- and Newark-like riots that people of Knight's way of thinking viewed
as rebellions against police brutality, structural racism, and colonial war. The
effort to craft a "TRINITY" powerful enough to undo the riot-causing
"melodies of madness" that climax in shots like the one fired from James Earl
Ray's rifle must indeed at times have left Knight feeling "scared and lonely"
and convinced that all "SONGS OF LOVE" were being not just drowned out,
but drowned in blood.

To some extent, Knight must have seen himself in *Born of a Woman* as a
man crying out, song by song, in a wilderness. ("In my personal life, he said
in 1989, "I stay scared a lot, from old hurts and new ones that I encounter
every day.")[21] The volume offers a spectrum of "songs of love" in which
everything from poetic friendship (as in the poem to Kinnell) to romantic
longing and romantic joy (in poems to McAnally and other lovers) to apocalyptic warnings (as in a revised version of "Dark Prophecy: I Sing of Shine")
become the burden of Knight's "WORD."

For example, in "On the Birth of a Black / Baby / Boy," a poem that is the
sequel to "Stretching the Belly" and, with "Stretching," is clearly a raison
d'être for the title *Born of a Woman*, Knight portrays a trinity formed against
a dangerous environment by himself, Charlene Blackburn, and the child, Isaac
Bushie Blackburn-Knight, whom she gives birth to after three days of labor.
As a family unit, this trinity embodies both the romantic love that led to the
pregnancy and the love-driven transit through generations that Knight evokes
in "The Idea of Ancestry." But this trinity is ringed round in the poem by the
sociopolitical and historical barbed wire that always hems Knight in—by "the
Ku Klux / Klan" marching "like locusts" just "short miles to the south" of the
Memphis hospital where the birth takes place, and by those who murder
potentially transformative leaders—leaders like San Francisco mayor George
Moscone, who in 1978 was shot by a conservative opponent—shot "like //
Martin, Malcolm, and Medgar Evers."

How can songs of love and the cries that attend hopeful births be heard over the noise of such murders? This is one of the questions *Born of a Woman* in particular, and Knight's oeuvre as a whole, strives to pose powerfully enough to summon if not solutions, then new interpretations of reality that might lead to solutions. In "We Free Singers Be"—perhaps the most joyous and defiant poem in *Born of a Woman*—Knight works to set the word "we" quivering like a tuning fork sending out a tone so strong that readers' and listeners' minds (and no doubt Knight's own mind) hum the same tone in a larger "we" that, in turn, strikes sympathetic vibrations outside Knight's immediate audience, thus creating a yet larger "we" that becomes loud enough, perhaps, to overwhelm not only "melodies of madness" but also unbridgeable silences, like those he accuses the IRA of maintaining with respect to non-Irish groups like the Native Americans. "We Free Singers Be," which sags in its rather uninventive center, opens nevertheless at a remarkable and memorable pitch of intensity:

> We free singers be
> sometimes swimming in the music,
> like porpoises playing in the sea.
> We free singers be
> come agitators at times, be
> come eagles circling the sun,
> hurling stones at hunters, be
> come scavengers cracking eggs
> in the palm of our hands.
> (Remember, oh, do you remember
> the days of the raging fires
> when I clenched my teeth
> in my sleep and refused to speak
> in the daylight hours?)
> We free singers be, baby

Again Knight is summoning his best self, and all those whom that self has power to move, to the battle against melodies of madness. The poem celebrates, above all things, a power of self-transformation and self-making that is emphasized by the enjambments that break the word "become" into "be" and "come," suggesting a state of being that arrives before the summoning of it is finished. In this poem all confinement is in the past, in memories of the "raging fires" of riots and memories of refusals to communicate or to even try to form a "we." When she ordered his tombstone, Knight's mother saw to it that the line "We free singers be" was carved upon it, and she was relentless in making sure the artisan made the stone the summa of her son that she wished it to be, according to Eunice Knight-Bowens.

Aside from the poet-word-audience trinity, Knight championed another, complementary trinity: that of love-freedom-birth. "And Tell Me, Poet, Can Love Exist in Slavery," *Born of a Woman*'s variation on the themes of "To Make a Poem in Prison," insists,

> . . . Poet, your tongue
> is split, and as still
> as the Stone
> In the Belly of the Great Mother.
> She has always known:
> *Love and Freedom are One!*

The "Great Mother" Knight invokes is likely the female divinity whose manifestations Erich Neumann chronicled and Robert Bly celebrated in his annual conferences. Knight fuses the Neumann-Bly account of her with his own concept of the belly to evoke—if not to achieve—a locus of transpersonal and transgenerational emotional wakefulness, communication, and communion: the never fully realizable locus in which love and freedom can truly be one, and the poet's tongue—and at times his heart—are not turned to stone by "the anxiety producing, psychically painful world."

CHAPTER 6

The Essential Etheridge Knight

The Essential Etheridge Knight, the last book Knight published during his lifetime, combines poems from *Born of a Woman* with a number of remarkable, previously uncollected works. This chapter will focus on a small group of new or reprinted poems in which Knight adds fresh political grace notes to the major themes of both his work and his life: the negotiation of dangerousness, both within and outside the psyche and its wounds; the effort to expand the array of possible futures; and the effort to sing a belly song powerful enough to fulfill the shamanistic ambition—itself a symptom of an insatiable thirst for utopian freedom—that Knight expressed in statements such as the following: "I see poets . . . as singers, as preachers, as prophets. . . . The things I call poetry—you know—speak about big things in human life—death, war, freedom, and birth. These kinds of things can only be spoken about in a way that you can feel them. They can only be spoken about in symbols, in myths. . . . When you are speaking of feelings, you can't present them in prose, in everyday English; they must be presented through symbols or myths. That's why religion has been so effective in speaking to people. The big questions concern economics, politics, medicine, etc. All of these things answer the question: Where did I come from and where am I going? Religion and poetry speak in symbols and try to answer big questions."[1] The effort to make poetry as consequential as economics, politics, medicine, and prophecy is part of Knight's effort to free himself and all who come under the influence of his words. In the service of this effort, the poem "My Uncle Is My Honor and a Guest in My House"[2] taps the same bloodline that, in "The Idea of Ancestry," reaches down through past generations and up through future ones and, thereby, escapes death, war, and other impediments to the utopian freedom Knight longed for:

In the center of the bloodvein
    is a kinkiss
    is a boiling
    and a calling
of your name
. . . .
. . . down the bone-filled alleys
where the bible
    and the blade lay
like lovers
the shadows flee . . .
. . . .
before the gold / bright teeth
of my Uncle
. . . .

The fakes, the unforgivers,
the fear-feeders, and the CIA
deny the kinkiss
. . . .
and point to the stones
falling from my tongue—
as I call out your name

The malefactors here are the enemies of poetry and of the kinship with self, family, and world that Knight wants prophetic poetry to foster: they are fakes, "unforgivers," fear-feeders—all who make the Bible and the sword into lovers. The pimps of this sword-Bible union include the CIA, with its penchant for toppling developing country governments during the 1950s and 1960s.

It seems at first glance odd—assuming that Knight is writing autobio-graphically and that the speaker of the poem is not a persona he creates—that he opposes his uncle to all this worldly might. But he makes his relative into the sort of mythological figure that for him embodies the mysteries of survival in the face of all that threatens it. Because of Knight's success in making it mythological, the smile of the uncle becomes more powerful than both Bible and blade: powerful enough to free Knight's tongue from the stones—the whole weight of injustice—that weigh it down. In the conclusion of the poem, the uncle has become so powerful that, like an apotheosis of Knight himself, he sings poems to "the short men" who "shake their fists // at the darkening sky." This conclusion revisits the themes of "I Sing of Shine." The "short men" watch the sky darkening in the same way that the passengers on the

Titanic watch the water rising around their ship. However, in "My Uncle Is My Honor," the singer's song is clearly what darkens the sky—both racially and, from the point of view of the "short men," in terms of dangerousness.

The poem makes it clear that part of Knight's mission is exorcism: the "short men" are not simply white, as one might suppose. "Short" in this context signifies withered, diminished, and self-diminished by refusal of the "kinkiss" that stretches a life beyond its beginning and its end. It is likely that Knight includes himself among the men shaking their fists at sometimes self-darkened skies.

"My Uncle Is My Honor" is bracketed by poems to McAnally. In "I and Your Eyes," the poem that follows "My Uncle Is My Honor," McAnally all but takes the larger-than-life place of the uncle:

> If I could hold your hillside smile
> Your seashore laughter your lips
>
> Then I
> Could stand alone   the pain
> Of flesh   alone   the time and space
> And steel   alone   but I am shaken
> It has taken   your eyes
> To move this stone.

Here McAnally is summoned to play the part of an anti-Medusa who can thaw a Knight frozen and silenced by pain and the very time and space in which his struggles unfold. Given what actually happened in the McAnally relationship, it is clear that the fragility of flesh and will were too much for even McAnally's eyes to overcome. Only the McAnally made superhuman in the lines of the poem—and the Knight made strong enough to "hold [her] hillside smile"—can free the speaker turned to silent stone.

New aspects of the petrifying environment that shakes and silences are revealed in "Poem for the Liberation of South Africa" (which appears in both *Born of a Woman* and *The Essential Etheridge Knight*) and "Various Protestations from Various People" (which appears only in *The Essential Etheridge Knight*). These poems dramatize in new ways the fact that what petrifies Knight are threats to the utopia of freedom he hungered for—whether the threats occur in apartheid South Africa or among associates who find Knight's idealism too uncompromising.

In the South Africa poem, Knight makes "ecstasy" and "Love"—meaning, in the context of the poem, indestructible communicative and liberating forces—into the equivalents, on a global scale, of McAnally's eyes and smile: "have danced in ecstasy," the poem begins,

> (That's all—all I got
> But for Love)
> That leaps and sings across the sea
> To the cell of Nelson Mandela
> Sitting with his / own / self on Robbins [Robben] Island

To strengthen Mandela—who during his decades of incarceration by the apartheid South African government grew steadily in moral stature and international prominence—with the rippling out among concentric audiences of Knight's lines, is to strengthen everything Knight himself battled for in the erratic behavior brought on, arguably, by his attempts to resist Stockholm authority. Mandela sitting "with his / own / self" and singlehandedly counterbalancing the power of the apartheid government—which he eventually defeated with the aid of voices like Knight's—twists the space of history in the direction of freedom and of ecstasy for a whole nation.

Knight goes on to both praise and mock "white mission / aries" whose voices, added to voices like his, did indeed strengthen Mandela: "They huddle in circles then hurry away // To demon / strate." Plucking the word "demon" out of "demonstrate" is an ingenious bit of poetry, though not necessarily an entirely accurate bit of political analysis. There are, of course many ways of reading this excavated pun: Are the "missionaries" spotlighting the demonic nature of apartheid? Or are they hiding, behind their demonstrations, the demonic intentions that people like Elijah Muhammad might have ascribed to them? The answer to both questions is "yes." Knight represents actual slogans the missionaries might have shouted but then inserts a fanciful—and very crude and even sexist—one that suggests that they despise the people on whose behalf they are demonstrating—and that they are demanding no more than a false freedom: "'Leaflet the banks.' // 'Down with the krugerrand." // "March on the [South African] embassies." . . . "Give 'em some white / pussy— // That's all them Africans want, anyways."

Here Knight's experiences with "prison/America" combine with the street corner man's expectation of doom to create an outburst of cynicism. Thereafter he turns his attention away from Mandela's triumphant self-possession and back to all that interferes with his desire to conquer distance and distill strength into Mandela's cell. He turns his attention specifically to "Pulling Charlie's [white authority's] foot outta / my / own / ass." For Knight the chance that Charlie and the demonstrators are linked cannot be ignored. Some demonstrators will inevitably have benefitted from the placement of Charlie's foot: from the civil death that has left a greater proportion of people like Knight with "no land" and "no job." Knight concludes by insisting that almost all he has is the land of the landless—the utopia (the no-place) of love.

As a special "no-place," love is reduced here to a spark of potential: a tiny spark that is nevertheless the most valuable product of self-confrontation and confrontation with the world. It becomes a spark that cannot be put out—a spark that, however seemingly dormant, retains the potential to fire resistance, whether that resistance takes the form of removing Charlie's "foot"— the whole legacy of slavery, discrimination, and poverty that is summed up in the phrase "no land at / all"—or building one's self-love to the point where it captures an ecstasy that can be communicated to the psyche of a freedom fighter across seas of racial conflict.

The effort to cultivate love's spark in an environment that seems to be working to put it out—whether with overt discrimination and incarceration or with their historical aftermath ("no land at / all")—can both be hurt by and require the sort of perverse obstinacy that Knight defends and celebrates in "Various Protestations from Various People":

> Esther say I drink too much.
> Mama say pray don't think too much.
> My shrink he say I feel too much,
>
> . . . .
>
> Philosophers say I wanna BE too much.
> Reagan say I talk about me too much,
> Singing songs 'bout being free too much.
>
> I say—sing about me being *free* too much?
> Say sing about me being *free* too much?

This poem is the most eloquent of several in which Knight, while not forgiving himself for his trespasses, argues that a man struggling to get a noose from around his neck must not be condemned for his sometimes grotesque and, for those near him, injurious flailing.[3] The noose can only be removed, this poem suggests, by a constant vigilance and resistance that, in their very constancy, become excessive, painful, and susceptible to breakdowns marked in Knight's case by drinking or drug-taking binges. The key lines in the poem have a which-comes-first, chicken-and-egg relationship: the wanting to "BE too much" while singing of songs about being free (and thus grabbing added being) constitutes a self-sustaining feedback loop. The sung songs themselves, including "Various Protestations," are attempted expansions of being, which here can be defined as expansions of possible futures and the power to choose among them. But the expansion of the possible is itself an expansion of being—an attainment of new knowledge about a part of the aleascape that the light of songs reveals.

In the relentless pursuit of (for others) excessive feeling, excessive critique and thought, excessive expression, and, ultimately, excessive escapism via bottle or needle, Knight comes to resemble Sartre's self-uprooting selves. And comes to resemble someone obsessively pursuing what another French philosopher, Jacques Derrida, calls *ipseity*.

Both Knight's drive to excess and his constant frustration—indeed, the apparent fear of permanence that manifested itself in everything from his sabotaging of his own university appointments[4] and relationships to his preference for conducting Free People's Poetry Workshops outside of institutional settings—are illuminated by Sartre's observation that "the writer knows that he speaks for freedoms which are swallowed up, masked, and unavailable; and his own freedom is not so pure; he has to clean it. . . . Every freedom, if one considers it *sub specie aeternitatis,* seems to be a withered branch. . . . It is nothing else but the movement by which one perpetually uproots and liberates himself."[5] If Knight achieved nothing else, he succeeded in perpetually uprooting himself. The very addictions that so damaged his life were themselves periodically uprooted at places like Daytop. Of course his uprootings were "not so pure." They were, as he confesses in works like "Another Poem for Me," sometimes the very withering that afflicted his creativity. But for a man who saw Stockholm authority infecting everything around him and within him, the uprootings, beginning with the insistence on more, more, and finally too much thought, too much feeling, too much being, were unavoidable. Some of the methods of uprooting could have, and should have, been avoided, as Knight admits in "Cop-out Session." But, again, the man struggling to tear a noose from his neck does things he may not be fully aware of. And the man who knows that the rope is woven of strands of his own thought and feeling, as well as strands of a mighty political system, flails about all the more and, at times, all the more self-destructively.

The flailing and the singing about being free—even with the needle of addiction through his throat—is part of what Derrida called the pursuit of "sovereign self-determination, of the autonomy of the self, of the *ipse*, namely, of the one-self that gives itself its own law."[6] What is ultimately involved in this pursuit is potency—the pursuit of the potency of a completely socially alive person in Knight's case—and human potential in general. The particular potency being pursued is, in Derrida's terminology, *ipseity.* With this term, Derrida explained, "I . . . wish to suggest some 'I can,' or at the very least the

power that gives itself its own law . . . its self-representation, the sovereign
and reappropriating gathering of self in the simultaneity of an assemblage or
assembly, being together, or 'living together,' as we say. . . . Each time I say
ipse, metipse, or *ipseity,* relying at once on their accepted meaning in Latin,
their meaning within the philosophical code, and their etymology, I also wish
to suggest the self, the one-self, being properly oneself. . . . I . . . wish to suggest . . . the power, potency, sovereignty, or possibility implied in every 'I
can.'"[7] In declaring "We free singers be," Knight issues a declaration not of
independence but of ipseity. He summons a free-singing assembly where the
ipseity of each member of the assembly can be enabled by the singing itself.
Declaring "We free singers be," Knight installs an "I can" in the mind of each
listener. The deaf-mutes Steve Stoller describes respoding to Knight's "The Sun
Came" with their own excited sounds is an example of this infectious "I can"
at work. The power of free singing—of freely expressing one's ipseity—is the
power of being properly oneself. It is the power Knight struggled for against
all odds throughout his life, and through all his yielding of sovereignty over
himself to addiction or to institutions. Uttering his own free songs in an environment that appears to have always sent back echoes which sounded to him
at least somewhat like those of a locked room, Knight remained determined
to pick the lock with words. "We free singers be" is, among other things, a
call for a utopia of legitimate sovereignty and unincarcerated ipseity.

Fully legitimate sovereignty, if such a thing is possible on earth, or possible within a single life, would be the opposite of Stockholm authority, which
is always backed by the implied threat of violence and always summons a
degree of sycophancy and self-policing. But, Derrida claimed, a person who
did achieve such sovereignty could *only* do so by wielding something akin to
Stockholm authority: "In its very etymology, [*ipse*] implies the exercise of
power by someone it suffices to designate as himself, *ipse*. The sovereign,
in the broadest sense of the term, is he who has the right and the strength to
be and be recognized as himself, the same, properly the same as himself.
. . . [The linguist Émile Benveniste pointed out that for] an adjective [*ipse*]
that means 'oneself' to become amplified to the sense of 'master,' one condition is necessary: a closed circle of people, subordinated to a central person-
age who takes on the personality and complete identity of the group to the
point of summing it up himself; by himself, he embodies it."[8] An example of
such sovereignty is a dictatorship that "gives orders and has no account to
render other than to itself (*ipse*)."[9] Knight, of course, wished only to fling off
such dictatorial sovereignty and the Stockholm hooks it thrust into tongues
like his.

This is surely one of the reasons why Knight, who claimed in one interview that he knew only how "to poet" or how to steal—and whose friends, Quinn says, were well advised to hide their checkbooks when he came to visit or to stay—obsessively questioned his own *ipseity* in its relations with *ipseities* around it that inevitably condition and shape it and create the aforementioned sense of hearing echoes within a locked room. Such an obsessive questioning and pushing of limits can account for both the generosity and the thefts for which he was known. Only in his poetry did he appear able to sustain the authority and self-possession he needed to approach a sustainable balance between his own and others' *ipseities*. This is because the poetry (and the workshops) is compatible with the pursuit of unbounded dialogue and communication that is the heart of his aesthetic: because the pursuit boils down to an effort to find a nondictatorial bridge from "I" to "we": "I believe that one has to move from the 'I,' subjective, through the verb, to the 'we,'" Knight once said. The three repetitions of "alone" that Knight rhymes with "stone" in "I and Your Eyes" signify the absence of "we"—the state of fright, isolation, and incarceration that he wants to break free of with the right connecting verb.

The "verb" for Knight is, more often than not, the poem performed before an audience that is the beginning of the larger "we": "If I verbalize, see, I am a Black male in this country and if I, through my own self-examination, expressed that, I bet you I'm pretty much going to be hitting what most other Black males feel."[10] But through the accurate expression of black male emotion, Knight expected also to touch the "bellies" of nonblacks and nonmales and to thereby begin to create the larger "we." A powerful poem, powerfully performed, thus ideally becomes a catalyst for a nondictatorial interlocking of ipseities into a larger and more legitimate "we."

Knight hungered for this sort of "we" and rejected all imitations or suspected imitations. His journey from prison to the pinnacle of American poetry, furthermore, left him uniquely prepared (in his periods of relative self-possession) to separate counterfeit from actually plural consciousnesses. The counterfeit for Knight is the universality that Giammanco declared to be stained with the blood of slavery and brutal colonizing invasions. In an unpublished review of Sonia Sanchez's book *Homegirls & Handgrenades*, Knight wrote of having to defend black poets against the charge that they are "not addressing universal themes"; that they "are singing about . . . black pains and pleasures, about rats and roaches and racism"; that they are producing "just 'protest' and 'hate' poetry." Recalling an exchange with an Ivy League professor who made just such a charge, Knight described himself retreating into the trickster mode he employed in "The Warden Said to Me": "I scratched my mississippi head for a minute and said. Well, sir, say that you're walking/down the street with your pretty wife here, and a crazy leaps outta the bushes and attacks her—and you kill him. Now, would you/ be/ killing him because you *hated* him, or because you *loved* your wife?"[11] The actual "we" for Knight is one that grows not out of the murderous universal Giammanco condemns, but out of what he called (translating the Dogon term *Nommo*), "the living word."[12] This living word lives—authenticates itself— as long as it feeds back, through a poem or other communication, between speaker or poet and concentric audiences.

"Feedback" here means both the sort of feedback a performer receives when an audience applauds—or boos—and the sort of feedback that emerges when an amplified note from an electric guitar emerges from the amplification system only to feed back into the "pick-ups" of the guitar and emerge again from the amplifiers as a powerful new sound. Such feedback was famously used by guitarist Jimi Hendrix to expand music's vocabulary and communicative potential. Hendrix did this by positioning "his body and his guitar relative to the amplifier's speaker cabinets so that the resulting feedback would modulate to the precise tone he wanted."[13]

Knight relied on standard applauding or booing (or more likely quiet postreading) audience feedback to tell him whether he was being true to his listeners' sense of things. But he also depended on the audience to function as an amplification system that would catch his message and make it into something stronger than the sound of a single voice or the impulse of a single consciousness. His changing of words or phrases in some poems on the basis of audience response is an example of the first kind of feedback at work. But (since, after all, the two kinds of feedback are not entirely separate or separable) it is also, together with his repertory of prosodic techniques, his equivalent of Hendrix's positioning of his body in such a way as to summon a special sound. Knight's parlaying of the resulting poetic achievement into the forming of Free People's Poetry Workshops and his insistence on the incorporation of a commitment to nonviolence into the creative process of workshop participants, are examples of the second kind of feedback at work. An equally consequential example of this second kind of feedback is the impact of Knight's poetry and poetics on people like Fran Quinn, Stephen and Francy Stoller, Dudley Randall, and Gwendolyn Brooks,[14] who became part of the "we" that nurtured Knight's poetic "I" and his poetic legacy. The careful dialogue implied by the first kind of feedback and the personal commitments cultivated by the second are a basis for the sort of "we" Knight wanted to make as large as possible.

Part of Knight's unconquerable sense of insecurity no doubt derived from his knowledge of just how fragile this sort of "we" is, and how difficult it is to empower, given the clash of *ipseities* that occur even within a single person. Knight's own life provides dramatic evidence of the clashes within the self. As we have seen, his mind was full enough of self-contradiction and self-destructiveness to qualify him as a victim of what Derrida called "the auto-immune." Derrida explained that the autoimmune "consists not only in harming or ruining oneself, indeed in destroying one's own protections, and in doing so oneself, committing suicide or threatening to do so, but, more seriously still . . . threatening the I [*moi*] or the self [*soi*] . . . it consists not only in compromising oneself . . . but in compromising . . . ipseity"—the very "mine-ness" of the self.[15]

Knight's "autoimmunity" was clearly an exaggerated response to his feeling of being squeezed in coils of Stockholm authority. But it also gave him insider insights into the worldwide workings of autoimmunity. These insights are memorably expressed in four poems. The poems, two of which appear only in *Born of a Woman,* and two of which appear only in *The Essential Etheridge Knight,* are "A Personal Letter to Eldridge Cleaver," "A Black Poet Leaps to His Death (for mbembe milton smith)," "Welcome Home, Andrew Young—I'm / sho / glad that you didn't get hung," and "At a VA Hospital in the Middle of the United States of America: An Act in a Play." The first of these works raises the issue of autoimmunity within the Black Freedom movement; the second, that of autoimmunity within a single psyche; the third and fourth, that of autoimmunity on a global scale.

"A Black Poet Leaps to His Death" treats the issue most nakedly, mourning as it does an actual suicide. In the course of the poem, Knight compares Mbembe Smith's pain to a slash across his own throat. He underscores the fact that he shares much of the pain when he writes of his own "October cry" at the wounding spectacle of a "yellow moon ringed with blood // of children dead in the lebanese mud."

Since the poem is dated October 1981, the reference appears to be to the Israeli invasion and occupation of a portion of Lebanon in 1978 and to the bombing of Palestinian Liberation Organization camps in July 1981. Knight's cry is not only against the deaths of children, but against the entire Middle East peace process, which, in a poem on the subject that appears in both *Born of a Woman* and *The Essential Etheridge Knight,* he characterizes as a process whose main outcome is the planting of future wars in the brains of children. Late 1970s Israeli prime minister Menachem Begin is made to contradict himself in the opening lines of "A Poem on the Middle East 'Peace Process'" by citing his love for peace as the reason "why we / drove . . . the Palestinians off

/ their / land— // With the help of america." It is under the umbrella of such reasoning that the next generation forms with war's spike in its brains: "In the Gaza strip an Arab boy sleeps, // his knees / are / drawn / up to his chest // . . . He dreams of grenades, // and machine guns." At the same time, an Israeli boy asleep in Tel Aviv dreams of "tales told to him by his / grand / father: // Nazi boots goosestepping on cobblestone. . . . He dreams too of blooming gardens // In the 'promised land' and of killing Arabs." The poem concludes with a condemnation of Middle East peacemakers who "Give guns to / one // And bombs to the / other // All contrary to the / cries / of the Mother." The Mother here is clearly the Great Mother whose lore and power Robert Bly wished in the post–Vietnam War era to infuse into a patriarchal culture he feared was entering a hypermasculine, war-making, autoimmune death spiral. As Bly put it in 1975, "Many seem to feel . . . that this patriarchal society is collapsing. It's collapsing partly because of poor decisions being made by males in government matters. From the point of view of consciousness, statesmen make these errors because they actually are living in an unbalanced consciousness, with much too much of father consciousness and too little of the mother consciousness. . . . Obsessive competitiveness is a right-sided [father consciousness] thing, involving domination of the earth . . . instead of living *with* it."[16]

War as autoimmunity is well illustrated in the dreams of Knight's Palestinian and Israeli boys. The children dead in the mud in the Smith poem, and Smith himself leaping to his death, are additional victims of the autoimmune. Knight's "October cry" expresses, in part, his fear of himself succumbing to the autoimmune.

Smith's suicide is portrayed as a desperate attempt by Smith to rid himself of an autoimmunity even more intolerable than the one that causes him to take his own life: the possible severing of poetry itself by pain "like a slash across the throat." Thus "it must have been a rush a great gasp // of breath // the awesome leap to your death // o poet . . . of the short song // and serious belief." The death leap as a "rush" like that given by a drug, the gasp of breath, like that made by a person who had almost drowned but suddenly breaks the water's surface, and, above all, the "serious belief" that remains admirable after the suicide and that Smith may have felt had to be preserved at all costs— these turns of phrase construct Smith's suicide as a final attempt to rescue a spirit and an interpretation of self and world that had been imploding.

Knight, with his "bullet-thru-the-brain" thoughts and "needle-in-[the]-arm problem," clearly identified with both the feeling of being under unbearable pressure and the temptation to leap "into the universe," as one line of the poem describes Smith doing. Yet Knight's lines also express the contradictions involved in Smith's leap:

                        can the poet belie
            the poem
                    old revolutionaries never die
            it is said
                    they just be born again
            (check chuck colson and his panther from folsom)

Since, for Knight, poems are intended to be tools for liberation from every
form of death, it is clear that the poet who kills himself belies the poem (and
fails to answer Knight's call for black poets to at all costs live as trumpets of
their people).[17] At the same time, however, there are fates that, in Knight's
view, may be worse than death.

A case in point is the fate of Chuck Colson's "panther from folsom." This
panther is the postrevolutionary Eldridge Cleaver. While on the run from
American authorities and living in France, Cleaver saw a vision of his own
past self and his Marxist heroes being eclipsed on the face of the moon by a
triumphant Jesus Christ. Cleaver became a born-again Christian and, later, an
associate of Colson, the infamous Richard Nixon administration hatchet man
who himself was born again in prison. The born-again Cleaver's born-again
pronouncements and friendships dismayed and angered many who had once
admired him. After his return to the United States, Cleaver found himself
shunned by old associates, some of whom denounced him as an FBI and/or
CIA tool being used to destroy black organizations.[18]

In light of this history, Knight's syntax speaks volumes by making Cleaver
a nameless Colson possession. The derisive tone of "they just be born again,"
furthermore, suggests that Knight was among those who dismissed Cleaver's
rebirth as the latest scam of a "turncoat opportunist."[19] Interpreted thus,
however, Cleaver's conversion, like Smith's suicide, serves as a warning of what
can go amiss in a personal fight for liberation from what Cleaver himself
called the "American nightmare"[20]—a nightmare from which Knight, as much
as Smith or Cleaver, was trying to awake.[21]

Another aspect of the frightening "there but for the grace of God go I" lesson that Knight seemed to perceive in Cleaver has to do with the fact that
some disappointed former associates and admirers concluded that Cleaver
had either abandoned or simply lost his grip on the world-famous *ipseity* he
built during his revolutionary period. Cleaver's former wife, Kathleen, said in
a 1994 interview that after his 1977 return to the United States (following his
period of exile), Cleaver had become "a very unhealthy person, unhealthy
mentally, and I don't think he's ever quite recovered. He became a profoundly
disappointed and disoriented person."[22] And he was not alone. Reflecting on

Cleaver's and others' metamorphoses, Kathleen Cleaver asserted that "tens of thousands of people during [the 1980s] sought some way to fill the void left after the destruction of those movements that had given meaning to their lives. Some joined religious cults while others turned to drugs, and although many navigated a transition into new careers and family lives, that proved elusive for Eldridge Cleaver."[23]

The fact that Knight was struggling with the same collapse of 1960s and 1970s movements and ideologies makes the disillusionment the poet appears to have felt about Cleaver's metamorphosis that much more poignant. A magnificent poem, included in *Born of a Woman* but pointedly excluded from *The Essential Etheridge Knight,* makes it clear that Cleaver was someone Knight admired and lionized at one point—someone whose footsteps Knight thought about following. One can only imagine Knight's shock at Cleaver's decisions to associate himself with the Chuck Colsons of the world and to endorse Ronald Reagan for president in 1980. The same Reagan inspired Knight to speculate thus in one poem: "When the doors/ close // On the Oval office // Maybe Reagan's nose // Grows . . . red (like Rage // And Sin and Blood)."[24] Of the conservative wave that Reagan's election helped unleash and and of a number of people with whom Cleaver (coincidentally) prayed, Knight wrote (in the tellingly titled unpublished poem "On the Removal of the Fascist American Right from Power"): "Take back the American Revolution/ From the big daddies and the little wives,/ You can do it, White man. . . . take it from them: // The American Ayatollahs: Jerry Falwell, // Billy Graham. . . . Encircle the lil wives of the Big Daddies in a Dance, // A Revolutionary Dance, confront the lil wives // With Revolutionary Songs."[25]

Smith, on the one hand, and Cleaver, on the other, figure for Knight as two different kinds of victims of the same autoimmunity—an autoimmunity hard at work within himself. Because he so admiringly mourns Smith's suicide, it is clear that Knight views Cleaver's transformation as something worse than zombification—as a hollowing out by Stockholm syndrome akin to that caused by the probiscus of an assassin bug that liquefies the insides of its prey before sucking those insides out.

This makes all the more intriguing the poem Knight chose *not* to include in *The Essential Etheridge Knight*—the poem called "A Personal Letter to Eldridge Cleaver." This "letter" addresses the preconversion Cleaver during the period of exile in France that ended (unbeknownst to Knight when he penned the lyric) with the vision of Christ. The letter opens with Knight warning Cleaver to look over his shoulder and face the fact that those who should be following Cleaver's lead "have snuck // Back to their homes" to sit in comfort with their feet stretched toward their hearth fires. Therefore "Brother you are alone (prove // Me wrong)," Knight writes.

The letter goes on to emphasize the most obvious common denominator between himself and Cleaver—the common denominator of prison experience. Did Cleaver, Knight asks, forget the pattern of prisoner-warden confrontations in which white and black Hard Rocks would lead from the front, facing the guns on the warden's side, and therefore fail to see those they were leading slink away? Did Cleaver, Knight continues, forget that those "wanting // Freedom for real" and leading from the front would find, after things "got hot," that they alone ended up shut away "in the hole"? Knight laments that, as Cleaver sits in his "paris cell" (his exile), people like Knight himself are sitting "in soft chairs." The final lines challenge Cleaver to somehow rouse lapsed rebels out of those chairs. Returning as the last line of the poem, the demand "Prove me wrong" becomes a plea for Cleaver to end Knight's disillusionment.

Cleaver, of course, proved Knight wrong in a way that neither Knight nor anyone else who had idolized the unbreakable Black Panther firebrand could have imagined. In his book *Soul on Fire*, Cleaver revealed that the prelude to his vision was a decision to commit suicide. In other words, he, like Smith, might have been the subject of a Knight elegy instead of a wave of shock and of derision from former associates and admirers. Knight's call in "Letter" comes back to him not as an *ipseity*-enhancing bit of feedback but as a kind of pulling of the plug on Cleaver's part in the "we" that "Letter" wants to enhance.

In another poem that appears in *Born of a Woman* and not in *The Essential Etheridge Knight*, the poet is more welcoming of another returning hero—Andrew Young, a former Martin Luther King Jr. lieutenant who was forced to resign as President Jimmy Carter's ambassador to the United Nations after meeting unofficially with a representative of the Palestinian Liberation Organization (PLO). Unlike the born-again Cleaver, Young is placed by Knight's poem in the pantheon headed by the Armageddon-beating protagonist of "Dark Prophecy: I Sing of Shine." "Welcome Home, Andrew Young—I'm / sho / glad that you didn't get hung" is in fact placed in *Born of a Woman* immediately before "Dark Prophecy," and Young is explicitly advised to be like Shine and abandon the "boat" of American policy. The opening lines of the poem, furthermore, endorse Young's view that the outraged response to his probing of Palestinian positions was designed in part to slow the Middle East peace process.[26] Given the content of his other poem on that peace process, Knight could only have been pleased earlier when Young courted controversery with comments on Israel's bombing of targets in Lebanon. Knight may even have agreed with the PLO's cry that Young's forced resignation was an instance of "mental terrorism and racist persecution." The then-president of the Southern Christian Leadership Conference (SCLC) expressed a widely shared African American sentiment when he declared that Young's meeting with the PLO official (condemned by some as defiance of the era's official U.S. policy) was part of the "'aggressive pursuit of peace and justice' endemic to the Black movement from which comes Andrew Young."[27] This sort of public pro-Young point of view—including the implied assertion that there are parallels between African American and Palestinian struggles—is the unstated axiom of "Welcome."

Knight adds his own associations, linking Young's case with that of previous African American leaders and rebels who ended up assassinated for their views. Risking sloganeering,[28] Knight collapses the forces that compel Young's resignation into a single archetypal "whiteboy"—"the killingest boy // History has / ever / known." No "right / on Preacher" should work with this "boy," Knight insists, so "do / like / Shine— // Leap off the boat."

The trick, as all Knight's work and life show, is to find a way to leap off the boat without plunging into the void—into a dangerousness that is beyond any person's (or any poet's or preacher's) power to interpret, act upon, and thereby survive with most of his or her sense of "mine-ness" intact. The deeper trouble, even here, is that Shine can only save himself, or inspire others to save themselves. But Shine cannot, as Knight ultimately wants to do, save the ship by transforming the minds of those who benefit from its inequities. What Knight can and does do is continue to record the costs of failed peace processes.

One of his most memorable efforts in this regard is "At a VA Hospital in the Middle of the United States of America: An Act in a Play." More like a monumental set of stage directions and a chorus than a play, this work appears to use "act" to mean "performative statement," like the sentence "I now pronounce you man and wife."[29] But, rather than pronounce the formation of man and wife, the poem pronounces the formation of peacemakers— and the formation, too, of makers and artists of inner peace. It does so by sketching a group of men who at first glance seem like no more than the remnants of the wars they fought. One was "gassed outside Nice" and has a "gracious grin" born of a "chemical high"; another is a black World War II veteran who suffers from "pains in the head"—pains no doubt both emotional and physical—that he tries to drive off with alcohol. A third veteran is, like Knight, an ex–Korean War medic, but, unlike Knight, is a quadruple amputee and "an amazement of machines // And bubbling bottles" whose loving wife cannot compete with his desire for sleep; a fourth is a Vietnam War veteran who is nevertheless a kind of Knight doppelgänger in the sense that he has been sent to the hospital as a condition of his bail for a "'possession and sale' // Of narcotics" charge. Like a Knight fallen off the wagon, the veteran seeks "an end to sin" and "a surcease of sorrow" by spending his pension checks "for ten grams of 'pure.'" He "nods the days away."

The fifth and final veteran sketched in the poem seems to have been broken without the aid of a war: his "war was the south side // Of San Diego" where he caught a "fifty/Dollar dose of syphilis" in a brothel. His mind affected by the disease, he spends his days performing "feats" of howling masturbation that cause doctors to "whisper and huddle in fours" while Knight and the other hospital inmates listen sympathetically, "patient patients." All five of the veterans and, of course, the poet who describes them have been dealt incurable wounds by the earthquakes in the parts of the aleascape they tried to cross. Knight ingeniously makes their tragedies a performative by turning the poem into a sing-along pledge—a sing-along impressment of those the poem captivates into the ranks of people who secede from war. He carries this impressment out by setting up a sing-along with words already known to many of the poem's readers—words from the powerful text of a famous spiritual:

> Gon' lay down my sword 'n' shield—
> Down by the river side, down by the river side—
> . . . .
> Ain't gon' study war no more.

NOTES

Chapter 1—Introduction

1. Robert Bly, "Hearing Etheridge Knight," in *American Poetry: Wildness and Domesticity* (New York: Harper & Row, 1990), 108.

2. Coleen Cowette, "Toast Teller Turned to Poet: Knight Writes on Prison Life," *Equinox* (Keen State College, N.H.), February 19, 1986, 19.

3. Bly, "Hearing Etheridge Knight," 102.

4. Fran Quinn, interview by the author, July 19, 2010.

5. Lamont B. Steptoe, "A Deity of the Spoken Word: Etheridge Knight 1931–1991," *Bride Unveiled* (newsletter of Philadelphia's Painted Bride Arts Center), Fall 1991, 2.

6. Yusef Komunyakaa, *Blue Notes: Essays, Interviews, and Commentaries*, ed. Radiclani Clytus (Ann Arbor: University of Michigan Press, 2000), 16.

7. Haki R. Madhubuti, "Etheridge Knight: Making Up Poems," *Worcester Review* 19, no. 1–2 (1998): 103.

8. Cowette, "Toast Teller."

9. Jared Carter, "Etheridge Knight: Return of the Rainmaker," otherwise unidentified newspaper clipping, Etheridge Knight Collection, Special Collections and Rare Books, Irwin Library, Butler University.

10. Etheridge Knight, "Things Awfully Quiet in America (Song of the Mwalimu Nkosi Ajanaku)," *Painted Bride Quarterly*, no. 32–33 (1988): 100. Note that, to preserve Knight's use of intralineal slashes, double slashes have been used to indicate line breaks.

11. Etheridge Knight and Other Inmates of Indiana State Prison, *Black Voices from Prison* (New York: Pathfinder Press, 1970), 9.

12. Gladys Keys Price, "Careers and Education: Biographical Sketch of Poet Etheridge Knight," *Indianapolis Recorder*, October 5, 1974.

13. Eunice Knight-Bowens, interview by the author, June 16, 2010.

14. "Poetry Bridges Great Gap," *Commercial Appeal*, February 26, 1980.

15. Nancy Bunge, "Etheridge Knight: A Poet Comes out of the People," in *Master Class: Lessons from Leading Writers* (Iowa City: University of Iowa Press, 2005), 32–33.

16. Knight-Bowens interview.

17. Komunyakaa, *Blue Notes*, 16.

18. Ibid.

19. "Biographical Sketch," Etheridge Knight Papers, 1964–1990, Ward M. Canaday Center for Special Collections, University of Toledo.

20. John C. Ensslin, "Ex-inmate Saved by Poetry," *Rocky Mountain News*, February 7, 1986, 70.

21. Stephen Salisbury, "Black Poets Open a Special Week," *Philadelphia Inquirer*, March 20, 1985, 3-C.

22. Thomas C. Johnson, "Interview with Yusef Komunyakaa," *Worcester Review* 19, no. 1–2 (1998): 122.

23. Knight-Bowens interview.

24. Chris Lavin, "Poet Shows Inner Self at Reading," *Burlington Free Press,* March 15, 1986.

25. H. Jack Griswold, et al., eds., *An Eye for an Eye: Four Inmates on the Crime of American Prisons Today* (New York: Holt, Rinehart and Winston, 1970), 115.

26. Knight-Bowens interview.

27. Powers in Griswold, *An Eye for an Eye,* 115.

28. Ibid., 116.

29. Ibid., 115.

30. Sanchez's letter is part of the Etheridge Knight Papers, 1964–1990, Ward M. Canaday Center for Special Collections, University of Toledo.

31. Giammanco letter to Knight, September 29, 1967, Etheridge Knight Papers, 1964–1990, Ward M. Canaday Center for Special Collections, University of Toledo.

32. Poet Francy Stoller has noted this insistence.

33. Dan Carpenter, "Another Hard Knock Saps Poet but Replenishes His Art," *Indianapolis Star,* February 26, 1989, C-1, C-9.

34. Dudley Randall, "Reminiscences of Knight," in *Poetry Criticism,* vol. 14, ed. Nancy Dziedzic and Christine Slovey (Detroit: Gale Research, 1996), 52.

35. Elizabeth Gordon McKim, "Freedom and Confinement," *Worcester Review* 19, no. 1–2 (1998): 146–47.

36. Mary McAnally, letter to the author, February 19, 2011.

37. Mary McAnally, "Family Chronology," Etheridge Knight Papers, 1964–1990, Ward M. Canaday Center for Special Collections, University of Toledo.

38. Letter to Dudley Randall, February 6, 1973, Etheridge Knight Papers, 1964–1990, Ward M. Canaday Center for Special Collections, University of Toledo.

39. Mary McAnally, "Family Chronology."

40. Mary McAnally, letter to the author, February 19, 2011.

41. Mary McAnally, letter to the author, March 14, 2011.

42. Mary McAnally, *Cosmic Rainbow: New and Collected Poems* (Norfolk, Va.: Partisan Press, 2006), 116.

43. Ibid., 113.

44. Etheridge Knight, "Letters," *Callaloo* 19 (Autumn 1996): 960.

45. Rodger Martin, e-mail to the author, February 2, 2011.

46. Mary McAnally, letter to the author, March 14, 2011.

47. Fran Quinn interview.

48. Fran Quinn, "The Worcester Poetry Scene and Etheridge Knight," *Worcester Review* 19, no. 1–2 (1998): 86.

49. Ellen Slack, "Trouble Over," *Painted Bride Quarterly, no.* 32–33 (1988): 23–24.

50. Ibid. Eunice Knight-Bowens testified, in another arena, to Knight's gifts, recalling him as a "kind, fun-loving type brother. . . . He was free-hearted with a gentle spirit and he always had a smile. . . . I wouldn't have traded my brother" (in an interview with the author, June 16, 2010).

51. Etheridge Knight, "Dearly/— Beloved/—Mizzee," *Painted Bride Quarterly,* no. 32–33 (1988): 141.

52. McKim, "Freedom and Confinement," 140.

53. Stephen Stoller, in a phone interview with the author, June 15, 2010.

54. Stephen Stoller, *Freedom and Fame,* by Etheridge Knight (Indianapolis: R. W. Haldane and Associates, 1990).

55. Stoller, phone interview.

56. Dennis Bernstein, "Hard Time: Etheridge Knight: Soldier, Thief, Junkie, Poet," *Village Voice,* March 28, 1989, 38.

57. Francy Stoller, e-mail correspondence with the author, January 3, 2011.

58. "Poets Honor Black History Month," *Keen (N.H.) Town Crier,* February 11, 1986.

59. The dates cited here are from "Etheridge Knight to Read Poetry at UVM in March," *UVM Record,* March 3–23, 1986.

60. Carpenter, "Another Hard Knock," C-1, C-9.

61. Etheridge Knight, "Behind the Beat Look Is a Sweet Tongue and a Boogie Foot," *Worcester Review* 19, no. 1–2 (1998): 131.

62. Bernstein, "Hard Time," 38.

63. Ibid., 37.

64. All quotations are from a June 15, 2010, telephone interview with Stephen Stoller.

65. Jo Ellen Meyers Sharp, "Master of Words Is Now Man of Letters," *Indianapolis Star* (November 2, 1990); Haki R. Madhubuti, "Etheridge Knight: Making Up Poems," *Worcester Review* 19, no. 1–2 (1998): 100.

66. Fran Quinn interview. About the sale of Knight's papers, the *Indianapolis Star,* September 29, 1999, 1–2, reported that "Quinn and Etheridge Knight's sister Janice Knight Mooney, as literary co-executors [at the time of the sale], carried out the poet's wish to have his papers sold and the proceeds disbursed to his three children and 17 nieces and nephews."

67. Letter to Dudley Randall, October 6, 1975, Etheridge Knight Papers, 1964–1990, Ward M. Canaday Center for Special Collections, University of Toledo.

68. Fran Quinn interview. The head of the Canaday Center at the time was not Noel Stock, who Quinn says would "have done anything for Etheridge."

69. Nancy Bunge, "Interview with Etheridge Knight" (transcript of interview done on February 21, 1986), Etheridge Knight Collection, Special Collections and Rare Books, Irwin Library, Butler University.

70. "A Letter to Lois," reproduced in a January 24, 1968, letter to Roberto Giammanco, Etheridge Knight Papers, 1964–1990, Ward M. Canaday Center for Special Collections, University of Toledo.

71. Hoyt W. Fuller, "Perspectives," *Negro Digest,* January 1968, 49.

72. Etheridge Knight, response to survey, *Negro Digest,* January 1968, 87.

73. Charles H. Rowell, "An Interview with Etheridge Knight," *Callaloo* 19 (Autumn 1966).

74. Ken McCullough, "Communications and Excommunication: An Interview with Etheridge Knight," *Callaloo* 14/15 (February–May 1982): 7.

75. Lou Camp, "An Interview with Etheridge Knight," *Painted Bride Quarterly,* no. 32–33 (1988): 41–42.

76. This joke appears in Margot FitzGerald, "Knight Reading," *Mass Media,* November 19, 1985, 11, 15.

77. Walter Ray Watson Jr., "Poet Etheridge Knight Discusses Life of Writing," *Pittsburgh Courier Entertainer,* undated clipping, Etheridge Knight Collection, Special Collections and Rare Books, Irwin Library, Butler University.

78. Richard Wilkinson, *Mind the Gap: Hierarchies, Health, and Human Evolution* (London: Weidenfeld & Nicolson 2000), 38–43.

79. Etheridge Knight to Noel Stock.

80. Jenifer Warren, principal author, *One in 100: Behind Bars in America 2008* (Washington, D.C.: Pew Center on the States, 2008), 5.

81. Devah Pager, "The Mark of a Criminal Record," reprinted in *Constructions of Deviance: Social Power, Context, and Interaction,* ed. Patricia A. Adler and Peter Adler (Florence, Ky.: Thomson-Wadsworth, 2006), 210; and Warren, *One in 100,* 3.

82. Angela Y. Davis, *Abolition Democracy: Beyond Empire, Prisons, and Torture* (New York: Seven Stories Press, 2005), 39–40.

83. The White House Conference for a Drug Free America, Lois Haight Herrington, chairman, *Final Report,* June 1988, 11.

84. Ibid., 63.

85. Paul Scriven, *The Medicine Society* (East Lansing: Michigan State University Press, 1992), 120.

86. Bunge, "Etheridge Knight: A Poet Comes out of the People," 32.

87. "Proposal. Submitted to: Flanner House; From: Etheridge Knight and John E. Sullivan," Etheridge Knight Collection, Special Collections and Rare Books, Irwin Library, Butler University.

88. See http://www.neh.gov/news/humanities/1998–01/knight.html.

89. There is no evidence that the vignettes were actually commissioned, written, or performed.

90. Maureen Hayden, "Indiana Prison Officials Push for Sentencing Reform," *Anderson (Ind.) Herald Bulletin,* June 6, 2010, http://heraldbulletin.com/local/x1996 915888/Indiana-prison-officials-push-for-sentencing-reform.

91. Ibid.

92. The actual verse, rather than the compressed, colloquial version of it, is "'Vengeance is mine. I will repay,' saith the Lord" (Romans 12:19).

93. Etheridge Knight, preface to *Born of a Woman: New and Selected Poems* (Boston: Houghton Mifflin, 1980), xiii–xiv.

94. Knight's column is reprinted in David Rohn, "Response to Unsigned Letters," *Indianapolis News,* December 8, 1986.

95. Amiri Baraka, "The Black Arts Movement," in *The LeRoi Jones / Amiri Baraka Reader,* ed. William J. Harris in collaboration with Amiri Baraka (New York: Thunder's Mouth Press, 1991), 496, 499, 502.

96. Etheridge Knight, "Lend Me Your Ear," *American Poetry Review* 6 (November/December 1977): 19–20. As Knight explains at the beginning of this essay, the passages in which he defines his concentric audience were written while he was serving his sentence at the Indiana State Prison.

97. Dudley Randall, preface to *The Black Poets* (New York: Bantam Books, 1971).

98. Both Genet and Knight strive to co-opt traditional aesthetics rather than reject them out of hand.

99. Jean Genet, introduction to *Soledad Brother: The Prison Letters of George Jackson,* by George Jackson (New York: Bantam Books, 1970), 5.

100. Ibid., 5–6.

101. "Mainstreamese," Gish Jen suggests, consists of popular turns of phrase that mark those who comfortably use them as insiders, and those who do not as outsiders.

102. Stephen Henderson, *Understanding the New Black Poetry: Black Speech and Black Music as Poetic References* (New York: William Morrow, 1973), 28.

103. Etheridge Knight, "On the Oral Nature of Poetry: A Talk by Etheridge Knight," *Colorado Review,* 1987, 5–6.

104. Ibid., 8.

105. Harold Bloom, *A Map of Misreading* (Oxford University Press 2003), 19.

106. The concept of "social death" is precisely defined by Orlando Patterson in his book *Slavery and Social Death* (Cambridge, Mass.: Harvard University Press 1982). A socially dead person has, to alter the infamous words of the nineteenth-century chief justice of the United States Roger B. Taney, "no rights which *a socially alive person* must respect." For more, see Patterson, *Slavery and Social Death,* 7–9.

107. Bruce Jackson, *"Get Your Ass in the Water and Swim Like Me": Narrative Poetry from Black Oral Tradition* (Cambridge, Mass.: Harvard University Press, 1974), x–xi, 3–4.

108. Etheridge Knight, "A Nickel Bet," in *Poems from Prison* (Detroit: Broadside Press, 1968), 25.

109. Liebow, quoted in Jackson, *"Get Your Ass in the Water,"* 16.

110. Jackson, *"Get Your Ass in the Water,"* 17.

111. Ibid., 14.

112. Etheridge Knight, *Belly Song and Other Poems* (Detroit: Broadside Press, 1973), 25; a slightly revised and improved version of the poem appears in Knight's third book, *Born of a Woman.*

113. Jackson, *"Get Your Ass in the Water,"* 186.

114. Etheridge Knight, "Junky's Song," *Callaloo* 19 (Autumn 1996): 949.

115. Bloom, *A Map of Misreading,* 13.

116. Harold Bloom, *The Anatomy of Influence: Literature as a Way of Life* (New Haven, Conn.: Yale University Press, 2011), 200.

117. William H. Grier and Price M. Cobbs, *Black Rage* (New York: Basic Books, 1968), 1.

118. Fred M. Harris, foreword to Grier and Cobbs, *Black Rage,* xv.

119. Jonathan Simon, "Managing the Monstrous: Sex Offenders and the New Penology," *Psychology, Public Policy and Law* 4, no. 1–2 (1998): 453–54.

120. A. A. Stone, "The New Legal Standard of Dangerousness: Fair in Theory, Unfair in Practice," in *Dangerousness: Probability and Prediction, Psychiatry and Public Policy,* ed. Christopher D. Webster, Mark H. Ben-Aron, Stephen J. Hucker (Cambridge: Cambridge University Press, 1985), 14.

121. Ibid., 18–19.

122. Ibid., 19–20.

Chapter 2 — Knight in the Aleascape

1. Knight's previously published poems in *Negro Digest* focus on the singing of Johnny Mathis and Ray Charles and elegize the vernacular mastery of singer Dinah Washington.

2. Etheridge Knight, "Lend Me Your Ear," *American Poetry Review* 6 (November/December 1977): 19.

3. Etheridge Knight, "The Belly Dance," in *Singular Voices: American Poetry Today* (New York: Avon Books, 1985), 147–48.

4. Harold Bloom, *The Anxiety of Influence: A Theory of Poetry,* 2nd ed. (New York: Oxford University Press, 1997), 100.

5. Ibid., 148–49.

6. Ibid., xvi–xvii.

7. There is no more polemical and political poet—and no greater or more complete poet—than Dante Alighieri. Dante without his politics is Dante without the inspiration for and the subject matter of the *Inferno* and much of *Purgatorio* and *Paradiso.*

8. Harold Bloom, *The Western Canon: The Book and School of the Ages* (New York: Harcourt Brace, 1994), 23–24.

9. Harold Bloom, *The Anatomy of Influence: Literature as a Way of Life* (New Haven, Conn.: Yale University Press, 2011), 100–101.

10. Harold Bloom, *A Map of Misreading* (New York: Oxford University Press, 2003), 40.

11. Bloom, *Anxiety of Influence,* 30.

12. Bloom, *Map of Misreading,* 19.

13. Friedrich Hölderlin "To the Fates," in *Selected Poems,* by Hölderlin and Eduard Mörike, trans. Christopher Middleton (Chicago: University of Chicago Press, 1972).

14. Ossie Davis, "Why I Eulogized Malcolm X," in *For Malcolm: Poems on the Life and the Death of Malcolm X,* ed. Dudley Randall and Margaret G. Burroughs (Detroit: Broadside Press, 1967), xxiv–xxv.

15. Ibid., xxiv.

16. See Ashby Bland Crowder, "Etheridge Knight: Two Fields of Combat," *Concerning Poetry* 16, no. 2 (1983): 23, 24

17. The hammering of nature is the hammering of our environment, which is ultimately the cause of natural selection: the philosopher Daniel Dennett (*Freedom Evolves,* New York: Penguin Press, 2003) theorizes that human evolution can be viewed as the result of a quest by brains (driven by natural selection rather than conscious choice) "to produce useful future." Specifically Dennett argues, "When the need arises, creatures evolve instincts for sprucing up their most intimate environments: their own brains. . . . The goal unconsciously followed in these preparations is for the creature to come to know its way around itself. . . . Along one of these paths, or many of them, lie the innovations that lead to creatures capable of considering different courses of action in advance of committing to any one of them, and weighing them on the basis of some projection of the probable outcome of each" (247–48). Once he makes his big choice to enter the military, Flukum does his best to move backwards along the evolutionary path.

18. Ashby Bland Crowder pointed out that the term has other meanings, among them, "a bundle of twigs for fuel," like the faggots used in "the Holy Inquisition, during which unorthodox persons (including homosexuals) were eliminated in great autos-da-fé." However, Knight's Christ figure is not portrayed as a victim but as a temporarily felled oppressor. Crowder's reading of the significance of "Black Relocation Centers" is not only more convincing but very illuminating: "The idea of black relocation, Knight's central metaphor," Crowder wrote, "brings to mind the relocation of Africans to southern plantations. It recalls the freed slaves who were relocated in Liberia in 1847. It suggests the Nazi relocation centers for Jews; the U.S. relocation centers for Japanese Americans during World War II . . . and even Urban Renewal's relocations of entire ghettos." Crowder, "Etheridge Knight," 23, 25.

19. The details of the events that sparked the Detroit riots are drawn from Max Herman's *Ethnic Succession and Urban Unrest in Newark and Detroit during the Summer of 1967* (Newark, N.J.: Cornwall Center Publication Series, 2002).

20. Bart Kosko, *Fuzzy Thinking: The New Science of Fuzzy Logic* (New York: Hyperion, 1994), 37.

21. Ibid., 85–87.

22. Ibid., 47.

23. Miriam DeCosta-Willis, "Etheridge Knight's Love Songs to Women: 'How / be / Thee, good Lady?,'" http://nathanielturner.com/etheridgeknightlovesongstowomen.htm (accessed September 24, 2011).

24. This unpublished poem is housed in the Etheridge Knight Collection, Special Collections and Rare Books, Irwin Library, Butler University.

25. Etheridge Knight Collection, Special Collections and Rare Books, Irwin Library, Butler University.

Chapter 3 — *Black Voices from Prison*

1. H. Jack Griswold et al., eds., *An Eye for an Eye: Four Inmates on the Crime of American Prisons Today* (New York: Holt, Rinehart and Winston, 1970), 118.

2. Etheridge Knight and Other Inmates of Indiana State Prison, *Black Voices from Prison* (New York: Pathfinder Press, 1970). Page references will be given parenthetically in text.

3. Roberto Giammanco, e-mail to the author, February 24, 2011.

4. June 8, 1967, letter from Giammanco to Knight, Etheridge Knight Papers, 1964–1990, Ward M. Canaday Center for Special Collections, University of Toledo.

5. Charles H. Rowell, "An Interview with Etheridge Knight," *Callaloo* 19 (Autumn 1966): 977.

6. Yusef Komunyakaa, *Blue Notes: Essays, Interviews, and Commentaries,* ed. Radiclani Clytus (Ann Arbor: University of Michigan Press, 2000), 17.

7. Elizabeth Gordon McKim, "Etheridge Knight in Conversation," *Worcester Review* 19, no. 1–2 (1998): 133–35.

8. Knight, *Black Voices from Prison*, 98.

9. Elias Canetti, *Crowds and Power* (New York: Farrar, Straus & Giroux, 1984), 315.

10. C. G. Jung. *Memories, Dreams, Reflections* (London: Fontana Press, 1995), 413.

11. Regarding the linguistic component of race, Ishmael Reed sees the expression of something ingrained in American culture when a Richard Wright character is called "a black ape": "Black men are animals, and the inner cities are the jungles we inhabit. . . . [In 1997, s]uch descriptions of African Americans are not limited to . . . ultra-right publications." Ishmael Reed, "Bigger and O. J.," in *Birth of a Nation'hood: Gaze, Script, and Spectacle in the O. J. Simpson Case,* ed. Toni Morrison and Claudia Brodsky Lacour (New York: Pantheon Books, 1997), 179.

12. Canetti, *Crowds and Power,* 328. My argument here deviates from Canetti's somewhat or, rather, somewhat extends his argument.

13. Griswold, *An Eye for an Eye,* 44.

14. Data Processing Office and Service Unit, Indiana State Prison, "An Analysis of 277 New Admissions to the Indiana State Prison, January 1–June 30, 1960," October 20, 1960, 6.

15. David Garland, *Punishment and Modern Society: A Study in Social Theory* (Chicago: University of Chicago Press, 1990), 172–73.

16. See Yusef Komunyakaa, *Blue Notes: Essays, Interviews, and Commentaries,* ed. Radiclani Clytus (Ann Arbor: University of Michigan Press, 2000), 17–18; however, had Hard Rock been able to spark the sort of inmate culture that the scholar David Garland describes, he would have created a space for more widespread rebellion. See Garland, *Punishment and Modern Society,* 172–73.

17. Charles H. Rowell, "An Interview with Etheridge Knight," *Callaloo* 19 (Autumn 1996): 976.

18. "Time Marches On . . . So Does Penal Progress," *Encourager Magazine* 13, no. 2 (Sesquicentennial Edition).

19. Griswold, *An Eye for an Eye,* 51.

20. V. H. Mark, W. H. Sweet, F. R. Ervin, "Role of Brain Disease in Riots and Urban Violence," *JAMA* 201 (September 11, 1967): 217.

21. The information in this summary of the riots is drawn from the Rutgers website on the 1967 Detroit and Newark riots, http://www.67riots.rutgers.edu (accessed November 20, 2011).

22. Joseph Boskin, "The Revolt of the Urban Ghettos, 1964–1967," *Annals of the American Academy of Political and Social Science* 382 (March 1969): 2.

23. Dr. Max Herman, *Ethnic Succession and Urban Unrest in Newark and Detroit during the Summer of 1967* (Newark: Cornwall Center Publication Series, July 2002), 9.

24. A. Louis McGarry, William J. Curran, and Donald P. Kenefick, "Problems of Public Consultation in Medicolegal Matters: A Symposium," *American Journal of Psychiatry* 125 (July 1968): 80–81.

25. Gabe Kaimowitz, "My Case against Psychosurgery," in *The Psychosurgery Debate: Scientific, Legal, and Ethical Perspectives,* ed. Elliot S. Valenstein (San Francisco: W. H. Freeman, 1980), 513.

26. Kaimowitz and a coauthor cite this passage, from Erving Goffman's *Asylums,* in a post-trial brief they wrote for the *Kaimowitz* case. The passage itself appears in Erving Goffman, *Asylums* (Garden City, N.Y.: Anchor Books, 1961), 38.

27. Kaimowitz, e-mail to the author.

28. (a) Etheridge Knight, "On the Next Train South," *Negro Digest,* June 1967, 87–94. (b) "Etheridge Knight Reading," Scranton Public Library, https://www.youtube .com/.

29. Etheridge Knight, *The Essential Etheridge Knight* (Pittsburgh: University of Pittsburgh Press, 1986), 114.

30. Herbert A. Simon, *Administrative Behavior: A Study of Decision-Making Processes in Administrative Organization* (New York: Free Press, 1976), xvi.

31. Ibid., xvii.

32. Sartre distinguishes between working-class Americans and middle-class Americans, but writes of the latter, "I don't dare call them bourgeois; I very much doubt whether there is bourgeoisie in the United States." Jean-Paul Sartre, *What Is Literature?,* trans. Bernard Frechtman (New York: Harper Colophon Books, 1965), 156.

33. Ibid., 106–10.

Chapter 4—*Belly Song and Other Poems*

1. Etheridge Knight, *Belly Song and Other Poems* (Detroit: Broadside Press, 1973), 13–15.

2. Nathan Hare, "The Black Anglo-Saxons," *Negro Digest,* May 1962, 53.

3. Knight, *Belly Song,* 15–16.

4. Jessica Mitford, *Kind and Usual Punishment: The Prison Business* (New York: Knopf, 1973), 237–38.

5. Ibid., 237–43.

6. Haki R. Madhubuti, "Etheridge Knight: Making Up Poems," *Worcester Review* 19, no. 1–2 (1998): 92.

7. Ibid.

8. Giammanco, e-mail to the author, February 24, 2011.

9. Madhubuti, "Etheridge Knight," 92.

10. Etheridge Knight, "Letters," *Callaloo* 19 (Autumn 1996): 957–58.

11. Juanita Johnson-Bailey, "Sonia Sanchez: Telling What We Must Hear," in *Conversations with Sonia Sanchez,* ed. Joyce A. Joyce (Jackson: University Press of Mississippi, 2007), 75.

12. "Police and Panthers: Growing Paranoia," *Time,* December 19, 1969, 16.

13. Eldridge Cleaver, *Post-Prison Writings and Speeches* (New York: Vintage Books, 1969), 101.

14. "The Nation: Huey Newton Freed," *Time,* December 27, 1971, 6.

15. Peniel E. Joseph, *Waiting 'Til the Midnight Hour: A Narrative History of Black Power in America* (New York: Henry Holt, 2006), 262–63.

16. "Hung Jury for Huey," *Time,* August 23, 1971, 11.

17. "Police and Panthers: Growing Paranoia," *Time,* December 19, 1969, 14.

18. Cleaver, *Post-Prison Writings and Speeches,* 41.

19. Ibid., 102.

20. Sartre's definition of "poets," however, is flexible enough to include Mallarmé. See Ann Jefferson, "Biography and the Question of Literature in Sartre," in Adrian van den Hoven and Andrew Leak, *Sartre Today: A Centenary Celebration* (New York: Berghahn Books, 2005), 184.

21. Jean-Paul Sartre, *What Is Literature?* (New York: Harper & Row 1965), 16–17.

22. Ibid., 225.

23. (a) Ibid. (b) Knight told his Scranton library audience that he began the poem the day after Sanchez phoned, announced she had divorced him, and hung up.

24. "King's Last March," *Time,* April 19, 1968, 18.

25. Nick Kotz, *Judgment Days: Lyndon Baines Johnson, Martin Luther King Jr., and the Laws That Changed America* (Boston: Houghton Mifflin, 2005), 419.

26. Ibid., 400.

27. "Drug Charges Made against 2; 1 Sentenced," *Hartford Courant,* March 14, 1971, 3.

28. From the Etheridge Knight Papers, 1964–1990, Ward M. Canaday Center for Special Collections, University of Toledo.

29. Charles Rowell, "An Interview with Etheridge Knight," *Callaloo* 19 (Autumn 1996): 969.

30. Ibid., 975.

31. Ibid., 975.

32. "A MELUS Interview: Etheridge Knight," *MELUS* 12 (Summer 1985): 23.

33. Jackie Robinson, as told to Alfred Duckett, *I Never Had It Made: An Autobiography* (New York: Ecco, 1995), 234.

34. Ibid., 231, 233.

35. Ibid., 232.

36. Ibid.

37. "Sloganeering" is Christopher Gilbert's characterization of a mode Knight sometimes slips into when his imagination cools. Christopher Gilbert, "The Breathing/In/An Emancipatory Space," *Worcester Review* 19, no. 1–2 (1998): 121, 128.

38. *The NIV Study Bible,* ed. Kenneth Baker (Grand Rapids, Mich.: Zondervan, 1995), 1270.

39. Ibid., 1270–71.

40. Knight, *Belly Song,* 15.

41. S. E. Anderson, "The Fragmented Movement," *Negro Digest,* September/October 1968, 5.

42. Etheridge Knight, "21," in "Brother: A Book of Poems: Works by Etheridge Knight" (typescript compiled by Eunice Knight-Bowens), July 29, 2000, 4, Indiana Historical Society. Used with permission.

43. Knight, *Black Voices from Prison* (New York: Pathfinder Press, 1970), 177–78.

44. George Breitman, ed., *Malcolm X Speaks: Selected Speeches and Statements* (New York: Grove Weidenfeld, 1990), 37–38.

45. Knight, *Black Voices from Prison,* 178.

46. Shaikh Muhammad bin Jamil Zeno, *The Pillars of Islam and What Every Muslim Must Know about His Religion* (Kingdom of Saudi Arabia: Dar-us-Salam Publishers, 1996), 26.

47. A. Ezzati, *The Spread of Islam: The Contributing Factors* (London: Islamic College for Advanced Studies Press, 2002), 94.

48. Elijah Muhammad, *Message to the Blackman in America* (Chicago: Muhammad Mosque of Islam No. 2, 1965) 163.

49. Etheridge Knight, "15," in "Brother: A Book of Poems," 3.

50. Etheridge Knight, untitled response to *Negro Digest* survey, *Negro Digest,* January 1968, 87.

51. Muhammad, *Message to the Blackman,* 37.

52. Elijah Muhammad, "Warns the Black Man!," *Muhammad Speaks,* December 3, 1971, 16.

53. Muhammad, *Message to the Blackman,* 32.

54. "Do you know? She was the best sister-in-law," Knight-Bowens says. "And we still love Sonia . . . and talk to Sonia." Eunice Knight-Bowens, interview by the author, June 16, 2010.

55. Reed Johnson, "From Prison to Poetry, Etheridge Knight Seeks Freedom in Words," *Rochester (N.Y.) Times Union,* August 19, 1986, 1C.

56. Knight met both poets in McAnally's New York City apartment, McAnally reports in a March 1, 2011, letter to the author.

57. Etheridge Knight, "To Keep on Keeping On," in "New Black Writing" special issue, *Nimrod* 21, no. 1–2 (1977): 135.

Chapter 5—*Born of a Woman*

1. Etheridge Knight, "On the Oral Nature of Poetry: A Talk by Etheridge Knight," *Colorado Review,* 1987, 4. "The logical end is not to have the poem published in some magazine, like the obvious end for a preacher that sits down and writes a sermon is to say that sermon to the congregation, not to publish it in a book," Knight once said (Unidentified clipping, Box 18, Folder 9, Etheridge Knight Collection, Irwin Library, Butler University).

2. See J. L. Austin, *How to Do Things with Words,* J. O. Urmson and Marina Sbisa, eds. (Cambridge, Mass.: Harvard University Press, 1975), 1–11, 32–44.

3. Wynton Marsalis, speaking in episode 8 of *Jazz: A Film by Ken Burns* (PBS/Paramount, 2004).

4. Walter Cohen, Jean E. Howard, and Katherine Eisaman Maus, eds., *The Norton Shakespeare* (New York: W. W. Norton, 1997), 825.

5. Daniel Berrigan, *The Dark Night of Resistance* (Garden City, N.Y.: Doubleday, 1971), 72–77.

6. *The Challenge of Crime in a Free Society: A Report by the President's Commission on Law Enforcement and Administration of Justice* (Washington, D.C.: GPO, 1967), 211.

7. Ibid. 212.

8. Avram Goldstein, *Addiction: From Biology to Drug Policy* (New York: Oxford University Press, 2001), 95–96.

9. Ibid., 104.

10. Ibid., 157.

11. "Chapter III: The Roots of the Problem," in *The Negro Family: The Case for National Action,* http:www.dol.gov/oasam/programs/history/moynchapter3.htm (accessed September 24, 2011).

12. Ibid.; "Chapter IV: The Tangle of Pathology," in *The Negro Family: The Case for National Action,* http:www.dol.gov/oasam/programs/history/moynchapter4.htm (accessed September 24, 2011).

13. Ibid.

14. Etheridge Knight, "Addiction: A Philosophical Problem," *Encourager Magazine* 13.1 (Spring edition [year unclear]), 21.

15. Ibid.

16. Jean-Paul Sartre, *Saint Genet: Actor and Martyr,* trans. Bernard Frechtman (New York: Mentor Books, 1963), 205.

17. Ibid.

18. Etheridge Knight, *Born of a Woman: New and Selected Poems* (Boston: Houghton Mifflin, 1980), xiv.

19. Ibid.

20. Galway Kinnell, "Brother of My Heart," *Painted Bride Quarterly,* no. 32/33 (1988): 59.

21. Dan Carpenter, "Another Hard Knock Saps Poet but Replenishes His Art," *Indianapolis Star,* February 26, 1989, C1, C9.

Chapter 6—*The Essential Etheridge Knight*

1. Charles H. Rowell, "An Interview with Etheridge Knight," *Callaloo* 19 (Autumn 1996): 974.

2. This poem appears in both *Born of a Woman: New and Selected Poems* (Boston: Houghton Mifflin, 1980), 8, and *The Essential Etheridge Knight* (Pittsburgh: University of Pittsburgh Press, 1986), 12.

3. Two other poems in this vein that appear in *The Essential Etheridge Knight* are "Birthday Poem" (p. 72) and "Apology for Apostasy?" (p. 92).

4. "Junior says that institutions—universit[ies]—stifle . . . the arts, in a way," his sister says. Eunice Knight-Bowens, interview by author, June 16, 2010.

5. Jean-Paul Sartre, *What Is Literature?* (New York: Harper & Row 1965), 61.

6. Jacques Derrida, *Rogues: Two Essays on Reason,* trans. Pascale-Anne Brault and Michael Naas (Stanford, Calif.: Stanford University Press, 2005), 10.

7. Ibid., 11.

8. Jacques Derrida, *The Beast and the Sovereign,* trans. Geoffrey Bennington, 2 vols. (Chicago: University of Chicago Press, 2009), 1:66, 68.

9. Ibid., 1:67.

10. Stephen C. Tracy, "A MELUS Interview: Etheridge Knight," *MELUS* 12 (Summer 1985): 16.

11. "Homegirls & Handgrenades: A Review," typescript, Etheridge Knight Collection, Special Collections and Rare Books, Irwin Library, Butler University. Knight eloquently makes the same case in his poem "On Universalism," which appears in *Poems from Prison* (Detroit: Broadside Press, 1968).

12. Ken McCullough, "Communications and Excommunication: An Interview with Etheridge Knight," *Callaloo* 14/15 (February–May 1982): 6.

13. Charles Shaar Murray, *Crosstown Traffic: Jimi Hendrix and the Post-War Rock'n'Roll Revolution* (New York: St. Martin's Press, 1991), 214.

14. While Knight may not have influenced Brooks's actual writing, her discovery of him inspired her to teach in penitentiaries other than the Indiana State Prison, as she told the journalist Mildred Ladner in an otherwise unidentified clip housed in box 5, folder 1, of the Knight collection at the University of Toledo.

15. Derrida, *Rogues,* 45.

16. Robert Bly, "About the Conference on the Mother: An Interview with Bill Siemering," in *Talking All Morning* (Ann Arbor: University of Michigan Press, 1980), 218, 220.

17. See "For Black Poets Who Think of Suicide," in *The Essential Etheridge Knight,* 52.

18. T. D. Allman, "The 'Rebirth' of Eldridge Cleaver," *New York Times Magazine,* January 16, 1977, 11.

19. Ibid. 11.

20. "I feel I am a citizen of the American dream," Cleaver said once, "and that the struggle of which I am a part is a struggle against the American nightmare" (quoted in ibid.).

21. "History . . . is a nightmare from which I am trying to awake," is an assertion made by the character Stephen Dedalus in James Joyce's *Ulysses.*

22. John Kifner, "Eldridge Cleaver, Black Panther Who Became G.O.P. Conservative, Is Dead at 62," *New York Times,* May 2, 1998.

23. Kathleen Cleaver, ed., *Target Zero: Eldridge Cleaver, a Life in Writing* (New York: Palgrave, 2006), xxiv.

24. Etheridge Knight, "Who Knows???," *Painted Bride Quarterly,* no. 32/33 (1988): 97.

25. Etheridge Knight, "On the Removal of the Fascist American Right from Power," Etheridge Knight Collection, Special Collections and Rare Books, Irwin Library, Butler University.

26. See "The Fall of Andy Young," *Time,* August 27, 1979, 10.

27. See "Foreign Policy, Black America and the Andy Young Affair," *Ebony,* January 1980, 118.

28. On Knight's occasional weakness for sloganeering, see Christopher Gilbert, "The Breathing/In/An Emancipatory Space," *Worcester Review* 19, no. 1–2 (1998): 121, 128.

29. Knight probably had Sartre's notion of "action by disclosure" in mind as well.

BIBLIOGRAPHY

Selected Materials by Etheridge Knight

BOOKS OF POETRY

Poems from Prison. Detroit: Broadside Press, 1968.

Belly Song and Other Poems. Detroit: Broadside Press, 1973.

Born of a Woman: New and Selected Poems. Boston: Houghton Mifflin, 1980.

The Essential Etheridge Knight. Pittsburgh: University of Pittsburgh Press, 1986.

Etheridge Knight and Other Inmates of Indiana State Prison. *Black Voices from Prison.*
   New York: Pathfinder Press, 1970.

The Lost Etheridge: Uncollected Poems of Etheridge Knight. Edited by Norman Minnick. Athens, GA: Kinchafoonee Creek Press, 2022.

PUBLISHED BUT UNCOLLECTED POETRY

"Johnny Mathis' Ruby / Ray Charles' Ruby." *Negro Digest,* January 1965, 61.

"To Keep on Keeping On—after the fashion of Alice Walker and Denise Levertov." In
   "New Black Writing," edited by Francine Ringold. Special issue, *Nimrod* 21, no.
   2/22, no. 1: (1977): 135.

"The Point of the Western Pen." *Iowa Review* 6 (Spring 1975): 12.

"Things Awfully Quiet in America (Song of the Mwalimu Nkosi Ajanaku)." *Painted
   Bride Quarterly,* no. 32–33 (1988): 100.

"Your Song Ain't Really Blue (for William 'Sonny' Ford)," "memo #50," "memo #1,"
   "(Untitled)," "All the Way Home," "Behind the Beat Look is a Sweet Tongue and a
   Boogie Foot (for those who see me as a tragic figure)." *Worcester Review* 19, no. 1–
   2 (1998): 129–31.

PROSE

"The Belly Dance." In *Singular Voices: American Poetry Today.* Edited by Stephen
   Berg. New York: Avon Books, 1985. 147–49.

"Lend Me Your Ear: A Column." *American Poetry Review* 6 (November/December
   1977): 19–20.

Letters. *Callaloo* 19 (Autumn 1996): 956–64.

"My Father, My Bottom, My Fleas" [fiction]. *Negro Digest,* August 1966, 64–71.

"Narcotics Addiction: A Philosophical Problem." *Encourager Magazine* 13, no. 1
   ([year unclear]), 21.

"On the Next Train South" [fiction]. *Negro Digest,* June 1967, 87–94.

"On the Oral Nature of Poetry: A Talk by Etheridge Knight." *Colorado Review,* 1987,
   4–9. Reprinted in *Painted Bride Quarterly,* no. 32–33 (1988): 12–16.

"Paducah." In "Poetry, Fiction, Articles, Literary News & Gossip: Etheridge Knight: typescripts, mss., hand-writ, the printed word." *11 x 30: A Publication of Toledo Poets Center* 3, no. 1 (n.d. [October 1990?]). Housed in Etheridge Knight Papers, 1964–1995, MSS-016, The Ward M. Canaday Center for Special Collections, University of Toledo.

"Reaching Is His Rule" [fiction]. *Negro Digest,* December 1965, 61–63.

"Response to Unsigned Letters." *Indianapolis News,* December 8, 1986.

CHAPBOOKS

Freedom and Fame. Indianapolis: R. W. Haldane and Associates, 1990. A chapbook of poetry written by Knight together with reproductions of paintings, as well as commentary, by the artist Stephen Stoller.

Archival Collections

Etheridge Knight Collection. Special Collections and Rare Books, Irwin Library, Butler University, Indianapolis, Indiana.

Etheridge Knight Papers. MSS-016. The Ward M. Canaday Center for Special Collections, University of Toledo, Toldeo, Ohio.

Etheridge Knight, Jr., Papers, 1955–2004. Collection M 0798 OM 0409. Manuscript and Visual Collections Department, William Henry Smith Memorial Library, Indiana Historical Society, Indianapolis, Indiana.

Interviews

Bunge, Nancy. "Etheridge Knight: A Poet Comes out of the People.' In *Master Class: Lessons from Leading Writers,* 29–33. Iowa City: University of Iowa Press, 2005.

Camp, Lou. "An Interview with Etheridge Knight." *Painted Bride Quarterly,* no. 32–33 (1988): 39–43.

Knight, Etheridge, Louis McKee, and Elizabeth McKim. "A Conversation with Etheridge Knight, Elizabeth McKim, and Louis McKee." *Calapooya Collage* 15 (August 1991).

McCullough, Ken. "Communication and Excommunication: An Interview with Etheridge Knight." *Callaloo* 14/15 (February–May 1982): 2–10.

Pinsker, Stanford. "A Conversation with Etheridge Knight." *Black American Literature Forum* 18 (Spring 1984): 11–14.

Price, Ron. "The Physicality of Poetry: An Interview with Etheridge Knight." *New Letters* 52 (Winter–Spring 1986): 167–76.

Rowell, Charles H. "An Interview with Etheridge Knight." *Callaloo* 19 (Autumn 1996): 966–81.

Tracy, Stephen C. "A MELUS Interview: Etheridge Knight." *MELUS* 12 (Summer 1985): 7–23.

Selected Secondary Sources

JOURNAL ISSUES OR JOURNAL SECTIONS DEVOTED TO KNIGHT AND HIS WORK

Camp, Louis, Joanna DiPaolo, and Louis McKee, eds. "Etheridge Knight Issue." Special issue, *Painted Bride Quarterly,* no. 32–33 (1988).

Johnson, Thomas C., ed. "Etheridge Knight 1931–1991." Special section, *Worcester Review* 19, no. 1 & 2 (1998): 79–147.

SELECTED BOOKS, CRITICAL ESSAYS, AND JOURNALISM ON KNIGHT

Alexander, Elizabeth. "Elizabeth Alexander on Etheridge Knight." In *Poetry Speaks: Hear Great Poets Read Their Works from Tennyson to Plath,* edited by Elise Paschen and Rebekah Presson Moody, 304–7. Naperville, Ill.: Sourcebooks, 2001. Alexander explores the links between Knight's prosody and the prosody of Whitman, on the one hand, and the prosody of the black church and the black community, on the other.

Anaporte-Easton, Jean. "Etheridge Knight: Poet and Prisoner: An Introduction." *Callaloo* 19 (Autumn 1996): 940–46. Introduces a selection of Knight's letters.

Bernstein, Dennis. "Hard Time: Etheridge Knight: Soldier, Thief, Junkie, Poet." *The Village Voice,* March 28, 1989, 37–38. An account of Knight's struggles and triumphs in the late 1980s.

Bly, Robert. "Hearing Etheridge Knight," In *American Poetry: Wildness and Domesticity,* by Robert Bly, 101–8. New York: Harper & Row, 1990. Makes the case for Knight's significance to American poetry.

Carpenter, Dan. "Poetic Feet of Clay: Etheridge Knight's Literary Reputation Bids Fair to Survive His Sometimes Sordid Life." *Indianapolis Star,* September 29, 1999, 1–2

Collins, Michael. "The Antipanopticon of Etheridge Knight." *PMLA* 123, no. 3 (2008): 580–97. Analysis of Knight's attempts to turn the tables on carceral culture.

———. "God—his uniqueness: Donald Hall Remembers Etheridge Knight." *Worcester Review* 36, no. 1/2 (January 2015): 133–44.

Crowder, Ashby Bland. "Etheridge Knight: Two Fields of Combat." *Concerning Poetry* 16 (Fall 1983): 23–25. A reading of "2 Poems for Black Relocation Centers."

DeCosta-Willis, Miriam. "Etheridge Knight's Love Songs to Women: 'How / be / Thee, good Lady?'" http://nathanielturner.com/etheridgeknightlovesongstowomen.htm (accessed September 23, 2011). A celebration of Knight as a lover of women—a man who "understood women, their promise and their pain."

Gilbert, Christopher. "The Breathing/ in / An Emancipatory Space." *Painted Bride Quarterly,* no. 32/33 (1988): 117–34. Explores the "genealogical" aspect of Knight's poetry.

Hall, Donald. "Learning a Language: Etheridge Knight." *Worcester Review* 19, no. 1–2 (1998): 95–96. How a three-hour Knight discourse on the word "funky" became a door to African American culture for Hall.

Hayes, Terrance. *To Float in the Space Between: A Life and Work in Conversation with the Life and Work of Etheridge Knight.* Seattle: Wave Books, 2018. A meditation on Knight as muse and literary role model that Hayes illustrates with his own drawings.

Hill, Patricia Liggins. "'The Violent Space': The Function of the New Black Aesthetic in Etheridge Knight's Prison Poetry." *Black American Literature Forum* 14 (Autumn 1980): 115–21. Explores Knight's use of "temporal/spatial [and other] elements" to "merge his personal consciousness with the consciousness of Black people."

Komunyakaa, Yusef. "Tough Eloquence: Poetry for the Free Peoples." In *Blue Notes: Essays, Interviews, and Commentaries,* edited by Radiclani Clytus, 16–30. Ann Arbor: University of Michigan Press, 2000. An account of how Knight's knowledge of the American psyche "makes him an expert signifier—playing the dozens with his reader."

———. "Foreword." In *The Lost Etheridge: Uncollected Poems of Etheridge Knight.*

Edited by Norman Minnick. Athens, GA: Kinchafoonee Creek Press, 2022. xvii–xx. A sketch of Knight as a man who succeeded in "embracing duality."

Lifson, Amy. "Knight: The People's Poet." www.neh.gov/news/humanities/1998-01 /knight.html (accessed September 23, 2011). A brief introduction to Knight and the impact of his poetry workshops.

Lumpkin, Shirley. "Etheridge Knight." In *Afro-American Poets since 1955*. Vol. 41 of *Dictionary of Literary Biography*. Detroit: Gale, 1985. 202–11. An overview of Knight's life, career, and work.

Nelson, Howard. "Belly Songs: The Poetry of Etheridge Knight." *Hollins Critic* 18 (December 1981): 1–11. Posits the nurturing of human relationships as the core theme and ambition of Knight's poetry.

Powers, Art. "The Prison Artist." In *An Eye for an Eye,* edited by H. Jack Griswold, Mike Misenheimer, Art Powers, and Ed Tromanhauser, 112–22. New York: Holt, Rinehart and Winston, 1972. An account of Knight's prison metamorphosis.

Steptoe, Lamont B. "A Deity of the Spoken Word: Etheridge Knight 1931–1991." *Bride Unveiled,* Fall 1991, 2. A prose-poem elegy on Knight and his impact on Steptoe and on poetry.

Werner, Craig. "The Poet, the Poem, the People: Etheridge Knight's Aesthetic." *Obsidian: Black Literature Review* 7 (Summer/Winter 1981): 7–17. An account of how Knight widened the definition of "the People" while remaining within the Black Aesthetic.

INDEX

addiction, 4, 9, 11, 13, 103, 108–10, 113–16

aleascape, 45–48, 127, 137. *See also* Borges, Jorge Louis; dangerousness; Knight, Etheridge: "Dark Prophecy: I Sing of Shine"; Kosko, Bart

Anderson, S. E., 89–90

Austin, J. L., 102

autoimmunity, 131–32

Baraka, Amiri (a.k.a. LeRoi Jones), 15, 21–22, 38–39, 43, 44, 55, 73, 83, 93

Berrigan, Daniel, 105–7

Biko, Steve, 9

Black Aesthetic, 16, 23

Black Arts Movement, 15–16, 21–22

Blackburn, Charlene, 8, 10–11, 99–101

Black Panther Party for Self Defense, 77, 106

Black Power Movement, 30, 51

Bloom, Harold, 22, 24, 28, 37–38, 116; on divination, 28; on the daemonic, 36; on literary study and politics, 37–39

Bly, Robert, 1, 38, 95; and "Great Mother Conference," 8, 121

Borges, Jorge Louis, 25

Broadside Press, 7, 15, 42, 82

Brooks, Gwendolyn, 6–7, 22, 43, 150n14

Bunge, Nancy, 3, 15, 19

Cabral, Amilcar, 9–10

Camp, Lou, 16–17

Cannetti, Elias, 57

civil death, 74, 91, 97

Cleaver, Eldridge, 77–78, 106, 133–35

cognitive horizon, 44. *See also* Dennett, Daniel; Simon, Herbert

Colson, Chuck, 133–34

Crowder, Ashby Bland, 144n18

dangerousness, 26–27, 29–32. *See also* aleascape; cognitive horizon

Dante, 38

"Dark Prophecy: I Sing of Shine." *See under* Knight, Etheridge

Davis, Angela, 18–19

Davis, Ossie, 42–43

Daytop, Inc., 82–85, 113

Dennett, Daniel, 144n17

Derrida, Jacques, 127–28, 131

Detroit riot of 1967, 30, 46, 64–65, 66, 119

Elkins, Stanley M., 111–12

Etheridge Knight Festival of the Arts, 154–55

Fanon, Frantz, 16

Free People's Poetry Workshops, 11–12, 18, 20, 127

Fuller, Hoyt, 6–7, 15

Garland, David, 146n16

Genet, Jean, 8, 23, 142n98

Genovese, Kitty, 92–93, 100

Giammanco, Roberto, 16, 23, 38, 74, 129, 130; advises Knight on writing, 7–8; writes introduction to Knight's *Black Voices from Prision* 51–52; translates and oversees publication of *Voci Negre dal Carcere (Black Voices from Prison)*, 51

Goffman, Erving, 68, 69

Hall, Donald, 8, 73, 95
Henderson, David, 23
Hound Mouth, 4, 24, 75

ipse, 127–28
ipseity, 127–29, 131

Jackson, Bruce, 24–26
Jackson, Jesse, 94
Jen, Gish, 23, 142n101
Jones, Leroi. *See* Baraka, Amiri
Jung, Carl Gustav, 2, 57
justice, 20–21. *See also* prison-industrial
complex; U.S. incarceration rates

Kaimowitz, Gabriel, 64, 66–68
*Kaimowitz v. Department of Mental
Health of the State of Michigan,* 64–
68
Keller, Anthony, 98
King, Martin Luther, Jr., 82, 105–6
Kinnell, Galway, 8, 98, 116–19
Knight, Belzora Kozart , 3, 13, 121
Knight, Etheridge: ambivalence about
Sartre, 16; on being desperate, 17–18;
on being "scared," 119; and the Black
Arts Movement, 16, 21–22; chame-
leonic tendencies of, 4; children of, 9,
14, 119; concentric conception of his
audience, 22; death of, 8–9; on freedom, 10; health problems of, 12, 13,
14, 17; on language, 23–24, 34; military service of, 4–5; *Negro Digest*
questionnaire of, 16; papers sold to
Butler University, 15; parole hearing
of, 72–73; "psyche wound," 4; sells
papers to University of Toledo, 14–
16; sent to Daytop, Inc., 82; in solitary confinement, 34–35; and toasts,
24–27; use of slash marks, 23; wins
American Book Award, 13, 17; wins
Guggenheim Fellowship, 9; wins Shelley Memorial Award, 12; youth, 3–4.
See also addiction; Black Arts Movement; Brooks, Gwendolyn;
Daytop, Inc.; Giammanco, Roberto;
Keller, Anthony; Knight-Bowens,

Eunice; Komunyakaa, Yusef; Lane,
Ward; Lincoln University; Madhubuti,
Haki; McAnally, Mary; McKim, Eliz-
abeth; Muhammad, Elijah; Quinn,
Fran; Sanchez, Sonia; Steptoe, Lamont
B.; Stoller, Francy; Stoller, Stephen
Knight, Etheridge, writings of: "Addic-
tion: a Philosophical Problem," 113–
15; "And Tell Me, Poet, Can Love
Exist in Slavery?," 121; "Another
Poem for Me (after recovering from
an o.d.)," 76–77; "At a VA Hospital
in the Middle of the United States of
America: An Act in a Play," 136–37;
"Behind the Beat Look Is a Sweet
Tongue and a Boogie Foot," 13;
"Belly Song," 82–86, 90; "The Bones
of My Father," 87–89; "Cell Song,"
40; "Cop-out Session," 92–93; "Dark
Prophecy: I Sing of Shine," 26–29,
136; "Feeling Fucked Up," 80; "For
Eric Dolphy," 101; "For Freckle-
Faced Gerald," 52–58; "For Lang-
ston Hughes," 107; "For Mary Ellen
McAnally," 95–96; "From the Mo-
ment (or, Right / at / —the Time),"
102; "Genesis," 76–77; "Green Grass
and Yellow Balloons," 85–86; "Hard
Rock Returns to Prison from the Hos-
pital for the Criminal Insane," 61;
"He Sees through Stone," 41;
"Huey," 77–79; "I and Your Eyes,"
124; "The Idea of Ancestry," 34–37;
"The Innocents," 55–58, 63; "It Was
a Funky Deal," 42; "Lend Me Your
Ear," 142n96; "A Love Poem," 96;
"My Uncle Is My Honor and a Guest
in My House," 122–24; "A Nickel
Bet," 48; "On the Next Train South,"
68; "On the Oral Nature of Poetry: A
Talk by Etheridge Knight," 148n1;
"One Day We Shall Go Back," 86–
87; "On Watching Politicians Perform
at Martin Luther King's Funeral," 81;
"A Poem for Galway Kinnell," 116–
19; "Poem for the Liberation of South
Africa," 124–25; "A Poem to Be

Recited," 29–30, 95; "Rehabilitation and Treatment in the Prisons of America," 69–71, 72; "Revolutionaries Live in Houses of Love," 50; "The Sun Came," 43–45; "Things Awfully Quiet in America," 2; "This Poem Is For," 92, 95; "Three Songs," 104; "To Gwendolyn Brooks," 33–34; "To Make a Poem in Prison," 58; "2 Poems for Black Relocation Centers," 45–47; "Untitled I," 89; "The Violent Space," 48–50; "The Warden Said to Me the Other Day," 59; "We Free Singers Be," 120–21; "Welcome Back, Mr. Knight: Love of My Life," 108, 109–13

Knight, Etheridge "Bushie," 3
Knight-Bowens, Eunice, 3–6, 13, 121, 140n50, 148n54, 149n4, 154–55
Knight-Mooney, Janice, 141n66
Komunyakaa, Yusef, 1–2, 4, 61–62
Korean War, 4–5, 41, 100, 136
Kosko, Bart, 47

Lane, Ward, 59–62
Levertov, Denise, 97
Lincoln University, 9, 13

Macbeth, 104
Madhubuti, Haki R., 2, 74, 98
"mainstreamese," 23, 142n101
Malcolm X, 7, 18, 21–22, 41–45, 52, 68, 91, 93, 94, 97, 105, 106
Mandela, Nelson, 9, 125
Marsalis, Wynton, 103
Martin, Rodger, 10
McAnally, Mary, 9–10, 13, 75, 76, 81, 82, 96, 97, 98, 102, 103, 109, 119, 124, 125
McKim, Elizabeth, 8–9, 10, 11, 13, 14, 16–17, 54
Middle East peace process, 131–32, 135–36
Misenheimer, Mike, 59
Mitford, Jessica, 74
Moynihan, Daniel, 111–12
Muhammad, Elijah, 93–94, 95, 96, 125

Negro Digest, 6, 15, 16, 73, 89–90
Newton, Huey P., 77–78
Nixon, Richard M., 81, 111, 119

panopticism, 63. See also prison-industrial complex
performative statements, 102, 136
Powers, Art, 5–6, 51, 58
"prison/America," 54, 70, 118
prison-industrial complex, 2. See also civil death; Davis, Angela; Mitford, Jessica; Simon, Jonathan; Stone, A. A.; U.S. incarceration rates

Quinn, Fran, 1, 8, 10–11, 13–15, 20, 129

Randall, Dudley, 7–8, 14, 22–23, 75
Ray, James Earl, 118–19
Reagan, Ronald, 32, 77, 134
Reed, Ishmael, 145n11
Robinson, Jackie, Jr., 83–84

Sanchez, Sonia, 7, 72–75, 80, 85, 96; possible influence on Knight, 23
Sartre, Jean-Paul, 16, 70, 79–80, 81, 115, 146n32, 147n20, 151n30
Simon, Herbert, 69–70
Simon, Jonathan, 30–31. See also prison-industrial complex
Simpson, Louis, 15, 16
Slack, Ellen, 11
social death, 91, 143n106. See also civil death
Steptoe, Lamont B., 1
Stock, Noel, 14, 141n68
Stockholm authority, 69, 125, 131
Stockholm syndrome, 63, 67, 91
Stoller, Francy, 12–14
Stoller, Stephen, 12–14
Stone, A. A., 31–32. See also prison-industrial complex

toasts, 24–27

U.S. incarceration rates, 18

Walker, Alice, 97
war on drugs, 19, 30–32
What Is Literature? (Sartre), 70
Whitman, Walt, 2, 22, 24, 80
Wilkinson, Richard, 18
Wright, Richard, 68, 79, 145n11

Young, Andrew, 131, 135–36